Left Hook

a Sideways Look at
Canadian Writing

Left Hook

a Sideways Look at
Canadian Writing

George Bowering

RAINCOAST BOOKS

Vancouver

Raincoast Books gratefully acknowledges the ongoing support of the
Canada Council for the Arts; the British Columbia Arts Council;
and the Government of Canada through the Department of Canadian
Heritage Book Publishing Industry Development Program (BPIDP).

Text design by Tannice Goddard

LIBRARY AND ARCHIVES CANADA CATALOGUING IN PUBLICATION
Bowering, George, 1935–
Left hook: a sideways look at Canadian writing / George Bowering.

Includes bibliographical references and index.
ISBN 1-55192-845-0

1. Canadian literature (English) — History and criticism. 2. Canada — Intellectual life.
3. Canada — Civilization. 4. Bowering, George, 1935– 5. Authors, Canadian (English) —
Biography. I. Title.

PS8077.1.B69 2005   C810.9'3271   C2005-902492-5

This collection published in 2005 by:

Raincoast Books
9050 Shaughnessy Street
Vancouver, British Columbia
Canada v6P 6E5
www.raincoast.com

At Raincoast Books we are committed to protecting the environment and to the responsible
use of natural resources. We are acting on this commitment by working with suppliers and
printers to phase out our use of paper produced from ancient forests. This book is one step
towards that goal. It is printed on 100% ancient-forest-free paper (100% post-consumer
recycled), processed chlorine- and acid-free, and supplied by New Leaf paper. It is printed
with vegetable-based inks. For further information, visit our website at www.raincoast.com.
We are working with Markets Initiative (www.oldgrowthfree.com) on this project.

Printed and bound in Canada.

1 2 3 4 5 6 7 8 9 10

These pieces are for my fellow essayer, Roy Miki. You come too.

CONTENTS

Preface

A Word with You

I USED TO like the idea of the well-made book of essays, based on the models encountered in U.S. and British collections. You could make a book of twelve essays, say twenty pages each. It would be neater still if the subject were defined, Canadian poetry, for instance, or North American fiction. See my books *A Way with Words* and *The Mask in Place*.

Then along came Kroetsch, and Barthes. And Warren Tallman. Essays did not have to cover the subject. They could be improvisations made of writing. The essayist could be trying something. He could see what would happen if he were to read a Kroetsch poem line by line, always stopping to see what we have so far. He could check out a word that sounds a little like a poet's name, and see whether the poet had noticed that.

1

He could write essays that are too long for their topic, or too short by half. I have of late been fascinated by the extremely short essay. Some day I want to write one-sentence essays about some of the major works in our perceived canon. After I published a book of short pieces called *Craft Slices* and a book of even shorter pieces called *Errata* (that title was chosen partly because I wanted to confound the bibliographers, who put book titles and Latin words in italics — would they feel that they had to mention my title in Roman type?) I found myself writing them still. Consider them an ongoing book.

But mainly I like the idea of the essay as a piece of writing. One often skims or skips essays in journals because the writing itself is not interesting. I will always learn more from Barthes than I will from Derrida, because Barthes is a writer and Derrida is a post-structuralist. I don't imagine that all readers will go gaga over my prose; but the nicest thing that bpNichol ever wrote about me was that my stories read like essays and my essays read like stories.

Why not? I am not an authority on anything. But I enjoy writing an essay as much as I enjoy writing a story. As for reading, I think that Kroetsch's essays are among our best fictions. I think that Gail Scott's book of essays should have been shortlisted for the Governor-General's award in fiction. I wonder whether Jorge Luis Borges ever wrote a short story, and what went through the minds of editors who included his works in their fiction anthologies.

No fiction writer (nor any artist) can ever put the world of nature into his text; all he can do is to employ the techniques of his trade, and to make something that resembles earlier fictions. So it is for the literary essayist. He can't deliver the goods on an Atwood poem or a Wilson novel. All he can do is to write words, resembling earlier essays, and trying not to, too much.

Doing Our
Own Reading

SEVERAL YEARS AGO I was talking with a woman who had been brought up in Saskatchewan but was now employed in the writing world and living in central Canada. Here's what she said: "If I have to read one more novel that starts with a prairie farmwife, old before her time, leaning on her broom on the unpainted porch and looking out at the blighted fields, I will puke!"

I was awfully glad to hear such sentiments from a person in the book world. There had been a time when I liked naturalism more than anything else in fiction. I mean when I was about twenty-one. And I do not begrudge writers and readers their love of the realist text with all its description and characterization and survival. Readers have been trained to expect description and so forth, and they want what they think is continuity between their books and their world. Writers do, too. When a Montreal shrink told Hugh

MacLennan that characters out of his newest novel were showing up in his clinic every day, MacLennan took that as a compliment.

That is, people who will never read a Henry James novel are enjoying conventions that James promoted. "What is character but the determinant of incident?" he asked. "What is incident but the illustration of character?" From this cause-and-effect system, the writer is supposed to be keeping a good distance. He is supposed to disappear from the reader's thought, and if possible, the book should seem to follow him. This kind of writer likes to say, "I just started these characters off, and then they took on a life of their own and all I could do was try to write down what they did and said."

We know that such a statement is seductive, but also that it is really equine manure. Any writer can, if she wants to, have a piano fall from the sky and finish off a character in chapter six. And she may even make a personal writerly remark about the musicality of the scene.

Henry James saw such a writer as a dead end. "The reality of Don Quixote or of Mr. Micawber is a very delicate shade; it is a reality so coloured by the author's vision that, vivid as it may be, one would hesitate to propose it as a model." He had even worse things to say about Anthony Trollope, who admitted that the events in his fiction did not really happen and that he could give his narrative any turn one would fancy. "Such a betrayal of a sacred office seems to me, I confess, a terrible crime," wrote Henry James.

He would not have liked Robert Kroetsch one little bit. We are supposed to be representing life, James would say, not a rime by Robert Service. He would not have liked Michael Ondaatje's *Coming Through Slaughter*, either. In that novel the author seems to be saying to the protagonist: "What ... made me push my arm forward and spill it through the front of your mirror and clutch myself? Did not want to pose in your accent but think in your brain and body ..." Keep your distance, my old creative writing teachers would have admonished. The mirror is an image for realists, my old English teachers would have said — we mirror life in our writing. Or we erect a window before the world, and so on, all that glass.

In *Coming Through Slaughter*, Buddy Bolden is forever escaping through windows or mirrors. In *What the Crow Said*, a newspaper guy can remember only the future. So much for history, James's model for serious fiction.

It has always bugged me that Robert Kroetsch and Michael Ondaatje manage to write novels and poems and non-fiction prose, but they do not write short stories. I have edited a lot of short story collections, and it bugs me that I can never include the two writers who most exemplify the kind of writing I am interested in. Maybe I should some day follow Ondaatje's precedent — he edited a famous and successful short story collection with a lot of things in it that are not short stories.

The relationship between these two writers and the general reading public can be seen in the different directions their careers have taken over the past few years. Michael Ondaatje has been writing longer and more conventional fictions of late, and they have made him world-famous and rich. He is still a wonderful writer, but now his books are not "difficult." They align themselves pretty well with history, whereas in *Coming Through Slaughter*, we got the "history of ice." Kroetsch writes very peculiar poetry, and every five years or more comes out with a novel that is very interesting in terms of the writing, but is ignored by the Canadian reading world, at least in central Canada, where reputations are made. In Germany and Australia they think that Kroetsch is the bee's knees. In Toronto they think of him as a regional writer — like Sheila Watson.

Daphne Marlatt — why the heck can't she write short stories?

There may be many reasons why the Canadian reading and reviewing and prize-giving public likes realist novels with descriptions and characters and so on, and no doubt some of these reasons would also apply in other parts of the world. But here is a thought that might be nothing but bushwa: Canada is a small, recently independent country that feels threatened by its big rich neighbour. Canada needs to get an identity and stick with it. Therefore, it needs a literature that shows us to ourselves. We read that notion in the prefaces to Canadian story anthologies all the time. They tell us that we need what people call a "national literature," and for many professors and reviewers that means a realist fiction with description and characters and history, however revisionist.

An example might be a central Canadian professor named T. D. MacLulich, who wrote of some "postmodern" Canadian fictions: "The games that these works play with Canadian themes may not announce the health of a national tradition, but may predict its death, crushed by the weight of excessive self-consciousness." We will leave aside for now our objections that one cannot crush a death and that self-consciousness does not weigh anything. MacLulich is interested in that central Canadian dream that we have heard so much of, the Canadian national tradition. He goes on: "When there is an emphasis on technical innovation in fiction — and a concurrent denigration of the straightforward mimetic possibilities of fiction — then our fiction may lose its capacity to mirror [see!] the particularities of culture and personality." Leaving aside our objection that a mirror prevents the straightforward, we note that MacLulich seems to agree with the kind of sentiments that emanated from the Robin Mathewses of the seventies and eighties, that Canadians should not seek to be innovators because innovation is USAmerican — that Canadians should remain hewers of wood and drawers of water, and sweepers of porches.

There are writers on the margins of the scene, and even toward the centre, who do not have a stake in the "national tradition," who do not view fiction-writing as an instrument of national cohesion, who might even think of such ideas as a kind of imperial brutality. Who wants to be told that their writing is supposed to promote non-literary ideas such as "The People's Revolution" or "The National Tradition"?

Look out. I am going to quote a writer who did not have a stake in the Canadian tradition. Roland Barthes wrote this about criticism: "its preferred material is this culture, which is everything in us except our present." That is why the criticism of jazz, for example, is notoriously unsuccessful. That is why Michael Ondaatje's *Coming Through Slaughter*, a book not "about" a jazz musician but like jazz itself, tells us to forget beginning and end, and to listen to the middle and all its possibilities.

You do that by paying attention to the innovative form that MacLulich fears so much. Charles Olson, the USAmerican, was right when he wrote "One loves only form,/ and form only comes/ into existence when/ the thing is born." Think about it. Can you love "content"? Are you enamoured of his small intestine, or recrystallized calcite, the material of Michelangelo's statues? Nicole Brossard, the truly wonderful North American poet and novelist (oh, why could she not have written some short stories?) made a simple discrimination that goes much further than I would dare to: "When it comes to reality, art does everything possible to really avoid it." One senses here that she has been driven to make an exaggerated reply to someone who has been insisting on Henry James's idea that we should "reproduce" reality in our works. In our play.

Of course when it comes to writing, maybe especially when it comes to the writing of fiction, there is no such thing as "content," as opposed to form or even as allied with form. What is there to contain? If a realist writer tells you that her characters "took on a life of their own," how can they be said to be contained? There is no content in a book of fiction. There may be lots of references. If Timothy Findley mentions the Duke of Windsor, he is making a reference, not to some human being once alive, but to his reader's experience of hearing about the "Duke of Windsor."

I think that the upholders of the "national tradition" believe that you ensure the survival of the country by referring to it.

I also think that people who want us to put our words to the service of their notion of a country are of the mistaken opinion that we own the words. We do not own the words we borrow to speak or write. The same is true for the rest of the world. As Guy Davenport, a USAmerican writer, put it while writing about a nowhere: "The world to an animal is food, to man a language of signs before which he is largely illiterate."

I do not want, as a reader or writer, to extirpate description and characters altogether. I just want readers to notice the writing. Ethel Wilson said that the most important thing in a story is the sentence. She was kind of a realist, but she loved form. Loved it. If you notice the writing, and the writing is good, you will love it. You might also notice in that moment of loving that the reader is the focus of the fictional act.

Let Me Get Back
to You on That

A CANADIAN IS a person who will probably be dumbstruck if you ask him the question: what is a Canadian?

And we will not be mistaken if we take that to be a good thing. It means that our country could use a sign overhead at all airports, border crossings, and ports of entry: UNDER CONSTRUCTION. It means that we cannot yet brainwash our schoolchildren and television-watchers that this is the country God picked to be the best, or the country that history had in mind, or the country that invented everything important.

We invented basketball, the potato peeler and the Jolly Jumper. That is enough to make a Canadian happy, but not enough to crow about. Canadians don't crow about Canada. Our young people put little Canadian flags on their backpacks, but not to boast. It's more that they want to show that they are not something else. For the

9

same reason, lots of young people who are not Canadians put little Canadian flags on their backpacks. That doesn't make us mad: we just smile and say "What a good idea!"

If a young person from some other country says, "What is a Canadian?" we might say, "I don't know. It's a beer, isn't it?"

Here is another good thing. If you ask a Canadian what a Canadian is, and she doesn't have a good answer, she is not filled with anxiety. There's no punishment for not knowing the answer. In some countries you can go to jail for not knowing the right answer. In the United States, as they say, of America, I'll bet that most people will tell you what an "American" is, but most people will not be able to locate the U.S.A. on a map of the world.

I do not imagine that I am a typical Canadian, but I might be viewed as a symbolic Canadian. One of my grandfathers was English and the other was USAmerican, from the Ozarks, of all places. I grew up naturally speaking our Canadian English, saying wrench rather than spanner, spelling it aluminum rather than aluminium, but traveller rather than traveler. One of my grandmothers was a Mennonite from Oregon and the other was a German-Canadian girl from an Ontario town so small that all that now remains is the building she went to school in.

What is a Canadian? A policeman once told me that I was not. Just before three policemen beat me up in the basement of the Vancouver "public safety building" one night in the early sixties, another policeman with a form to fill out asked me my nationality. I said "Canadian." He said there was no such thing unless you were an "Indian." I guess that he wanted to know my great-grandfather's nationality. According to your logic, then, I told him, I must be an

"Indian." That's when they beat me up. Apparently if you were an "Indian," policemen beat you up. Who knew?

He wanted me to say "English," I guess. Maybe there was a rule against writing down a colour, so they needed code words. But I was not going to say "English." I had been struggling against the English all my life, even though where I grew up in the South Okanagan Valley, my grandfather and my girlfriend and her parents were all English. The Southern Okanagan Valley had a lot of English immigrants in it, because land grants were made to veterans of the First World War, as long as they were "British subjects," a phrase I loathed. I lived just fourteen miles north of the International Boundary that lay invisible across the valley, separating our Okanagan from their Okanogan.

So I was three thousand miles from Ontario and Quebec, where all the Canadian stuff came from, and fourteen miles from the U.S.A., land of my dreams. The USAmericans are among the most expert people in brainwashing their children and children-like adults, and many of the techniques by which they do so are available to curious boys just barely inside that country to the north, whatever it is. I listened to U.S. radio stations, watched U.S. movies, read U.S. comic books and sports magazines, and listened to U.S. music. I could hardly wait to grow up and become an "American" citizen. If I were an "American" citizen, I reasoned, I would be able to redeem my Popsicle wrappers for great prizes. I would be able to travel the world and have foreigners admire me and my country.

The alternative was English stuff. The English were the colonizers. They had all the good jobs around my home town. In the late eighteenth century they had stupidly worn red coats and fought against the valiant freedom-seekers they were suppressing. Their automobiles were dicky little things that looked as if they belonged in the thirties. They spoke in an accent whose purpose seemed to be to put you in your place.

So at the movies you had to sing "God Save the King" (or Queen). They left the lights on to make sure you were standing still. Any Canadian magazines that made their way into the Southern Okanagan Valley (*Star Weekly*, *New Liberty*) had someone from the British royal family on the cover, usually the princesses. A couple weeks before I graduated from high school the new British queen had her coronation. Time for me to head for college in the States. But then my English girlfriend went to normal school in Victoria. I followed her, enlisting as an artsman at Victoria College, gnashing my teeth at the irony in the name.

Well, I was not successful at college, so I went to work for the provincial (oh, how I resented the fact that my province was called "British") government in the topographical survey up north. But I was not successful at that, either, so I joined the Royal (gnash gnash) Canadian Air Force and got shipped to the province of Quebec for basic training, Ontario for trades training, and Manitoba for my regular posting, from which I went to Alberta for temporary duty.

In the RCAF we had a lot of contact with other NATO air forces, including the USAF. We always felt superior to these latter, calling them Semis, pronounced "Semeyes," and noticing that while it took five Canadians to service an F-86, it took twelve Semis to handle the same job. It was while I was in the air force in mosquito country south of Lake Manitoba that I began to be a Canadian.

For a young man from the far southern interior of British Columbia, being a Canadian was a matter of choice. Okay, I said more and more, I will not choose to become a Yank; I will choose to be a Canadian. I will now spell flavours with a "u", even if there are not as many available to me as there would be in California.

Three of my grandparents chose to be Canadians, I remembered. And the fourth had relatives in Buffalo, New York, I think, so she made that choice, too. Even my grandfather who was born in England was scheduled to be a preacher in Idaho, but chose his church's request that he go to Alberta, instead. I do not know whether my parents chose to be Canadians; I know that my father's older brother Llew got married to a USAmerican girl in Seattle, but he eventually came home. I decided that I would follow a family tradition and chose Canada. Maybe, I began to think, because I was becoming an artist-academic, and such people are paid to perform slick-sounding theories, maybe all Canadians make that choice.

I don't really think that. I have met a lot of pickup-truck-driving guys in sideburns who actually believe that ice hockey is preferable to baseball. On the negative side, I know a writer who was going to move across the line until he developed a medical condition that would be terrifically expensive down there where medicine is a business. But while I still do not particularly like having Queen Elizabeth's profile on my coins, I also believe that "the land of the free" is a slogan that is no more historical than "the home of the Whopper."

So I know for sure that I am a Canadian. Now, if I could figure out what I am, I might have a step up to figuring out what a Canadian is.

I said that we do not tell our children that God picked Canada to be the best country in the world. But in recent years it has become a habit for Canadian newspapers to look around for any survey that ranks Canada as the best country in the world to live in. If the Yanks can sing or say "God Bless America," maybe we can be taught to sing "The UN Recommends Canada." I don't particularly want to live in a country that considers itself the best in the world. I want us to look around and see what needs fixing. We do not want to be smug; smugness is the benign form of a mental disease that results in nationalism, the delusion that other places were the failures on the path to your own perfection.

I like the fact that a Canadian, asked what a Canadian is, will likely say, "Let me get back to you on that."

That is why you should not be surprised to hear someone say, "I have looked all over, and I can't find a Canadian."

Here's your obvious reply: "That's okay. Give me a Blue."

BACKYARD BURGERS

A Letter to the U.S.A.

about Transborder Culture

I AM PROBABLY not a typical Canadian. I have endeavoured all my life not to be, I suppose. The things that I have endeavoured to be have changed from decade to decade. But I have always wanted not to be a typical Canadian. There was not much chance that I would be, in any case, because I did not grow up in Ontario, where the typical Canadians are thought to come from. You might say that the slightly rancorous anti-centrism suggested in my words so far makes me a typical Canadian. I hope not.

But you might call me an archetypal Canadian. Or a metaphorical Canadian. You see, USAmericans are USAmericans. It takes hardly any time at all for an immigrant to become a USAmerican. Ethnic Vietnamese in golf hats are USAmericans. Canadians do not become Canadians that fast, not even the hordes of refugees from the U.S. that took the underground railroad north during and after the Vietnam war. We have third-generation Alberta farmers who still speak with a bit of a Ukrainian accent. My own mother, born in Alberta but brought up with a father from the Ozarks, was teased for the way she talked when she was a schoolchild, and one of my linguist friends tells me that she has an identifiable accent, and that furthermore there are times when I show the influence that influenced her. I say "roof" [rime with "could"] rather than "roof" [rime with "aloof"] for instance. I say "route" [out] instead of "route" ["root"].

My childhood was a battleground where the armies of the United States and Great Britain continued the conflict they had been conducting for a century and three-quarters. I lived in a valley where British war veterans grew tree fruits. So there were English accents all around me. I hated them. The reason I hated them was that the valley extended across the border, and so did radio waves. Most of the narratives I knew were from the U.S. From Donald Duck to Walt Whitman, they were my compatriots. The comic books I got, the novels I found in the drug store, the radio serials, the movies on Saturday afternoon, the sport magazines, the hit parade, the popsicle wrapper — they were all made in the U.S.A., and they were not presented as anything but USAmerican stuff speaking to USAmericans.

Things have not changed all that much. At the video store I go to they regularly list movies made by Canadians among the "foreign films." The movie theatre closest to my house bears a (relatively) permanent sign that declares its fare as "American and foreign movies." In the neighbourhood chain drug store that advertises itself as "Canadian-owned" you can get two hundred different paperback novels, but you can not find a Canadian novel among them unless Margaret Atwood has been recently reprinted. It took me years to persuade my daughter that the U.S. president is not legally our president. I took me longer to persuade her that we do not have a president.

I like to ask people from the U.S.: how would you like to go into a bookstore and find no USAmerican books? How would you like to go to a record store and find no USAmerican music, unless the musicians had become famous in another country? How would you like to buy a popsicle, and read the rules about saving up popsicle wrappers, and see in fine print at the bottom: "This offer not valid in the U.S."?

When I was a kid I read everything I could get my hands on. Most of what I could get my hands on was printed in the United States. I read the popsicle wrappers. They told me "This offer not valid in Canada." I found that phrase in magazine coupons, in my beloved Batman comic books, on candy wrappers. They should have put it in giant letters suspended in the Canadian sky just north of the longest undefended border in the world.

Margaret Atwood has told about her similar childhood disappointment and alienation due to the popsicle wrapper. As a young woman studying in Massachusetts, she wrote a poem called "At the Tourist Centre in Boston" (Yep, she spelled it that way):

There is my country under glass,
a white relief —
map with red dots for the cities,
reduced to the size of a wall

and beside it 10 blownup snapshots
one for each province,
in purple-browns and odd reds,

the green of the trees dulled;
all blues however
of an assertive purity.

Mountains and lakes and more lakes
(though Quebec is a restaurant and Ontario the empty
interior of the parliament buildings),
with nobody climbing the trails and hauling out
the fish and splashing in the water

but arrangements of grinning tourists —
look here, Saskatchewan
is a flat lake, some convenient rocks
where two children pose with a father
and the mother is cooking something
in immaculate slacks by a smokeless fire,
her teeth white as detergent.

Whose dream is this, I would like to know:
is this a manufactured
hallucination, a cynical fiction, a lure
for export only?

I seem to remember people,
at least in the cities, also slush,
machines and assorted garbage. Perhaps
that was my private mirage

which will just evaporate
when I go back. Or the citizens will be gone,

run off to the peculiarly-
green forests
to wait among the brownish mountains
for the platoons of tourists
and plan their odd red massacres.

Unsuspecting
window lady, I ask you:

Do you see nothing
watching you from under the water?

Was the sky ever that blue?

Who really lives there?

So we advertise ourselves to each other, but we Canadians have
to spend more attention at it. As audience-victims we are just the
overflow. So I wanted to be an USAmerican when I grew up. As it
says in one of my books, when I was a kid I was upset that I was in
the one-eleventh who were not born USAmerican. Of course when
I grew up I changed my mind, and in fact consider myself lucky.
In fact I no longer want to have the offer valid in Canada. I want
a wrapper that is printed in Canada. I want to be able to find my
friends' books in a book store, and maybe even in a drugstore. One
of my novels was published in a mass-market paperback by Penguin
Books. In the drugstore in my home town they had one copy of
it for sale. My niece, who worked in that drugstore, bought it. In
that drugstore they had fifty copies of a new paperback by Danielle
Steel.

There is a reason for that ratio. It is not an aesthetic reason, nor a reason that reflects the small town Canadian imagination. It is an economic and political reason. The company that delivers paperback books to Canadian drugstores is owned by people in the U.S. That is the result of what people in the U.S. call "free enterprise." Two things about that phrase bother me, and maybe they are connected. One: people in the U.S. think that the word "free" in "free enterprise" is as denotative of something good as the word "free" in "free elections." Two: people in the U.S. think that private enterprise capitalism is both natural and inherently good for people. They think that everyone in the world really wants to have USAmerican-style private enterprise capitalism, or that if they don't, they just need to be educated enough to see that they do.

I love many things about the United States, but I would not want to be part of that country. I love southern Arizona. I can't live without the Boston Red Sox (sorry!). I have to buy and read the novels of Gilbert Sorrentino. In the 1960s John Coltrane saved my intelligence from despair. Until May 25, 1987, I smoked Winston cigarettes. When I was twenty years old I *became* James Dean. Seattle is probably the nicest city in the U.S., and I am so glad that it is just three hours away on the highway, even though I don't go as often since the Canadian dollar got sabotaged.

Now you know from the rhythm just set up that there is a "but" coming along about now. Yes. But.

But. I am the grandson of the youths who left England and the U.S. and came to Canada, to western Canada. They came because of difference. I want to stay in a place that is different from England and different from the U.S. For this reason I am not in favour of quote free unquote trade.

Neither are the people who live in my home town, where they
had only one copy of my book in the drugstore. I am from the
Okanagan Valley, a semi-desert that runs a little over a hundred
miles south of the boundary, and a little over 160 kilometres north
of the boundary. What we do there is raise tree fruits and grapes.
Tree fruits and grapes ripen first in the south. At the north end of
the valley the peaches ripen a few weeks after they have ripened in
the south. In my country we had a tariff forbidding the dumping of
the earlier (and more cheaply produced) Washington fruit in
British Columbia until it had been off the trees and vines for ninety
days. Anyone can see the reason and necessity for such a precau-
tion. But it is the opposite of free trade. Now we have free trade, as
long as the U.S. sees that free trade is to its advantage. A lot of
orchards have disappeared.

Who is in favour of free trade? I mean in Canada: who is in
favour of free trade? The business people, merchants, who think
that they can make a profit if not a killing by selling their stuff and
services in the States. The politicians, especially in the west, who
are the friends of those business men, who believe that government
is an outgrowth of business. (You will hear them say, without irony,
that a person who wants to run good government should be
someone who has demonstrated proficiency in business.) And those
regular people who think they are going to pay significantly less for
vegetables and gabardine slacks.

Who in Canada is against free trade? The workers and their
unions, who see a threat from foreign goods produced by cheap
labour. In this way Canadians feel about the U.S. the way the U.S.
auto-workers feel about Korea, let us say. Canadian patriots: there
are Canadians who reflect on the balance, and look at the real price

for California carrots. And the artists: I have been crossing the country for years, listening to painters, writers, movie makers, and others, without hearing one voice in support of free trade with the U.S. Margaret Atwood makes a lot of money in the U.S. but she is not in favour of free trade. The artists, let us say, might fit into the two earlier categories. Some of them might be seen as Canadian workers, and others might be seen as Canadian patriots. They might say with the labour unions that they are in favour of freer trade but not in the wide open free trade as presently handled by the governments involved, except when it would appear unpleasant to businessmen.

Lionel Kearns is a noted Canadian patriot, a gentle and passionate poet, and an old friend of mine. He expresses the sentiments felt by many of our artists in his somewhat bitter poem, "International Incident":

I was drinking the American's beer
and talking loud and saying things
that seemed unpleasantly true
I was drinking the American's beer
and shouting we should legislate against
foreign take-overs and U.S. control
of colleges, media, land, us
I was drinking the American's beer
and telling him it was all his fault
yes I was drinking the American's beer
and reminding him that it sure takes guts
to be so hostile to your host, but he
thought I was talking about myself

Let's go back to those California carrots. The southern suburbs of Vancouver, B.C. are built on land that was made from the deltas of silt brought south by the Fraser River, one of the most powerful rivers on the continent. The islands formed in the mouth of the Fraser River are made of the best agricultural soil in the world. But in the past three decades the farms there have been replaced by apartment buildings and condominiums and shopping plazas. The stores that used to buy vegetables and fruit from this area now get them from the refrigerated trucks that drive north from California and Mexico. The price of vegetables in our stores is now a lot higher than it used to be. Yet at the same time it is so low that the few remaining local farmers cannot make a living on their produce.

My point is that the businessmen who build concrete on farmland, and the politicians who permit that to happen, are the same kind of unreflective folk who do not see the long-range dangers of free trade with the U.S. Sure, there are people who want an apartment in Richmond. Sure, these people probably like watching *Jeopardy*! on their Japanese TV's. Sure, I know that the MC on *Jeopardy*! is a Canadian, or used to be.

Is that culture? Anthropologists would say that it is. Politicians haggling about borders and tariffs would say that it is. Personally, I am old-fashioned. I don't like to see the word "culture" slipping into such a usage. I like to call Henry James culture and Henry Winkler entertainment.

I am one of those people in Canada who has carried on a double battle for half their lives. First: I want to save culture against the onslaughts of popular taste, to preserve culture against the expansion of mere entertainment. In recent years people such as I have been exercised by the democratization of musical taste and talk-show content at the Canadian Broadcasting Corporation. The CBC has been more and more coming to resemble just a commercial radio station, like a USAmerican station, let's say. Second: I want to save both Canadian entertainment and Canadian culture from the "manifest destiny" of the U.S. industries.

I, this person who is uttering these words, was targetted all through the seventies as an agent for the invasive USAmerican culture, as a threat to the survival and integrity of something called the Canadian Tradition. This because I was a spokesman for and practitioner of poetics enunciated by poets such as Robert Duncan and Charles Olson. I do not repent. I think that these were great poets. In fact I am proud of the fact that they have had a higher reputation among Canadians then they have had among USAmericans. I believe that the zealots who called me a traitor were as mindless as the dinks who see free trade only as a selfish opportunity to buy cheaper objects.

That is, if the USAmerican is Robert Creeley I am pro-USAmerican. If the USAmerican is any of the Bushes I am anti-USAmerican. I want to be able to oppose an economic union while being able to buy Yankee books; and I will pay high prices for Yankee books as the condition for being able still to buy ours. That is what I am doing now. I recently, for instance, paid 28.95 of our dollars to buy a book that is priced here at 18.95 Yankee dollars. This was a book about cooking with chili peppers. Now *that's* American culture!

Let me tell you an instructive little story about books and tariffs and U.S. dollars. USAmerican publishers think of Canada as another area in which to dump books or magazines. If you are to be a big publisher you always have to manufacture more books or magazines than you will be able to sell. Therefore, if you already have the objects on hand, it is a windfall to look at that English-speaking area up here as a place to get rid of some surplus.

Well, you notice that you do sell a lot of copies up here. (For instance, the best market in the *world* for Archie comics is Edmonton.) So you need a distributor. If you are selling novels by Philip Roth you make a deal with a Canadian publisher, paying them to distribute your books. Then you think further and tell yourself that it makes sense to simply buy that Canadian publisher and distribute your own Roths up here. If you are selling magazines and mass-market paperbacks up here you might as well buy the rack service suppliers. That is good sensible expansionist quote free unquote enterprise.

Now let us for a moment look at these events from the point of view of the Canadian poet or novelist. Before I was a Canadian poet or novelist, I wanted to be both, and so I looked around at Canadian publishers, first at the professional publishers in, of course, Toronto. (We long ago made our accommodations about free trade with Toronto.) There were not many, and the ones that published some books of poetry were few. I am talking about the situation in the late fifties and early sixties. The professional publishers who produced a few poetry books were McClelland & Stewart, Oxford University Press, Macmillan, Clarke Irwin, and Ryerson. Of all these, the most important for the history of Canadian poetry may have been Ryerson.

In the fifties and sixties, Canadian publishers began to disappear, as did Canadian magazines. Eventually the voices raised by Canadian patriots were in the seventies to persuade the Canadian government to do at least a little in a symbolic way to preserve some of our publishers. Some takeovers were in fact forestalled. But first we had to lose Ryerson. This is a famous story in Canada, but only among the literati, not among carrot-eaters in Richmond apartments. Ryerson started as the publishing arm of the United Church of Canada, a union of Presbyterians and Methodists. Then it became one of the leading literary houses in the country. It published great books of poetry that I am glad I have copies of. I never published with Ryerson, but I would have been proud to, as my heroes and friends did.

Then one day an outfit we knew from our school days, McGraw-Hill, arrived on the scene, and announced that soon it would be providing stability to the house of Ryerson. Lovers of Canadian culture were alarmed, having seen this happen before, and they alerted their fellow Canadians in the government business. McGraw-Hill of New York responded by saying that there would be no new editorial policy toward Canadian texts in the new McGraw-Hill Ryerson. Now we are some years older and we know that professional presses such as McGraw-Hill Ryerson do not publish books of Canadian poetry. They distribute USAmerican textbooks to Canadian schools.

So who publishes poetry in Canada now? As in the United States, mainly poets' presses and regional presses. They are not good examples of free enterprise. They exist mainly on government subsidies.

I wonder how many U.S. backbones stiffen a little when I mention government subsidies. You know, there are even people in my country who think there is something wrong with government subsidies to writers and publishers. One does not hear from these people, however, when it comes to concessions made by government to large mining consortia and oil-explorations. It is thought, by some, that if you write or publish poetry and fiction and non-fiction, and take money from the Canada Council, for instance, that you will have to refrain from writing or publishing anything that might seem unpleasant to, say, the Liberal Party of Canada. Others think that it is just wrong for public money to go into the making of things. In the U.S. there is a lot of public money that goes into essential things such as the mysterious B2 bomber, but not much that goes into ephemeral things such as volumes of leftist concrete poetry.

Subsidies. That is a word that we in Canada hear from USAmericans in all discussions of free trade. And we are taken aback for a moment by its odd usage, and then we are reminded that our USAmerican cousins have minds that have been made completely different from ours. For instance we have a lot of families on the east coast of Canada who depend on fishermen for their lives. These fishermen fish for part of the year, making barely enough to survive, and for the other part of the year they receive the benefits of the Employment Insurance system they have been paying into.

The USAmerican negotiators at the free trade talks refer to this system as unfair government subsidy of Canadian fishermen. U.S. fishermen, who do not have such a progressive system of unemployment insurance, are seen to be placed at a competitive disadvantage. Calling such a basic fact of Canadian life a "subsidy" raises eyebrows right into our norwester hats.

Then we hear something even stranger. The U.S. negotiators complain about our public health system. U.S. workers who get sick and have to go to hospital will be placed at a disadvantage because they will have to pay for their own medical expenses or private health schemes, while hospitalized Canadian workers will be taken care of by socialized medicine.

Can you blame some people up here for being a little afraid of free trade when such an issue is raised?

The first North American government to bring in a comprehensive public health system was that of Saskatchewan. I had the good fortune to be spending some summer time in Berkeley and San Francisco while the last virulent debates were being waged over the issue. I had my eyes opened wide in amazement. California doctors and newspapers proclaimed every day that godless communism had set foot in North American soil and that people of brave hearts should do all in their power to combat this threat. I began to look around carefully before crossing streets, afraid that I might be recognized as a Canadian. We think of Berkeley and San Francisco as pretty enlightened parts of the United States. I am glad that I was not spending that summer in, say, Mississippi.

Well, we had our own opposition to socialized medicine in Canada. There are a lot of free enterprisers up here, and a lot of businesspeople, many of them doctors. But by now we have come to see medical service as a universal right, not as something tailored to the pocketbook. An occasional horror story in our press is the story of some Canadian who got into an auto accident or the like in the U.S. and was presented with a bill for many thousands of dollars by the good Samaritans who kept her life together. My late wife's aunt, who lived in the California of John Steinbeck, spent all the years of her widowhood trying to pay the medical bills that were laid on the corpse of her husband.

In my province there was a furor a few years ago when the right wing provincial government raised the price of a hospital room from one dollar a day to four dollars a day. Worse, the cost of a room in intensive care was raised to eight dollars. We don't understand a system in which one of the first amendments to the constitution says you can own a gun, but there is no amendment that says that you should not have to pay thousands of dollars to get fixed up when someone shoots you with one of those guns.

What I am trying to say is that Canada is not just some more United States. We are quite different, and we think that we are often on the right side of that difference. We think Yanks should be able to have their own opinion about that, too. We do not expect you to become Canadians as the price of free trade. We do not think that we should be considered wrong to be Canadians. Employment insurance and public medical insurance are not incorrect economics. They are, we think, a step in the progress of democracy.

I am not against trade between our countries. In fact I am not sure that I am against free trade, though I probably am. I am against the idea of forfeiting my Canadianness in order to get free trade for some Canadian exporters. Canada is a trading nation. We cannot get away from that. We share seven or eight thousand kilometers of borderland with the U.S.; we are going to have to continue to do a lot of trading with you. In terms of geography we are larger than you are, but we have only one-tenth of your population. When people compare North American free trade with the European Common Market, they forget that France and Germany and Britain and Italy are all about the same size. Being one-tenth the size of your neighbour does not always feel comfortable. Ask Finland. Ask the mouse in bed with the rhinoceros.

I do not have a lot of facts and figures here. My usual job is fictions and figures of speech. But try this one: in the free trade agreement any new U.S. takeover of Canadian resources and indus-tries that exceeds 150 million dollars in value must be negotiated with the governments involved. Any USAmerican entrepreneur knows how to cut a deal into 149 million-dollar pieces. I don't have 149 million dollars. I will bet that there are lots of U.S. companies that do.

Try this one. It concerns my own industry. Among the protectionist U.S. laws we come up against is the one that says you may not import into the U.S. more than 199 copies of a book. After that you have to have a U.S. publisher. The wonderful and inventive Coach House Press of Toronto used to have this kind of address: Toronto and Buffalo, or Toronto and Detroit. So a little book of poems by a little-known U.S. poet could conceivably swamp the U.S. market. Did this happen?

No. But have a look at the drugstore racks in Canada. Stephen King's books are on the top rack and the second rack and the third rack. In one block in downtown Winnipeg you might be able to find 199 copies of the latest Stephen King book. Did this happen?

Some book stores in Canada have little sections labelled "Canadian." Have you recently gone into a bookstore in the U.S. and seen a little section called "American?" Did you look around the store and see that it was filled with books by authors who are more familiar than the ones in the tiny little section called "American"?

If you are a USAmerican, I just wanted you to get a hint of what a Canadian reader feels like.

Before I was born the idea of free trade had another name. It was called reciprocity. We signed a reciprocity treaty in 1854. You will remember that the U.S. was beginning to split into north and south about then. Can you imagine how Canadian nationalists felt? How would any USA feel about the north if the south split away? Wouldn't it want an economic and then a political union, just to be significantly larger and more powerful than the Confederated States?

In the nineteenth century the Liberals were for greater continentalism, and the Tories were for continued ties with Great Britain. Now we see that the Tories are officially for continentalism and the Liberals, who used to be in favour of nationalism and against free trade, are now continentalists, too. In the nineteenth century the whole issue was part of the continuing rivalry and warfare between Britain and the U.S. Nowadays Britain is out of the question. The struggle is between nationhood and economics. An oil man in Alberta says that if Ottawa will not give him what he wants he will see what they have to offer in Houston. But an assembly line worker in Ontario will tell you about the U.S. free trade measures with Mexico. U.S. industrialists were happy to move the assembling part of their business to Mexico, where they could employ non-union labour to make objects that could then be shipped back to the U.S. without tariff. (Until cheaper labour in China complicated matters.)

I am writing as an ardent baseball fan. U.S. ballplayers played the game shortly after it was invented in Ontario. Do you know about workers in Haiti who made baseballs for 90 cents a day until it was cheaper to have them made in Asia? Do you wonder why Haitians crowd onto rafts and hope they get blown toward the Florida coast? Have you seen an outfielder flip a baseball into the crowd? That is called good public relations. José, can you see?

But I am a poet and a novelist. I am not an economist. You have to be an economist to have a creditable opinion about the merits of protectionism or open markets, don't you? You have to be a lawyer to understand anything about drafting legislation, no matter what the poet Shelley had to say about the matter. You have to be a businessman to make sure that you are handling national resources correctly.

Then what is the writer's job? What is the imaginative writer's job, and why am I going on about business and jobs?

Well, for every legislator there are fifty thousand legislatees. For every economist there are fifty thousand mortgage-payers. For every ten USAmericans there is one Canadian. We call our country Canada. We get a little scared when we hear Yanks calling theirs America. That always sounds to us like the sports promoters who call the last game in the U.S. season the "world's championship."

For every fifty thousand Canadians there is one artist. I read this week that in every fifty thousand births there is a case of Siamese twins. Can that be right? Are we artists such prodigies? Are we unrepresentative of our population? Don't we think that we are the reflective voices of our populations? Some artists, such as Ibsen, have said that the artist's responsibility to his country is to pay total attention to his art. But listen: to create great art you also have to create a great audience. In our world the first step in creating a great audience is to control the means of production. Some individual artists can leap over the barrier and become a star in the Imperial center. There are USAmericans who think of Margaret Atwood as a USAmerican. There are entertainment fans who think that Bryan Adams and Michael J. Fox and Shania Twain are USAmericans.

In our world, though, the first step in creating a great audience is to control the means of distribution. In Canada foreigners control the means of distribution. This is true in movies and books and magazines. The jobbers tell the drugstore managers which magazines to put in the front of the racks. They put *People* magazine in the front row. They put *Canadian Forum* in the back row, along with *Knitting Today*. Most Canadians have never heard of *Canadian Forum*. Most of our television advertising is for USAmerican products, because USAmerican megabusiness can afford advertising and governments give them a tax benefit for advertising. So we have a lot of Canadians who watch U.S. television. They can sing the commercials for USAmerican beer. In Canada the teenagers drink USAmerican beer. It is a lot weaker than our beer, and maybe that is one reason why teenagers drink it. But I think it is also because of television advertising.

Don't get me wrong. I am a big fan of the old Miller Light television ads. I would never drink Miller Light because regular U.S. beer is already light, but when I am in the U.S. I drink regional U.S. beer. One of the big stumbling blocks to free trade was the intransigence of the Ontario premier, who did not want to see cheap U.S. beer and wine flooding his province. I don't blame him. His province has the country's biggest beer and wine industry, and more important, the most workers in those industries. He didn't want to have to pay a lot more Employment Insurance benefits to workers put out of work by the taste of teenagers who watch a lot of foreign television.

Okay, that is what the Ontario premier didn't want. What do Canadians want? Rather, what do Canadian artists want? To be more exact, what do Canadian writers want? What do I want, let's say.

What I would like to see, in terms of television and books and magazines and movies and digital tapes, is the world. The technology is there to show me Argentine and Sudanese television. I would like to see it. I would like to see movies from all over the world, not just the big successes from Australia. I think I should be able to lay my hands on all the foreign reading material, and not have to pay huge prices for it. That is what I would like. In a perfect world that is what I would get.

Capitalism is all about what someone wants, what some "I" wants. The capitalist says that what he wants is the basis for all activity. Further, when it comes to others, he says that either those others deep in their hearts want what he wants, or if not, they can be persuaded that that is what they want. The capitalist believes that. It is what animates him. Even people who live under relatively unrestrained capitalism believe that. From my experience I think that most USAmericans believe that other people would like to live the way USAmericans live.

Well, I think that my values and desires are probably the best. I have a hard time not looking down on the human being who does not read. There is nothing intrinsically wrong with the person who does not read. But I have a hard time not feeling superior to him. So I understand to a certain extent how capitalists and USAmericans feel. But we are not right, you know, not always right.

The progressive person believes that what he wants is just one of the integers. What other people in his community or civilization want is also important. That means that if I want to be able to go to the store and buy cheap U.S. beer but another Canadian will lose his job because he bottles more expensive Canadian beer, then I should start weighing. His job is a lot more important than my Saturday night beverage. I say put a tariff on beer.

Here is something that speaks more of long-range loss. First that worker would lose his job. Then we would lose that beer. Then we would all be drinking Miller Light. Right now a lot of us are eating McDonald's hamburgers, and the younger people actually think that hamburgers are supposed to taste like that. In *Maclean's*, a Canadian magazine that is still alive, I read that McDonald's of Canada said that their hamburgers in the Moscow McDonald's taste exactly like the hamburgers in the McDonald's in Toronto or Atlanta. They said that *proudly*.

Well, that is not my point about McDonald's of Canada. McDonald's is one of those U.S. multinationals that is always making a big noise about their sensitivity to the local reality. In Canada, for instance, they always tell us that they use a hundred percent Canadian beef. But they make a ritual of taking down the Canadian flag in their parking lot at sundown. Well, USAmericans take down their flag at sundown. We Canadians do not. We fly our flags at night.

As a literary person I want to suggest that truth comes along with form a lot more than it does with content. But I want both. The best frankfurter I ever ate was sold to me with flourish and relish in a station of the New York subway. The first time I ate a truly tasteless hamburger was the first time I ever ate a McDonald's hamburger in Boston. This will never catch on, I said.

The best hamburgers you can eat are the ones you make in your own back yard. That is true. But the same thing is not true about poems and short stories and novels. For the past three decades I have been pestered by certain Canadian jingoists who want to prevent any U.S. poem from showing its face over the border. One of the unfortunate results of the Canada Council's support of our writing is the disappearance from our university campuses of U.S. writers. The Canada Council gives money to universities and art galleries to pay for visits from Canadian writers. The result is that the universities and galleries get stingy and lazy. They know that they do not have to hustle for poetry; all they have to do is send in a request to the Canada Council.

Before the Canada Council supported these visits I was going to a university on the west coast of Canada. The first poets I ever saw and heard were Marianne Moore, Stephen Spender and Kenneth Patchen. The students there now see the same Canadian poets over and over.

But there are some people in my country who are happy about that situation. They are also virulently against free trade. They are also vehemently against me, because I took as my poetry father William Carlos Williams instead of some bard from Ontario. So you see, though I am not in favour of free trade, I am not against U.S. culture. I am simply in favour of Canadian culture. I think that U.S. books should be available in Canada. I also think that Canadian books should be available in Canada. Further, I think that Canadian books should be available in the U.S. So far only the first of those three possibilities is a sure thing.

I say let us have as much trade as possible. It would be stupid to look at the geography of this continent and ignore the rivers and mountain ranges and coast lines and weather patterns that run north and south. But USAmericans should not be so terribly concerned about our pockets of protectionism. The United States is very active in protecting itself militarily against very much smaller countries. USAmericans should understand our desire to protect ourselves against a giant capitalist market.

But whatever happens, let the words cross the border. Let us keep on talking with each other. Let us write to each other. I am deeply grateful that early in my writing career I could sit in a friend's living room and talk about poetry with Robert Creeley. I am also, on this late date thankful that I can get on a plane to read my poems and talk about writing and things with people in Cleveland or Toronto. I do it almost for free.

Let me end with what I take to be a beautiful poem by Jack Spicer, a U.S. poet honoured more in Vancouver than in any city other than his own San Francisco. The poem speaks of a community that is not based on adversarial trade. You will see why I like it so. This is the first of his "Seven Poems for the Vancouver Festival." It makes mention of the great Canadian game:

Start with a baseball diamond high
In the Runcible Mountain wilderness. Blocked everywhere by
    stubborn lumber. Where even the ocean cannot reach its
    coastline for the lumber of islands or the river its mouth.
A perfect diamond with a right field, center field, left field of
    felled logs spreading vaguely outward. Four sides each
Facet of the diamond.
We shall build our city backwards from each baseline
    extending like a square ray from each distance — you from
    the first-base line, you from behind the second baseman,
    you from behind the shortstop, you from the third-baseline.
We shall clear the trees back, the lumber of our pasts and
    futures back, because we are on a diamond, because it is our
    diamond
Pushed forward from.
And our city shall stand as the lumber rots and Runcible
    Mountain crumbles, and the ocean, eating all of islands,
    comes to meet us.

Off Their Map

I WAS REALLY lucky in 1963 to be in Vancouver when that legendary poetry event happened in the summer: when Allen Ginsberg came back from India, and Charles Olson and Robert Duncan and so forth were there for that event that Warren Tallman invented. I was lucky about three years later to show up in London, Ontario, which of all the places in Canada is probably the most famous in terms of its use of the word "region." That place was the home of James Reaney, the most famous regionalist writer in Canada, who openly espouses the term and always has. It was the home of Greg Curnoe, who, when I arrived there, was publishing a magazine called *Region*. I think it had been three years between *Region* 3 and *Region* 4, but he was still the publisher of *Region*. I was struck by the word. What I did was go back to my training and find out what the hell the word means. Somehow or another it seemed to me that the people in

London were talking about something that I was interested in, but they had a far different idea on what being there meant.

So I did as I usually do ... when you go to word origins, do you go to Skeet or Partridge? I go to Partridge and Audrey Thomas goes to Skeet. I know that. So I went to Partridge to find out what the word "region" was connected with. I realized before that the difference between me and somebody like James Reaney in western Ontario. That had to do with the word "dust." James Reaney was asked in an interview what his idea of heaven would be. Being James Reaney, he said that his idea of heaven would be to go into a big library archive and down into the lowest depths of the archive and be told he could do anything he wants with any of that stuff in there, and he described it in terms of dust having collected on those archives. I thought, that is not what dust meant to me, a little kid growing up in Oliver, B.C. I moved to Oliver, B.C. in 1943, and when I arrived, the town I came to was twenty-one years old. That was how long it had been since the first white people had settled in that part of the valley and made that town. For me, dust meant what happened when a wind came down the valley and picked up the main surface of the ground at that place: dust. One of the differences between us was that in James Reaney's hometown dust settles, and where I came from, dust was always in motion and you turned your back on it if you did not want it in your eyes.

Then I began to say, what are some of the other differences? James Reaney — I sat in his house one time with him and his wife Colleen Thibadeau, a wonderful regionalist poet as well, and we were looking at a photo album. We were looking at photos of his grandparents and their parents and their cousins and their aunts and uncles. They said that they had been over looking at other people's albums, they had been other places in Middlesex County looking at other people's photo albums, and the same people were in them. In some cases, the same photographs were in them. They thought that they could probably do that in a large percentage of the homes in southwest Ontario, in Middlesex County. They lived in Middlesex County and they knew that they lived in Middlesex County. When I was a little kid in grade three, we were told that we lived in Yale County. I do not even know what a county is in British Columbia. I do not even know whether there still are counties in British Columbia. I know that they had something to do with sheriffs. These were people that took prisoners from here to there. I never learned the names of any other counties in British Columbia.

Another big difference is names. If you go to southwest Ontario, around London, where James Reaney and Greg Curnoe and the Nihilist Spasm Band and all those people lived, they know what county they live in, they know what township road they live on and they know the names of clumps of trees. If they see a little clump of trees, they say, "Oh yeah. That woodlot has been in the McReynolds family for four generations." Their street names are the same names that are in all other Ontario towns, Dundas, King, Dufferin, Queen. I grew up in a town where the only things that had names were waterfalls, mountains, rivers, and stuff like that. Sometimes different people called them different names. What we called Car Mountain, other people called something else. Streets did not have names. There were no street names at all. We lived on streets, and I think technically down at the town hall or maybe somewhere in Victoria there was a piece of paper that said the names of those streets, but there were no street signs.

If you are living in southwest Ontario where they proudly use the word "region," what they are talking about is something that is a collective pride and a collective obedience to something that they recognize as plural, as "something we do." When I was a kid and as I grew up, my context was what "I" and this dust are doing and what those other "I"s are doing. All the other people that I knew were "I"s. We were not Jamaicans at all, but we all would recognize that we were all called "I."

That leads me to my poetic; it was derived from Charles Olson, and still is. What I want to do is make an argument with the word "region." Not simply because I grew up in British Columbia, which is mostly made of valleys that are nowhere near the ocean or any goddamn arbutus tree. I grew up in cactus country. I am really glad that my friend Colin Browne has made some films up there, showing what God's idea of nature is like. Here is Olson as opposed to "region." This is in a lecture he did once called "THE AREA, and the DISCIPLINE of, TOTALITY."

"I knew no more then that what I did, that to put down *space* and *fact* and hope, by the act of sympathetic magic that words are apt to seem when one first uses them, that I would invoke for others those sensations of life that I was small witness to, part doer of. But the act of writing the book added a third noun, equally abstract: *stance*. For after it was done, and other work in verse followed, I discovered that the fact of this space located a man differently in respect to any act, so much so and with ..." and on and on.

I pretty well concur with Olson's idea about a special view of history, that history is something that you enact while you are doing it. It is not something that you are caused by or something that you are a victim of or something that you are the proof of. It is something that you enact while you are doing it. So is place. So is the spot that you are in. There can be no spot that you are in unless you are in it. Any awareness of place has to include awareness of awareness, but if you are in a region, that doesn't matter. It doesn't matter whether you are there or not. The word "region" is connected with the word Raj, that guy that used to run "Inja" for the Brits. That word is related to "region." And so is the "rect" in the word correct. So is the "reg" in the word regal. See what I am coming to? That "region" all has to do with rules.

And what is a region? I was talking one time to a famous Canadian novelist. I will not say who it was, but his initials were Hugh Hood. His Canada included a small town in Ontario, and Toronto and Montreal. I said to him, and I meant it seriously because I really admire his writing, "Hugh, you are maybe the country's best regionalist writer." He would not speak to me for a week after that. He hated that thought. It had not entered his mind. You know why? He lived in Montreal and before that he went to school in Toronto. What is the other half of the phrase? Toronto and the regions. *The Globe and Mail* and the regional versions of *The Globe and Mail*. Or the CBC and the regional stations. As Daphne Marlatt has said, if you consider yourself a regional writer, it seems to me that you either have to do it with a great deal of irony, as Greg Curnoe did, or you have to totally agree that you are going to be colonized. That you are not going to be in place, but put in that place. You will be seen as one of the functions of that place, which is exactly what thematic criticism and that aspect of Canadian nationalism was all about. Regionalism — they really liked that a lot.

Remember the little introduction that Sheila Watson made the first time she ever read *The Double Hook* at Edmonton, at MacEwan College? She said, I wanted to write something that takes place in this little place in the West, but I did not want it to be a regionalist novel and I did not want it to be a western. She wanted it to be a book that somehow or another offered a consciousness of that place. Not a subjugation to that place.

According to *Ana Historic*, Daphne Marlatt too, when she lived on the North Shore, spoke one language inside the house or was encouraged to speak one language, or let's say her character was. One dialect inside the house and another dialect outside the house. Maybe that was just a function of living in North Vancouver. Actually I did too: at home we had to say, "Oh, I have thrown it out," but on the street we were allowed to say, "I thrun it out."

The Struggle for Pork in Real Canadian Poetry

The Example of
Mrs. Buchanan

by Starling Mattress

AS I HAVE stated correctly elsewhere in my just struggle for a real expression of true consciousness in the proper terms of our people's social being, almost all Canadian poets have been conditioned by the swine in power to express ideas that champion the predator class in this country in order to serve the interests of a foreign hegemony situated in an anarchistic imperial power that has major territorial proximity to Canada. Those poets who endeavour to create a true consciousness of the class struggle by shifting the mirror of poetic investigation to the shores of our unique roots have always been savagely suppressed by the comprador interests dedicated to colonial rule and individualist fragmentation. An obvious and undeniable example is the suppression of the heroic verse drama written by members of the Arnprior chapter of the Lavrenty Pavlovich Beria Society in the mid-seventies. In a very real sense the exploiting class, in the persons of the editors of every newspaper and magazine in Ontario and eventually the other provinces, suppressed this example of real independent Canadian literature by closing ranks and refusing to publish it in their pages, those pages habitually covered with the false consciousness perpetrated by the imperialist elite whose rulers are safely ensconced in the cockpit of the U.S. stock exchange.

Meanwhile, hundreds of poems and plays are produced in Canada by the unwitting or fawning pawns of foreign editors and writers and critics who are employed by the U.S. State Department to infiltrate our culture and plant the seeds of anarchism, driving out our necessary drama of unique history.

We must, however, be aware of our literature, flawed as it might be, because our literature is the absolute expression of our consciousness as a people. In such U.S. beachheads as Vancouver, B.C., the majority of citizens travel to work with the anarchistic individualist verses of U.S. poets running through their heads. In fact the city of Vancouver is occupied by U.S. poets and recent "immigrants" who go from house to house instructing Vancouverites in the imperialist expansionist rhetoric of U.S. poetry. In a very real sense the battleground is the streets of Vancouver and the other Canadian cities threatened by the lyrical falling of U.S. foreign policy. We must bring the struggle to the streets of cities such as Vancouver. Before we can bring the agents of U.S. poetry to the people's courts where they belong, we must bring the poetry of birthright Canadians to the people of our metropolises and rural enclaves. Flawed as are the verses of Mrs. Walter Buchanan, for instance, we must see to it that Vancouverites, Haligonians and Thunderbayers hear poems such as

"Piggy" passing through their heads as they travel to work, be it menial or intellectual.

But a consciousness of our unique cultural production does not preclude a necessary sociological and class-conscious critical analysis of the writings that our cultural workers have left to us. For as I have correctly stated elsewhere, to understand our poetry is to understand the ruling ideology of the time in which it found expression. Mrs. Walter Buchanan, like every Ontario housewife of her time, was in many ways the willing spokeswoman of both major colonialisms vying for political and poetical power over Canada. Yet she was at the same time the possessor of true Canadian aspirations and spirit. Real literary critics in our own time can both appreciate an often suppressed example of Canadian expression and, by reading the literature correctly, defend our country against the expansionist ambitions of the giant dragon on the other side of the national demarcation situated midway between the shark-infested Caribbean Sea and the gentler and more noble waters of our far and true north.

Though the *vendu* editors and critics in Canada have conspired to suppress the facts, "Piggy" is Mrs. Buchanan's valiant response to an inferior but highly lauded U.S. poem, the often anthologized "Richard Cory" by Edwin Arlington Robinson, who was an agent of expansionist U.S. poetry from the time of the so-called Spanish-American War until his death during the Great Depression, an event brought on by the glut of bourgeois individualist poems in the boom years following the First World War, which was entered by Canada two years and more before U.S. involvement. In the Norton anthologies that celebrate hegemonic canons, Robinson is designated as a poet who "surpasses" all contemporary poets except Yeats. He attended Harvard University, as did many Black Mountain poets, such as Robert Creeley and Stephen Scubbie.

In "Richard Cory," a little poem whose title character bears the same initials as the aforesaid Robert Creeley, Robinson, ten years before Mrs. Buchanan's "Piggy," unashamedly praises the type of U.S. anarchic individualism. He is described as "imperially slim." Furthermore, he "glittered when he walked," an obvious reference to the "heroic" U.S. men of the "gilded age," praised incessantly by the renowned U.S. writer Mark Twain. In the third stanza Robinson lauds his hero for being "rich — yes, richer than a king." In other words Richard Cory personifies the U.S. ambition to replace British Imperialism with a U.S. brand, richer and completely free from the order of the British model. Cory is the epitome, though Robinson does not see this, of the falseness in the so-called American Revolution, by which the supposed revolutionaries became individualist exploiters of the duped workers who were manipulated into the delusion that each individual could rise to power: "In fine, we thought that he was everything/ To make us wish that we were in his place."

Finally, Richard Cory, the self-made man, hero of the narrator who speaks for his fellow citizens, and hero too of Edwin Arlington Robinson, goes home and commits suicide, the ultimate act of individualism, and he does it with a pistol, the emblem of U.S. rugged individualism in a thousand stories of Western expansionism. U.S. readers, and the international hostages of exported U.S. culture, are instructed to admire authors who kill themselves rather than learning to live in a peaceful community. Ernest Hemingway, Sylvia Plath and Hart Crane — whose poem "Cape Hatteras" takes place only a few miles from Black Mountain, are but three or four examples.

As I have correctly indicated earlier, Mrs. Buchanan's "Piggy" is an unambiguous Canadian response to the U.S. author Robinson's poem, which would have found its way to her farmhouse within a year or two of its publication, among the trainloads of U.S. poetry that were imported by the Canadian lackeys of their masters in New York and Boston and rural North Carolina.

On the one hand one can see the attempt by Mrs. Buchanan, whose last name is identical to that of an idle rich woman who loves and adulates the title character in U.S. novelist F. Scott Fitzgerald's (who was named after the poet who wrote the imperialist "Star-Spangled Banner") *The Great Gatsby*. Fitzgerald's kowtowing after the powerful bourgeoisie can be seen in his choice of title. In this way he is only another in a long line of U.S. writers, such as Edwin Arlington Robinson, content to idolize the robber barons who typify the aspirations of the American "Revolution."

Mrs. Buchanan, obviously calling upon her native ability to differentiate the true Canadian consciousness from the U.S. Imperialist ethos, produces the details that will mark her protagonist off from the foreign model. Where Richard Cory is elevated to more than royal proportions, the Canadian hero will be correctly praised "be he little or big." While Cory "was a gentleman from sole to crown,/ Clean favored," the Canadian benefactor "cares not a fig to be neat or trig," and indeed often wears the soil of honest labour. As we have seen, the well-dressed U.S. *poseur* is "imperially slim," but his Canadian rival carries on his working class body "meat — juicy meat."

And although the U.S. ideal ends alone, turning his back on his fellow citizens for his own anarchistic purposes with his beloved pistol, "the pig is a friend that will last to the end." Mrs. Buchanan does not relax in her demonstration of the inherent Canadian desire to seek harmonious community with emphasis on a whole people rather than on individualists. We see in the over-praised U.S. poem that its hero "went without the meat, and cursed the bread" during his pursuit of glitter and "crown," but Piggy will respond to the needs of his community "[i]f his trough we but fill with plenty of swill." Unlike the self-absorbed U.S. hero, "the pig nobly shares, and our burden oft bears."

Such a trenchant challenge to the canon imposed by the ruling liberals of Canadian politics and culture, shaped as it is by their foreign masters, was bound to be suppressed and censored by the satraps in the country's academic elite. That is why our students will not find the works of Mrs. Walter Buchanan in such anthologies as liberal Gary Geddes's *Fifteen Poets Times Twenty*, in which a patriot will look unsuccessfully for my own epic, for instance, nor encounter them in the few paltry courses devoted to "Canadian" literature in our universities. An equal to Mrs. Buchanan's challenge will not be met in Earle Birney's sycophantic approval of U.S. highway billboards, or E. J. Pratt's deification of the U.S. robber barons who were hired by the arch continentalist John A. Macdonald to build a falsely Canadian railroad to the West Coast.

Perhaps the finest moment of Mrs. Buchanan's poem comes at the moment that it begins its second half. That positioning itself perhaps serves as a wry attack upon the U.S. reverence for the exploitative frontier. Here the Canadian poet exposes the grandiosity of the U.S. culture of banditry and piracy by introducing the only moment at which her juicy protagonist shows any tendency to larceny. It is a masterstroke to superimpose the pig's looting of her garden against the far greater threat of U.S. designs upon our entire country. In a very real sense this is a very real comparison. At the same time the poet suggests the busy creature as the model for true Canadian scholars and artists: "[h]e may dig, he may root." Not only do those verbs rhyme correctly with "pig" and "loot," unlike the anarchic poetry imported of late from the administrative offices of Black Mountain, but they present images of earth and roots, a beacon for following generations of labourers at the loom of our history and literature.

NOTE ON CONTRIBUTOR

Starling Mattress is professor of Patriotic Studies at Simon Fraser University, and a member of the Burnaby chapter of the Lavrenty Pavlovich Beria Society. He is the author of several books of poetry published by the Mattress Press, and the ground-breaking volume *The Struggle for Correct Real Canadian Literature.*

British Columbia

What Did You Expect?

CANADIANS LOVE THEIR stories about USAmerican tourists and the questions they ask when they get to, say, Vancouver.

"No, that's not Japan, Sir; that's Vancouver Island."

"No, Ma'am, our flag doesn't come in any other colours."

Most Canadians live pretty close to the U.S. border, so they get to see lots of USAmericans. I grew up by Highway 97, for instance, about fourteen miles from the border. Whenever we saw a brand new car going really fast, we would shout "AmAIRicans!"

Canadians love their stories about what USAmericans bring with them when they come across the line. During the summertime school vacations I used to hang out with my friends at the Highway 97 border crossing, glugging down Coca-Cola on a bright 90-degree day, counting the California station wagons with skis on their roof-racks.

"What do you mean, we can't bring our .357 Magnums into Canada? How the hang are we supposed to protect ourselves against polar bears?"

As anyone can see, this kind of fun is really a kind of alloy. Part of it is made up of the famous USAmerican ignorance of their neighbour. The other part is made up of Canadian envy and hurt feelings that they don't matter enough to their neighbour. Anyone can imagine the complex of feelings in 1979, when the Vancouver Whitecaps were all set to play some New York team for the North American Soccer League championship, and a New York television station referred to Vancouver as a "village" on the coast north of Seattle. Naturally, the Whitecaps beat the New Yorkers, and six years later the North American Soccer League went out of business. Insulted Canadians had to wait a few years, until the USAmericans in Atlanta carried our flag upside down in a little military parade in Turner Stadium shortly before the Toronto Blue Jays won the World Series there.

It happens the other way round, of course. Years and years ago my future wife Angela and I were up in the Okanagan Valley visiting my parents during the wintertime university vacations. I suggested that we spend New Year's Eve in Oroville, Washington. Angela made me change out of my canoe moccasins into black leather shoes, because she didn't want me to stand out as a rube in the night club in which we would be consuming martinis. She had never been out of British Columbia, and she was from a town halfway up Vancouver Island. Her idea of Oroville, Washington came from movies starring Cary Grant and Olivia DeHavilland. She thought the skyline of Oroville would be something like the skyline of, say, Detroit, and that when midnight came we would be

in a room with white tablecloths on the banquette tables, and
confetti falling from the high ceiling.

Oroville is a sweaty little border town in the summer and a
parking strip for pickup trucks on New Year's Eve. The drummer
for the little band in the Happytime Bar went ticky ticky ticky all
night. I just loved it, sitting there drinking beer you can see through
and smoking cigarettes that burn up in about five minutes. This was
the town where I used to buy bubble gum when we couldn't get it
on our side of the border just after the war, and where I waited till
I was nearly at the drinking age before getting into the Happytime
Bar. My wife wound up with a fond memory of that night, too.
And when we finally went to Detroit in the sixties, she didn't say
anything about my cowboy boots.

But some things run in the family, and the times do change.
When I drove south with my thirteen-year-old daughter years and
years later, she just holed up during our one night in San Francisco.
She wanted to get out of town before the earthquake hit, and she
didn't want to look around town because there might be serial
killers with .357 Magnums out there.

I guess you could say that some people don't get enough information about other people, and some people get too much information
about other people.

But here in British Columbia we are the Canadians of Canada.
When I talk to Canadian nationalists in Toronto, I always tell them
that all their talk about USAmerican imperialism is very familiar to
us people out in the far west. We always feel as if folks in Toronto/
Ottawa/Montreal sound a little too much like the great USAmerican
poet Walt Whitman, who wrote "And what I assume, you too
shall assume." Everyone remembers Walt Whitman, who was truly

a great poet, and who spent time in London, Ontario with his literary executor, the great psychologist Richard M. Bucke. Walt said that one day Cuba and Canada would be part of the United States.

This was around the time that British Columbia sort of decided to be part of Canada. In 1866 the colonies on Vancouver's Island and the mainland were joined. A year later, Canada was invented back east, and the USAmericans snapped up Alaska. Pretty soon there was a political battle going on among B.C.'s twenty-three legislators and their special interest groups. The new Crown Colony had a most promising ocean to its west, but it also had USAmericans to the north and the south, and since the gold rush of 1858, an awful lot of them right up close. A post-colonial British Columbia had three alternatives: become an independent nation, join the new Canadian confederation, or say yes to Walt, and join the United States. There were supporters of each alternative. There still are.

The Canadian government offered a railroad as a signing bonus, and that did the trick. We decided to play for the Canadians. We became Canada's Alaska, a new province halfway to China, a really hard walnut in the USAmerican nut-cracker. We thought that those people back east had better show their appreciation. Now we have been complaining about them ever since. If you will look at political representation in the province, you will sometimes find the leftist New Democratic Party holding a majority provincially, and the fundamentalist or opportunist right wing party holding most of our federal seats. That means that some areas of the province sent both left and right to power. When B.C. voters are not electing social democrats to run the province, they elect the lunatic right.

When party politics entered the West Coast scene during the second provincial election of 1903, some people thought that the Liberals and the Conservatives, the parties back east, would

naturally contend out here. But soon the real nature of the elec-
torate became known. A few decades later these two parties joined
to fight off the leftist workers, and then practically disappeared as
the fundamentalist right arose in the era of the 1950s as something
called Social Credit. People thought of the Tories and the Liberals
as eastern parties that were pretty well interchangeable. In B.C. we
went for polarization. Nowadays the right wingers call themselves
the Liberals. Selfish voters don't care what they are currently called,
as long as they oppose social programming.

We were more-or-less saying: you people back east don't have
a clue where we are coming from anyway, so we will run our
own circus. Often we focused our sense of alienation on specific
issues — manufacturers out here faced exorbitant freight rates to
get merchandise to Ontario; national elections are over before
voting gets to our time zone, because most parliamentary seats
are in Quebec and Ontario; the Vancouver Canucks have to travel
twenty times as far as the Montreal Canadiens do just to complete
an NHL schedule, and then what if they were to get into the play-
offs, eh?

The answer from Ontario always seems to be: who cares? Who
knows anything about the other side of the mountains? In effect we
get portrayed in two contradictory ways. We are the repository of
all the nut cases, all the cuckoo trends, all the bizarre ideas, all the
loose stuff that piles up here when someone lifts Canada up by
the Atlantic handle. On the other hand, our difference is never
acknowledged as part of the Canadian makeup.

On the one hand easterners think that we fill our hot tubs with
Perrier water. On the other hand, here we are in January, wearing
shorts and sandals and carrying umbrellas, looking up at a billboard
designed in Ontario. It shows the latest rugged winter tire crunching

through the deepest snow of a "typical" Canadian winter.

So we send back contradictory images of ourselves. For decades Vancouver artists, poets, dance companies, and musicians have provided an avant-garde that periodically tromps eastward. Yet Vancouver is still a company town, just as British Columbia is still a company province. It's a big logging town, and logging towns are not known for being hip.

Toronto is, of course, the centre of the universe, as we so often say in our envious cynicism. It is the centre of Canada, and the people there are naturally centrists. They like the middle of the road and the middle class in their entertainment and the arts. The famous Canadian novelists who seem to be winning all the international prizes these days live in Toronto, and the big publishing houses are in Toronto, and the literary agents and publicists and critics and reviewers and professors. Those novelists write middle-of-the-road novels, the kind that people like to read, the kind that have stood the test of time.

As far as the literary crowd in Toronto is concerned, Atlantic Canada is from an earlier time, and British Columbia has not been around long. Writers from what Toronto calls "the regions" should fulfill certain stereotypes. East Coast writers should be purveyors of quaint Celtic tall-stories told in somewhat archaic forms. British Columbia writers should be rough romantic logger poets and outdoorsy writers of novels about bush-crazy gun-toting giants. If a poet from B.C. wants to get taken up for a while by the book crowd in Toronto, he or she had better show up in logging boots and a plaid shirt.

The truth is that the most interesting literary and artistic communities in Vancouver have always been impatient with both stereotypes and the middle distance. So they have created stuff that communicates with underground far-out literary and artistic work in New York and San Francisco and Paris. Eventually the existence of this incomprehensible avant-garde gets rumoured a little in Toronto, and another stereotype is born — the *artiste* from outer space who lives in the shadows and emerges from time to time in a purple coffee shop to recite poems that will never make sense to more than twenty-eight readers.

No wonder easterners don't know what to expect here, any more than USAmericans know what they're going to find in Canada. But if they come here to stay they know that they will have to learn to live with the Klingons. I have known several writers, famous for representing their neighbourhoods in Montreal and Toronto, who came out, had a look at the mountains and bicycles, and announced that they could not comprehend the possibility of human life in such a place. Not enough subways, not enough highly salted sandwich meat, not enough industrial grime on the windowsills. I have known other eastern writers who decided to come here and stay, but in order to do so they had to burn all their old clothes and learn to cook with tofu.

But really, back east they have just the vaguest idea of this place. Let me give you an example from the literary world, from the people who designate themselves the cultural nation builders. In 1959 a major Toronto publisher, McClelland & Stewart, finally broke down and published Sheila Watson's short novel *The Double Hook*. For a year or two the reviewers and critics argued about what this strange B.C. book was. It was unlike anything written in Canada before its time, but it has become canonized. When eastern academics persuaded McClelland & Stewart to publish a useful series of literary texts in paperback, they included *The Double Hook*. In a style part-fable, part-realist, part-lyric, it tells about the lives of figures who live among the rolling hills and sun-dried mud of the lower Cariboo-Chilcotin, cattle country. For edition after edition, the New Canadian Library back cover touted "[t]his compelling and imaginative first novel with its locale in the Rockies."

No, sir, that isn't Japan, and those aren't the Rockies.

After I wrote to the main editor, and then went to Ottawa and spoke with him, M&S removed that annoying piece of misinformation. But those literature professors are joined by a lot of other easterners who think that the Rockies can be seen from downtown Vancouver. Maybe they should talk with my nieces' geography teacher. My nieces went from our side of the line down to Oroville, Washington to go to school. One day their geography teacher mentioned the Rocky Mountains, and my nieces (they're twins) said that they had visited the Canadian Rockies. No, said their friendly geography teacher, the Rockies are in the United States. I think she probably said "America."

Well, there *are* a few little Rockies in Canada. But they are along the Alberta-British Columbia border. They are perhaps a twelve-hour drive from Vancouver, and not much closer to the south-west corner of the Cariboo. You have to pass through or over about five other mountain ranges to get to them.

Do I sound as if I am giving voice to regional complaint? Yes, I have heard people in Texas and Western Australia grousing about those damned know-nothing power mongers back east. Sure, I am getting off what my pals in Montreal call a *kvetch*. But I am also leading into a little survey of difference. I have said in my history book about B.C. that people back east live in history and expect us to, but we live instead in geography. It might also be argued that we find it more comfortable to live in myth and legend than in history.

What would you expect of a province that once had a premier who had legally changed his name to Amor de Cosmos? Or a later premier whose home was literally a castle in the middle of a tourist theme park operated by his wife? What about the province's first chief justice, Matthew Begbie, known as the "Hanging Judge?" He liked to mete out his own punishment. Once he was staying in a hotel upcountry, and he heard two ruffians discussing him in unfriendly terms just below his window. So he emptied his chamber pot on their heads. Justice could be swift in pioneer days. The punishment fit the crime, as they say.

Easterners shake their heads when they hear stuff about what they call the Left Coast. We just say "what's wrong with that?" We have a highways minister who loses his driver's license after his twentieth speeding ticket? What's wrong with that? Our stock exchange is a cross between a motorcycle gang and a one-ring circus? What's wrong with that? We once went to war with the United States because someone shot one of our pigs? What do you expect?

What do you expect? That's my question just about every time I talk with someone about my home province. Yes, we laugh at USAmericans because they expect us to be living in igloos. We laugh at easterners because they will not drop their idea that what's good for Ontario is good for Canada. But we are not satisfied with that. We also harbour strange notions about *each other* in British Columbia. I have mentioned that I'm from the Okanagan Valley. If BCers can say to Ontarians that they are *our* USAmericans, we Okanagan people can say to the powers that be on the Coast that they are *our* Ontarians. We have had it up to here with Coast chauvinism.

We vote for the fundamentalist right because those city slickers vote for the left and the centre. The big television stations are in Vancouver and Victoria, so we all buy satellite dishes and watch stuff from Detroit. When I was a kid growing up alongside highway 97, we sent a small percentage of our high school graduates to university. Half of them went to Vancouver, and the other half to Spokane. (Canada's most famous children's poet, who lives in Toronto, pronounced it "Spokain," to rime with something like rain.)

Here's the main thing that ticked us off about the Coasters. Just as Ontario figures that it is by and large Canada, so the Coasters figure they are by and large British Columbia. They encourage outsiders to refer to B.C. as the "West Coast Province." Actually, a tiny percentage of the province is at the coast. It should be called the "Mountain Province." They refer to rain as "typical B.C. weather." Typical B.C. weather is more likely to be a succession of a hundred hot suns over a landscape made of brown grass and twigs that snap when you step on them.

But pick up a magazine in Illinois or Manitoba, and if there is an advertisement from the British Columbia tourism branch, here is what you will see: a big white ferry boat gliding past some cedared island on its way into the setting sun. A few killer whales arcing out of the salt water. A husky guy with a big smile standing in a powerboat and holding up a huge salmon. A romantic couple with umbrellas, walking arm in arm along a misty seawall.

Coast chauvinism.

Those people from California drive up highway 97, air-conditioning at the max, staring forward into a series of heat mirages rising from the pavement, and wondering when they will be able to use their skis and when they will have to get out the waterproof gore-tex. When I tell people in Louisiana that I grew up on the desert, they get a funny evasive smile on their faces. They're thinking: oh, I wonder what those *Canadians* think a desert is?

But we do know, of course. We grew up in geography, not history, after all. History has always held up impossible dreams. The sun will never set on the British Empire. The North American Indian is fated to disappear as Darwinian principles take their course. Cuba and Canada will take their places as states in the U.S. federation. The twentieth century will belong to Canada.

Everyone knows that the explorers were always being surprised by what they found. The popular schoolroom myth used to be that Christopher Columbus thought that he had arrived in the East Indies, so he called the indigenous people of the Caribbean islands Indians. That's the paradigm. What were explorers expecting to find around here? The Spanish, who were to leave their names on most of the islands along our coast, were looking for something they had been lucky enough to find in the New World for over two centuries. They were looking for people who had never heard about *Jesus Cristo*, people who could be taught to wear crosses around their necks. While they were at it, the Spaniards would confiscate the paraphernalia of the savage superstitions that had kept these people in their abject condition. That these items were often made of gold was certainly a welcome bonus. The gold that once decorated the heathen walls of Tenotchtitlan, the capital city of the pagan Aztecs, was now shining on the walls of a church in Spain, a lustrous symbol of God's incorruptible bounty.

The USAmericans, too, would later be up here looking for converts and gold. When Benedict Arnold entered Quebec with U.S. troops in 1775, he was expecting the people there to rush to his side, naturally eager to escape the British yoke. Who in his right mind would not leap at the chance to become USAmericans? But that war of liberation did not work, and Arnold went back home. Later, of course, he became a famous prodigal son, returning to the British cause in North America, and today his name is symbolic of renewed patriotism.

A hundred years later the United States had grown in size, thanks to the petitions of neighbours to the south and the west who had long dreamed of joining the Union. What could be more natural and historically logical than to offer opportunity to the people who lived at the westernmost reach of British North America? The politicians and their lobbyists in Washington, D.C., were of course claiming that the southern half of the colony rightly belonged to the United States. "Fifty-four forty or fight!" was a popular slogan around the time of one presidential election. Thank goodness neither was to occur, and the border remained at forty-nine.

But ever since the California gold rush of '49 had salt-petered out, and the gold-dust boys had come north for the Fraser River gold rush of 1858, there was a kind of USAmerican fifth column operating all through the island colony and the mainland colony. Boatloads of prospectors and real-estate sharpies and saloon ladies came by ship from San Francisco to Victoria, turning that remote little colony of a few hundred Englishmen and natives into a developer's dream come true. In six weeks 225 buildings suddenly appeared, hotels and bars and lawyers' offices, all the signs of a seamier life come to replace the genteel frontier administration of James Douglas, the Hudson's Bay fur boss who had become Her Majesty's governor. Land prices shot up by 3,000 percent, mixed news for the English government men who had been putting away a few lots for themselves. Now there were ten recent USAmericans for every proper Englishman in town. And these people just took it for granted that they were acting out an extension of their own gold rush.

All these robust people from the south, pockets bulging with money, made Governor Douglas nervous. But he had his little army detachment, even if they were only the Royal Engineers. And he had the Hanging Judge. The Hanging Judge was usually hanging native men, but he had a lot of scorn for USAmericans. He was not about to see his bailiwick turned into the wild west, and he made a hobby out of taking handguns away from the foreigners. While sentencing a USAmerican rowdy to three years for mayhem, he pronounced, "We have a law which prohibits the use of bowie knives, pistols or other offensive weapons, and in those countries over which the British flag flies there is no necessity for carrying or using offensive weapons." How are we going to protect ourselves against grizzly bears, asked the visitors.

Not many gold rush people stick around when the boom is over, but some did, becoming pioneer British Columbians, operating barber shops or raising cattle on what used to be Indian land. When the new gold rush people came tromping through the province on their way to the Yukon gold rush in the late nineties, the recent settlers said look at all them barbarous Yankees. There ought to be a law.

The Spaniards and the USAmericans might have been looking for souls and gold, but what were the English looking for? When George Vancouver was sent to our serrated coast in the 1790's, he was disappointed that he had not been sent to the Atlantic or Caribbean to fight the French, but he did what King George III told him to do: make a detailed survey map of the entire coast, explain our interests to the Spanish, pick up any loose gold or diamonds the

Indian people might have to sell — and while you are at it, find the western entrance to that damned Northwest Passage.

That's what the English were expecting to find. One of those deep inlets along the northwest coast was sure to be the way to the passage that would allow the English navy and English merchants to get to England fast from the extensive English mercantile territories in Asia. Everyone knew there was such a passage. God would not have laid out solid land from ice to ice. The Spanish could continue to court storm and death around Cape Horn; the English would run the north Pacific as soon as they found that damned Passage.

They had been trying for a long time from east to west. The sea captain who found the way would win £20,000 from the British Parliament. Small ships spent whole winters locked in ice. Valiant sailors became the heroes of Canadian literature manufactured centuries later. They were buoyed, you might say, by two certainties: Britannia ruled the waves, and there was a Passage up there, waiting for the men who could navigate the right path among those thousands of islands. It even had a name — the Strait of Anian. Earle Birney and I, a couple of B.C. poets, enjoyed writing about the Strait of Anian. It is such a British Columbia thing, if you follow me.

The name was given around 1500 by a Portuguese sea captain named Gaspar Corte-Real, who claimed to have found the Northwest Passage and named it after his brother. Soon the Strait of Anian showed up on the world maps of Italian grand dukes and Spanish dons, as Europeans spread their merchants' arms to welcome the pelf of the entire globe. And sailors from every seagoing European nation kept discovering the Northwest Passage. Juan de Fuca, a Greek from Italy, found it for the Spanish, at about where the Fraser River meets the sea. Naturally, it led to enormous fields of gold and jewellery. Then a Spaniard named Admiral de Fonte found it, and travelled eastward until he met a ship from Boston. Even the French, whose Pacific adventures tended to happen around the tropics, claimed to have gone eastward to Hudson's Bay.

The trouble was that the Strait of Anian kept getting lost. It was worse than El Dorado. It was worse than the Fountain of Youth. It was worse than all those famous lost goldmines in Arizona. If an Englishman could find the Northwest Passage, Britain would beat out Russia, Spain, France, Holland and the United States in the Pacific trade. So George Vancouver, wintering in the tropics and exploring fathom by fathom northward in the summers, spent half a decade making precise charts of the Pacific rim from San Francisco Bay to the Aleutians. He never found the Northwest Passage, but he made maps that are still being used by sailors such as the U.S. Coast Guard.

Of course somebody did eventually find the Northwest Passage. But you don't see many British merchant ships using it. The Northwest Passage has too much north and not enough west in it. And it is a long way from British Columbia. There are some waterways that traverse the province, but it took idiot-heroes to negotiate transportation links along them.

Great expectations. For some reason this land was called Gold Mountain in China. And the Vancouver suburb of Richmond has become a city of Chinese-language malls and restaurants surrounded by new homes lived in by recent Chinese-speaking immigrants who came to settle there, so the story goes, because Chinese real estate salespeople translate the city's name literally. Of course Richmond, like Surrey, got its name because it is on the other side of the river, just as in London, England. But there was a time when Richmond was literally made of rich earth — the lovely silt that was carried down the long Fraser River, and became for a while the best vegetable-and-fruit-growing soil in North America. Expectations. British Columbia has for a few hundred years been a place to which people come. All my life I have been surrounded by people who came from another country. It's normal. One of my grandfathers came as an orphan from southwestern England. The other came as an economic refugee from the Ozarks. An awful lot of the B.C. voters who recently sent a majority of fundamentalist right-wingers to Parliament did so because they felt surrounded by immigrants who got here later than the families of these voters did.

But there was a nation that was here before any of these Europeans or Asians were. In fact, there were twenty-four nations, maybe more if you count more meticulously. There were as many languages as there were in Europe. The land that would be called British Columbia was about as big as Europe. And it was as diverse. In the sparse forest of little trees in the northeast, the Dene-thah and the Dunne-za needed a lot of land because they were hunters and gatherers. The gathering season was short, and the hunting often happened over snow. They did not have time to settle down and build palaces. On the coast there were people who lived on the bounty of the sea and the rivers and the cedars. They built towns with large houses and poles and boardwalks and marinas. These people were a big surprise to the eighteenth-century European tourists.

The eighteenth-century Europeans and the nineteenth-century Europeans were highly conscious of the differences between Germans and French, English and Spanish, because there were always alliances and wars. But for them an Indian was an Indian.

You could hardly blame the Native Nations, trade partners or political enemies, if they did not take the time to discriminate between the various pale visitors. (Nowadays it is pretty normal for a citizen of the state of Washington to refer to his northern neighbour's place as "Canada." Still, I guess that is better than hearing it referred to as "More Washington.")

The various Native Nations have paid a price for the indiscriminate policies of the white usurpers. When the reserve system was set up, for instance, the Native people were allotted ten acres a family, usually nowhere near valley floors. A Dene-thah family could not live on ten acres. In any given ten acres of the northeast there were likely to be no animals to hunt and no berries to gather. The fashioning of Indian policies went on at the southern coast.

People ought to know more about each other. In order to do so, they should not read advertising, but they should read. If they are curious they will never run out of interesting things to find out. The most interesting things are always the ones that relieve a person of her misconceptions.

If you were a California tourist or an Ontario adventurer driving north on Highway 97 into British Columbia, I could offer you a tip that will do away with at least two misconceptions. After getting through customs you could turn right, into the town of Osoyoos. There you would be next to an ecological preserve called the Pocket Desert. This Pocket Desert is a special place within the regular desert. It is the last and only place on earth for lots and lots of species. One of them is the northern scorpion. As far as the entomological world knows, the northern scorpion is the only insect in the world that suckles its young.

Who would have expected that?

Vancouver as
Postmodern Poetry

*The text is a tissue of quotations drawn
from the innumerable centres of culture.*

— ROLAND BARTHES

THE FIRST TIME some Vancouver poets heard the term "postmodern"
it was from the American poet Charles Olson, and appeared to
be a continuation of the New World's westward drift away from
Europe. Heroic International Modernism had been a story being
written, often by Americans, in old European cities, where the
persistent layering of myths could be seen in the architecture,
centuries standing (especially before the World War II bombard-
ment) before the present eye. The ancient world lies in the earth
below Paris and pushes its way up through history.

European capitals, like those of the Middle East, are inland,
beside rivers, where the oldest myths were first made into chronicles.
The oldest cities were *centres*, beside the ever-arriving. Heroes were
men who dared to depart, especially the stable earth. But a return,
of the heroes or social rewards, was the aim, an ending at home, a

closure. Charles Olson and the young Vancouver poets of 1960 were conscious more than anything else of living by the sea, at the edge, on a margin.

For the sake of the pages to come, we will assume that there is such a thing as postmodernism in poetry. It may have been glimpsed by a very few people in Toronto in the fifties, and then seen to re-enter Canada by way of Vancouver at the end of that decade. It came from New England, New York, San Francisco, Mexico City, and a lot of smaller places, some of them inland. When the more academic, Freudianized, Marxianized version arrived in the New World a couple of decades later, it spread itself out at the university faculties, but learned to accept hybridization among the poets who had learned New World ways.

If the historical fiction of the first person singular may be entered here, I was among the new Vancouver poets in 1960, and wish to admit that if I am writing an essay about Vancouver poetry, I am experiencing the embarrassment of the dead author — still standing, like the ninth letter of the alphabet. I, like most of my companions of 1960, went away from the city in the early sixties, and like some of them, returned in the seventies. In my view, Vancouver poetry became very lively in the sixties, slacked off in the seventies, and became interesting again in the late eighties.

Living in Vancouver in the late fifties and early sixties, the young poets (to be) knew first void and margin, saw the ocean every day, and then looked for tradition, that is for the trade. There was, as far as they could see, no tradition of Vancouver poetry. As far as they knew there was no tradition of Canadian poetry. The tradition they knew was to be found in the high school English 91 anthology: Chaucer and Shakespeare, Milton and Keats. These poets, at the *centre* of what would become a maritime empire, lived thousands of miles from the west coast of any America, in a pink hardcover textbook with Big Ben keeping time on the cover.

As for the U.S. poets — they were generally studied as a Yankee preoccupation, practicality and honest cunning. Hence Emerson and Frost and even Cummings. The young Vancouvers were aware that a few *eccentric* relatives were hidden in the attic or cellar — William Blake in England, Emily Dickinson in New England.

So the young Vancouvers did not choose the margin. They grew up in small towns beside rivers in the Interior. When they came to the city in 1957 and 1958 they were eager for poetry and they were naive about its domicile. They were, you might say, green, or ripe for postmodernism. They were thousands of miles from history. Vancouver was a big city, it seemed to them, but it had no skyscrapers. Downtown, among the tallest buildings, they could still smell the sea's salt and creosote. From West Point Grey, where the university was, they could see more forest than city, mountains with ocean at their feet.

They sensed, beneath their new sophistication, that the ancient world was not theirs, but the Quaternary was. As for *history*, they had to arrange it themselves. In a bit of gentrified forest on the edge of the UBC campus, one could kick leaves aside and discover a plaque on the ground, on which was inscribed the information that late in the eighteenth century there occurred here a meeting between a Spanish captain and an English captain, known to the young poet only as a nearby geographical denomination.

Around here, history, like most things, was makeshift, amateur, in comparison with what we knew was back East. Like a plywood cafe in Kispiox as opposed to a wise-crack deli in New York.

It was in a lecture about history that we first read Olson's use of the term "post-modern." Earlier (August 1951) Olson wrote a wonderful long letter to Louis Martz and Robert Creeley about "the very *expansions* which post-modern life have [sic] involved us, severally, in." Some of the expansions involved ontological time: "the job now is to be at once archaic and culture-wise — that they are indivisible — then where is the principle of function from which verse (anyway) can be written so that the balancing on a feather which make [sic] this simultaneous act possible can be achieved" (Olson and Creeley, 63-80). Certainly, in Olson's view, not in the *personae* adopted for a while by Eliot and Pound.

Some of the expansion involved what the critics three decades later would call the trespassing of genres, though they would often be misusing that noun, where they should have used the one Olson uses: "so far as verse goes, this seems to me so huge a thing that the old three — lyric, epic & dramatic — don't serve at all: that is, a novel has already shown that these descriptions are only such, that they don't isolate modes nor do they any longer cover such a function as the increase of critique in verse establishes." For Olson that critique is a necessary response to the huge increase in quantity of information characteristic of "post-modern life." It is what carries us beyond the hermeticism and detachment of Modernism: "the function of critique is more than the mere one of clarities (as, say, Flaubert & Mme Sand), it is even showing itself in the very form of our address to each other, and what work goes along with it."

Compare Rilke's view of Cézanne, whom he praises for his inability to theorize the social or even aesthetic implications of his work: "Whoever meddles, arranges, injects his human deliberation, his wit, his advocacy, intellectual agility in any way, is already disturbing and clouding their activity. Ideally a painter (and, generally, an artist) should not become conscious of his insights: without taking the detour through his reflective processes, and incomprehensibly to himself, all his progress should enter so swiftly into the work that he is unable to recognize them in the moment of transition" (75).

There are still many poets in Canada who would agree in their less elegant fashion with that beautiful romanticism. But when the tyros in Vancouver began to produce *Tish*, their "poetry newsletter" in 1961, they filled it with their youthful theorizing, in both prose pieces and poems, which were often addressed to one another or a master. A poem by Fred Wah will illustrate:

FOR R. D.

as Pound to you
you to me
I hear the final word
fear false admittance

    'a blind bird in a bird bath'

the paths lead backwards in time
word mimicry of magical minds
come to me through the open window
cool September breeze remember me?

not forgetting your truthful angels, Rilke
but they seduced my thoughts a few years back
and I roved too far by their bewitchery
which walking of the mind was with

'darkness behind closed eyes'

led into back tracks of the past
seemingly a blind bird bathing
just a few days ago ...

(in Davey, 1975)

From other parts of Canada, mainly the centres called Montreal
and Toronto, these tyros received messages mocking their seriousness, especially their notion that the activity of poetry was
something other than instinctual. Even bill bissett, whom many
readers would place among the *avantgardistas* of sixties Vancouver,
called one of his books *What poetiks* (1967).

No Canadian critic has produced more titles concerning
Postmodernism than has Linda Hutcheon, of the University of
Toronto. Like the Europeans, she has found it more rewarding
to work with fiction than with poetry (though she always reminds
readers that the condition includes a blurring of the boundary
between them). Her favourite subjects are parody and what she
terms "historiographic metafiction" (Hutcheon, 124-140). Charles
Olson, in 1956 at Black Mountain College, gave a series of lectures
with the Einsteinian title "The Special View of History," in which
he radicalized that last term. He counters the post-Trevelyan drift
of the discipline toward science and then the social sciences, by
redefining: "Let me try it this way: that a life is the historical
function of the individual. History is the intensity of the life process
— its *life value*" (Olson, 1970, 18, 47, 49). A human is not an
object of a force called history, not an example of "mankind." A
man is "no trope of himself as a synechdoche of his species, but is,
as actual determinant, each one of us, a conceivable creator" (49).

Elaborations of such a position will be seen in the writings of several important Vancouver poets and critics to come.

Says Olson for the age that was learning to live after Einstein's 1904 special view: "it does need to be noticed that the present is *post* the Modern." For Olson the present proposes something after Einstein closed the Kosmos, something human and political, an argument to be taken up in the eighties by the Language Poets, forty long years after the RAF bombed the treasure-house of Dresden. Olson: "art was never any more, and can be nothing other than the order of man, specifically man, and not nature, not history, not a creator God ... a concept of order which is different from that one which the attention to Kosmos involved man in, succeeding phases, from the 6th century B.C. to the 20th A.D." (47).

In the early sixties the young Vancouvers were reading Olson as much as they could, quoting him innocently, holding discussions about his pronouncements. They found him very difficult to read, this huge Yankee, but they knew that he was announcing the "new." They saw him as a development of what they admired in Ezra Pound and William Carlos Williams (whom their professors discounted). They did not fret much about Modernism and Postmodernism.

But Olson's poems, especially the last poems, were a lot different from Ezra Pound's (though there was something interesting in the fragmentary strophes or syntax in the very last poems of Pound and Williams). They seemed to trail away, often, into bits of music or argument over the night waves. Scornful academics called them "notes for poetry." It became impossible to tell where Olson had "broken" into verse out of, say, a letter or an essay. At a reading it was hard to tell when Olson had "broken" into poetry out of the talk between poems. All of it, verse and other, seemed perpetually unfinished, perhaps always ready to be taken up again. His early

Maximus poems are called "letters" to his townspeople and others. For my magazine *Imago* I received a poem from Olson, part of a handwritten letter. He asked for its return because it was his only, spontaneous, copy. So it appeared (because I took the care to commit it back to the mails) in the collected *Maximus Poems*.

The European theoreticians, Barthes and Benveniste, for instance, have taught their subscribers to pay attention to the written more than the oral use of language, to the discourse without the moment of uttering. People began writing letters to make the latter possible. Olson, in conceiving his task as personal *écriture*, at once casts aside the Modernist's mask and the lyric voice of poets like Dylan Thomas and Marianne Moore. The most enigmatic of his early poems, "The Kingfishers," is an attestation of constant change:

But the E
cut so rudely on that oldest stone
sounded otherwise,
was differently heard

and ends with an image of the poet as reader: "I hunt among stones" (1960, 11).

In reading, says Olson often, the individual can situate himself all through the Pleistocene. History seen as objective science suggests an order characterized by end, by aim. There are ideologues, for instance, who include the future in their structuring of historical pattern. Giving oneself over to a sense of history as "the intensity of the process" is to imagine living in the Quaternary, not, for instance, the "post-war" world. Vancouver poet Frank Davey used to counter eastern Canada's historical marginalization of the West

Coast by saying that while the piled stones of Montreal may be hundreds of years old, the rocks on his favourite sea cliff were Precambrian. Not a house in sight; only readable signs left by the ice age.

For a while Davey called his view "myth," an old usage running counter to "history," and started a late-sixties poem called "Sentences of Welcome":

Where there are rocks in the valleys of the waves.
Lichen, seabirds, cling to my words,
cling for air. There are dolphins, porpoises,
whales within my breath. Their green flanks
are staind with oil. The small fish
& plankton in their bellies
send strange odors to their mouths.

These words
would find their form around the planet,
make sentences of welcome.

(1970, n.p.)

The spatial equivalent of history is geography, and while the young Vancouvers were fascinated with maps, often putting them on the covers of their books and magazines, they felt about geography the way Olson did about history. Consider a section from Davey's ironically titled "A Light Poem":

I want you
to see.
To see that darkness, cast beside you

by 20,000 feet of green water
standing. The shadows
cast by the fish, swimming there —
one, on one, on one:
from wave to seabed
these shadows & shadows
on square inches
falling.

I want you to see.
Miles beneath your feet
there is light of unprotruded
volcanoes glowing.
I want you to worry for your feet,
for your earth,
for its awkward turning there on,
that silent fire . . . .

(1970, n.p.)

In what way is this stuff postmodern? I will let you come back to that question; but consider the "speaker's" position in that passage, and the one he is urging for "you." Not the poet as authority, not even the poet as muse-driven scribe, but the poet as reader, and the text as something that can throw light not on a topic but on the readers themselves. A few years later another young Vancouver poet-editor will call this business "context."

Though as early as the first decade of the twentieth century conservative Catholic theologians were denouncing Modernist thought in the church, and by the middle of the second decade they were already inveighing against "post-modernism," the young Vancouvers were innocent of such issues. They had only rough and uncanonical notions of authority, hence of tradition. It was foreign, for one thing, or other-place, or learned in suspicionable school, and in any case disparate. It was not *in place*; so the young Vancouvers' poems and declarations began to work on their (adopted, usually) place, Vancouver, the coast. Till then the main freight, when it was delivered, was the decayed romantic poem (see any poetry magazine from Kingston or Fredericton), a dream of representation, in which the represented is diminished by its passage through anecdotal verse:

> Against the scrawny comfort of the crane-legged pier
> the ship shudders, feeling the shore coils tighten.
> Sullen, she subsides and the brackish port-locked water
> touching tentatively, laps her sea-knowing hull.
>
> (in Sylvestre and Green, 519)

In such verse we are supposed to notice the uncommon descriptive language painting an impressionistic picture of an object, of a scene, to try to get at its *essence* the way a photograph or a quick look could not.

Somehow we feel that that does not work. Our suspicion begins when we perceive a kind of staginess, some kind of conversion. We know that the words misrepresent the ordinariness of the ship, that they are "poetry" words such as your high school teacher would pretend to like for the length of a class. Yet they are employed to get you past the surface of the scene. You know that there is a

contradiction here, a misdirection. Maybe the hope of representation is wrong. Roman Jakobson seems to make it simply so: "poetry
deepens the dichotomy between signs and objects" (Scholes, 26).

To return us to history, we can see that Claude Simon said something similar about time: "Proust's 'Recherche' didn't lead him to
regain time, but to produce a written object which has its own
temporality" (Janvier, 29).

So did the Vancouver poets of the sixties understand this
autonomy of the written text? Certainly they were hostile to the
New Critics' objectification of the poem, probably because it did
not work for anything but the lyric, partly because the poems
written by some of the New Critics were boring, and partly because
New Criticism had been the hot system for the earlier generation
who had become their teachers at UBC.

Still, the young Vancouvers, if they did not know the nomencla-
ture, and if they had encountered Saussure only in their linguistics
classes, were persuaded by their reading of Williams and Creeley
that the action in the poem was the phenomenon their readers
would encounter, that the human poet, not the landscape, was
what would be represented. Perhaps more than one of them took
Robert Duncan's advice and went to Gertrude Stein to read what
she had to say on the topic:

> If poetry is the calling upon a name until that name
> comes to be anything if one goes on calling on that name
> more and more calling upon that name as poetry does then
> poetry does make of that calling upon a name a narrative it
> is a narrative of calling upon that name.
>
> (Stein, 48)

Gertrude Stein is the Modernist who has remained most interesting to the newest postmodernists. That is interesting, of course, for reasons of gender, and also because she made and makes an alternative, say, to the totalizing James Joyce: "A great deal perhaps all of my writing of The Making of Americans was an effort to escape from this thing to escape from inevitably feeling that anything that everything had meaning as beginning and middle and ending."

Not all the poets around *Tish* or their associates downtown were reading Gertrude Stein in 1962, but they *were* reading Olson, and he had his own way of renouncing the classic beginning-middle-end formula: "If there is any absolute, it is never more than this one, you, this instant, in action" (1967, 58). Olson's famous open parenthesis is probably the most recognizable — and aped — orthographic signature of the movement he seemed to lead.

What distinguished the poets of that movement, the New York ones and the Vancouver ones, was their instantism, as it has been called, compositional decisions made (and seen to be made) in and by the poem too quick to be shaped by a will that would put poetry at the service of an already held opinion or program, yet made by the linguistic suggestions there in the poem-so-far. Poetry that races to elude the authority of the poet herself. Not poems made to express the poet's point of view. Poems trying to trace their own autonomy. Such poems, like any, can be good or bad. The postmodernist's skill resembles the post-swing jazz player's improvisation, bop to free to whatever they are playing now. Playing the work.

Consider the instantism, and consequent delicacy and accuracy, in part of a 1973 poem by Daphne Marlatt (who as a high school girl came to the Vancouver region from another English discourse):

Somehow they survive, this people, these fish,
survive the refuse bottom, filthy water, their choked lives,
in a singular dance of survival, each from each. At the
narrows, in the pressure of waves so checked & held by
"deep-sea frontage" it's the river's push against her, play of
elements in her life comes rolling on, hair flying. In gumboots,
on deck with rubber apron ("it's no dance dress"), she'll take
all that river gives, willing only to stand her ground (rolling,
with it, right under her feet, her life, rolling, out from under,
right on out to sea ...

(1974, 75)

Ellipsis leads as does the river, this poem that is three decades later
yet undergoing change. In a previous long poem, *Rings*, which is
concerned with marriages, births and other departures, Marlatt
said: "There is no story only the telling with no end in view ..."
(1971, n.p.).

Marlatt is likely the best example of the postmodern Vancouver
poet of the seventies, always doubling back and backing doubles.
She delights in ambiguity, not to deploy Empsonian erudition so
much as to show the writer as a person in the excitement of
composition, provisional and open to qualification and increment
rather than revision. Conversely, any reader reading the last pages
of *The Waste Land* suspects that Eliot had in mind from the beginning bringing his fisher king to the shore with the arid plain behind
him.

Some say that Modernism came to an end, or became a relic, with
the 1945 atomic bomb. Some of the Bauhaus's buildings survived
the Allied air raids, of course, and some were erected after the war,

especially at the edges of empires. So in poetry. There are poets in Canada, including Vancouver, who are even writing and publishing poems in the Hardy mode or the Frost method, leaving off the end-rime that gave them their music. Some poets fancy a dichotomy between the avant-garde and their politics, what they call progressive poetry. As Hardy stood against Modernism, so they stand Neruda and themselves against postmodernism. The highly political Language poets will counter that any poetry that does not criticize the conventions of poetic utterance is a perpetuation of the *status quo*. What of the readers who want poems they can "understand"? Their poets run the political risk of remaining satisfied to restate stuff the managers have managed to live with, no threat, comfortably discounted.

One might ask: when you seize the means of production, why would you keep it going as it has been going? The Georgian poet who wrote "Nay, nay, sweet England, do not grieve!/ Not one of these poor men who died/ But did within his soul believe/ That death for thee was glorified" (de la Mare) would probably not have or pretended to have held quite such sentiments if he had figured out as Eliot did, why poetry in the twentieth century had to be difficult.

Had to be new. Roland Barthes once put the question into clear anti-perspective: "The New is not a fashion, it is a value, the basis of all criticism ... There is only one way left to escape the alienation of present-day society: *to retreat ahead of it*: every old language is immediately compromised, and every language becomes old once it is repeated ... The stereotype is a political fact, the major figure of ideology" (1975, 40). Make it new, said Ezra Pound, way back when, and for the poets that would mean make it a way newer than Pound's.

Twenty years after "a particular group of young people who were writing" (Pound, 52) and inventing Imagism in 1912, Pound insisted on the moving image rather than the "handiest and easiest" stationary image. Twenty years later again Olson wrote, you will recall, "If there is any absolute, it is never more than this one, you, this instant, in action." We have looked at the instant; now let us look at the "you." Readers of Olson's "Projective Verse" will know that he is not suggesting the ego as absolute, but rather the "you" that can be perceived only as it is *in* action, what would become known in the Olson lexicon as proprioception.

That sense is treated very well in one highly intuitive essay about the first wave of postmodern Vancouver poets, Warren Tallman's "Wonder Merchants" (1972). Tallman tends to use his own terminology, he calls the young Vancouver poets "modernists," and his writing is innocent of the taxonomy of the European-influenced discourse crowd — but his essay is marvellously precognitive of the inventions to be made a decade or two later by the domestic poststructuralists.

"Wonder Merchants" is an interesting phrase. It may, to some ears, appear to be an oxymoron. The second term might be seen, though, as related to the word tradition. Tallman is interested in the community fashioned by the young Vancouvers, the *Tish* poets and others such as David Bromige, bill bissett, Roy Kiyooka, Gerry Gilbert, *et al.* He begins by relating Vancouver to Olson's Gloucester: "Eventually the city looks out through his eyes, speaks through his voice, remembers through his memory, has its meetings in his person. Having no whisper of influence at city hall, his voicings nonetheless were the politics of the place" (175).

I do not know whether Tallman is right, but I certainly think that this trope is more like the experience of making a city and its poems than the typical noticing or wilful lyric, say "With the coming of night,/ Vancouver has donned a garment of stars" (A. M. Stephen, "Vancouver"). Young David Cull would compose a book of verse entitled *The City in Her Eyes*. A very early Marlatt poem about the Georgia Viaduct says: "i'm all bridge/ today, even rail/ road we somehow/ more than leaving indicates/ both love ..." (1980, 84). Fred Wah's title poem "Among" begins "The delight of making inner/ an outside world for me/ is when I tree myself" (Wah, 7). That odd verb is the perfect rejoinder to the sensibility intent on describing.

Of course there are at least two Vancouver cities, and one of them is inhabited by crooked stockbrokers and car dealers, hustlers and illiterates, a million people who do not know about the city that has been built stone by stone in the poems. There are also other kinds of poets. Tallman takes Irving Layton as a prime example of the poet who is egoceptive rather than proprioceptive: "he has concentrated on himself as object and scarcely at all upon the language innovations necessary in order to enter Modernist writing." That kind of poet celebrates individuality, alienation and humanism. His sentence might be "I placed/ my hand/ upon/ her thigh."

Tallman reparses the sentence this way: "Self is subject, writing is verb and the object is life, to be as fully alive as one can manage by way of sight, hearing, thinking, feeling, speaking — that is, writing. The reader becomes the respondent, hopefully the correspondent." Poems as letters — in later years Frank Davey and Fred Wah would invent an electronic literary journal for e-mail poetry.

Davey, a West Coast poet who took the margin to "central" Canada with him, quite early saw the explosion of electronic information as a wild updating of Olson's observation that quantity created postmodern life. In his introduction to *From There to Here* (1974) Davey sees that the proliferation of "micro-electronic technology" has "disappointed rationalist views of reality, and decentralized rather than centralized political and cultural power" (1974, 11-23). Little presses sprang up a long way from Toronto, and there was a revolution in printing costs. The means of production were no longer to be controlled by a few "professional" publishing "houses" in the old centre. At the same time the expansion of opportunity led to artists crossing formal boundaries, poets taking up video cameras, novelists designing books, painters mixing media. Then, if the boundaries between media were assailable, what chance did the borders between genres have? Art movements themselves became many and elastic; once they were said to succeed their parents as Vorticism succeeded Imagism — now they could spring up as siblings, parallel and multifoliate. Many observers see that development as a main feature of postmodernism in the arts.

Davey recalls Eli Mandel's 1966 declaration that the new writing is "beyond system." Mandel's words signalled his desire to escape his reputation as a poet who had learned from Northrop Frye, or had been created by the Frye circle in the heart of the university in the heart of the city in the heart of the country. He was beginning to write as a marginalized poet, a short, football-loving Jew from rural Saskatchewan. Davey welcomed Mandel's move, and said that criticism should not be "systematic analysis and explication," but a (perhaps) irrational response "which does not attempt to impose on individual works or on art itself a structure of reason or indeed a pattern of any kind except that of perception." That would be the response of Tallman's "correspondent," the person who extends the text rather than making conclusions from it. Such a vision insists that the text is not just an autonomous piece of writing. Tallman had said that the Vancouver writing he was interested in differed from Eastern (central) writing in this way — that it was writing not as a literary activity but as life-living.

Davey also invokes Marshall McLuhan, of course, and calls his time "a decentralized, 'post-electric,' post-modern, non-authoritarian age." As soon as the centre will not hold, some people in the centre regret that instability, while some people on the edge welcome the change. Robert Scholes has a nice way of describing the former feeling, especially as it affects teachers: "The entire edifice of American instruction in written composition rests on a set of assumptions much like Ezra Pound's. We have all been brought up as imagists. We assume that a complete self confronts a solid world, perceiving it directly and accurately, always capable of capturing it perfectly in a transparent language: bring 'em back alive; just give us the facts, ma'am; the way it was; tell it like it is; and that's the way it is" (in Blonsky, 310). (Scholes has a flair, and his remarks are useful, but he does seem to have missed Pound's remarks about the stationary image.) Tallman was right to imagine the revolution as a revisioning of grammar.

As fans of the postmodern say, multiplicity replaces unity; difference replaces authority. In 1973 Davey put the change neatly. In opposition to Modernism's complex unity, "in the postmodern world of counterpointing influences, centres, and traditions, the claim that a single tradition can be central or orthodox has become meaningless." But just such a claim was being made all through the seventies. It was called "The Canadian Tradition," and it was being touted in English departments in Ontario and the Eastern Townships, where the stones were at least a hundred years old. "The Canadian Tradition" involved enduring of snow and fear of wolves, and leaned toward Frye's picture of Protestant enclaves in the landscape deep freeze. From the west edge, at least, it is not hard to see that such unitary myth-making is exclusionary. What did it say to a person such as Roy Kiyooka, whose father stood on whales in the winter rain of the northern B.C. coast? Kiyooka was the first Vancouver postmodern poet, partly because he was also deservedly celebrated as a painter, sculptor and photographer, and he tried to persuade his audience that he was also a musician.

A typical Kiyooka book is his *Stoned Gloves*. Kiyooka had gone to Osaka to install his brightly-coloured sails at the Canadian pavilion of Expo '70. While there he photographed gloves discarded by workers at the site. The photographs and some of his words, rendered large, made a travelling exhibition in Canadian art galleries, and were translated into a book by Coach House Press, becoming another "object" of art produced by a poets' publishing outfit that illustrates Davey's point about counter-authority. The book is undated. This Saskatchewan-born poet, whose first language was Japanese, is excluded by that "Canadian Tradition" that boasts offshore Protestant E. J. Pratt. Even if the glove fits it will be discarded or lost one day:

I search'd another man's painting for
the glove   & found it, where
my hand's shadow fell across his painting
(n.p.)

Subject is self, verb is writing, object is life. Modernist detachment was a corrective, now corrected. Kiyooka did let pieces of things lie as they fell, or rose, but in making his art he did not stand back. In *From There to Here* Davey wrote: "The classical artistic concept of the totally integrated whole [see *Ulysses* — GB] has no incarnation in a sensory reality that is everywhere fragmented, discontinuous, post logical." The postmodern long poem, Ed Dorn's *Gunslinger* or bpNichol's *The Martyrology*, keeps abandoning its nature of address and shape, doing inside itself what Kiyooka started when he walked onto the site at Osaka. "Culture and the universe," claimed Davey, "are randomly interacting cooperatives continually evolving new relationships and forms." He might have been anticipating a 1988 page by Vancouver poet Dan Farrell:

> plus   tell   sharp

> cutting   shallows   palace

> lacerating   tens   addressed

Our postures improved with each dedication. Cornice
bye. Mass times mass pushing for a predicate.

(n.p.)

Dan Farrell is associated with a group of writers, painters, video artists and movie makers who in the eighties began to create a Vancouver as dynamic as the city bricolaged by their forebears of the sixties. These new people, including more women than one remembers from the earlier wave, have a space called, with humour, The Kootenay School of Writing, a nod to one of their origins in Nelson's short-lived David Thompson University [ahem!] Centre. Most of their first books were slim volumes published by Tsunami

Editions, organized by fisherman Lary Bremner. It may be a sign of the economic times that until very recently, most of these poets did not hold or expect academic jobs. But they do engage in theory. They are smart enough to know that they must confront by *difference*, by technique — so they do not, as "work poets" do, relax into the forms that the institutions have vouchsafed them.

The KSW poets, like those of the sixties, share interest and venues with the poets of the U.S. avant-garde. As the sixties group found sympathy with the poets who appeared in Donald M. Allen's anthology *The New American Poetry* (1960), so the later group is often associated with the poets who were collected in the L=A=N=G=U=A=G=E anthologies, Charles Bernstein, Lyn Hejinian and Robert Grenier among them. Frank Davey's counterpart among the KSW poets is Jeff Derksen, an intense and serious poet well grounded in theory, aware of the political inevitabilities of his craft, and given to essay-writing as part of his job description. His pronouncements bear the signs of his having learned Bakhtin and Bernstein, but they also speak for a development of local principles — there are interesting similarities between Tallman's "Wonder Merchants" and Derksen's essay, "Sites Taken as Signs: Place, the Open Text, and Enigma in New Vancouver Writing" (Delany, 88).

Tallman's essay is intuitive, lyrical and taxonomically individual, while Derksen's is aware of its place in the recent syntheses of discourse theory. Tallman saw Olson's proprioception as the way to the "politics of the place." Derksen is interested in just that problem, and like Tallman before him he goes to the English sentence to work transformation. As Tallman saw self as subject, etc., Derksen sees "the writer (as subject) correlating with place." He praises Barry McKinnon's Prince George book *The Pulp Log* for "making landscape of self." Tallman saw the reader as correspondent and the poems as letters welcoming letters. For Derksen the poet's act is social — the subject moves out of "linguistics" into "context." Remember that Tallman saw his writers as preferring not literary activity but life-living. Bakhtin and Kristeva gave Derksen some language he could use to his purpose. So the contextual performance of poetry is "dialogic meaning." Subject alters context. The reading becomes a contextualizing act or a social evaluation of the information. We are some distance from the stationary Imagism that Pound saw becoming inadequate.

The Language poets and the KSW poets have no qualms about knowing European discourse theory, and have moved further than had their predecessors away from poetry as individual expression. They treat the event of the poem as a social-political act, and often use the language of the social and economic sciences. Wary of language arts as "commodity exchange," they oppose the low modernist poem that would view with detachment any experience, lyric, horrible or historicized. They are still, as were their predecessors, interested in constructing the local, but they stress a local that leans toward a "social context," rather than a topography. Language, said Bakhtin, as quoted by Derksen, is "ideologically saturated." State capitalism, for instance, will tolerate and encourage homogenization, "verbal and ideological unification and centralization."

The thematic criticism fostered in the Canadian Literature academy after 1967, and which made its way into the smiled-upon poetry of the seventies, was nationalistic; unfortunately, a criticism that concentrated on recognizable Canadian images and paradigms played into the hands of U.S. institutions (like the British ones during Empire) that are happy to see their language and forms spread through the white geography north of the border. Derksen's essay addresses the problem right away: "The schema of a unitary language, either as a system or as a national language, begins the search for a unified individual to speak it."

Hence Derksen's poetry, for example, will break down the convention of image as example, as specific that can be, by metaphor, generalized. Remember that Olson did not like the idea of an individual as synecdoche of his group. No model English sentence about the mute Canadian entering the snowy forest. Derksen understands the first task of the avant-garde, the responsibility of "eccentric or idiosyncratic" poetry:

I mean a writing that would be open to breaking
linguistic rules of representation and reception: a
writing that promotes an eccentricity of both
the writer and the reader so that there can be a
specific engagement of a social context that the push
for universals can [not] steamroll over. This would
not view writing as a condensation of images and
information into a discrete linguistic package for the
reader to correctly decode in order to have the text's
truths revealed, that is, it is not driven by intentionality.
Reading would be a correlation of information within
a social frame, a social evaluation, that allows for the
specifics of the reader's time and place.

One wonders, even an old-time avant-gardist wonders: will it work? Will obviously "enigmatic" poetry make for perception of a correlative social context? At a typical KSW poetry reading, with noisy Hamilton Street traffic below the windows, one could see some of the audience sporting faces trying not to show incomprehension, and lots of people, poets and others, responding enthusiastically. There are, it appears, Vancouver ears that know how to enjoy the mixture of personal and local events as *semes*, the play and slippage of signifiers (readers, listeners, as context, not even Saussurean decoders), rather than metaphors for a general human condition. The "I" is socially constituted, and during a reading the audience is doing its job. When it is tempted toward metaphor, but has to fall back on the signifiers that only *seemed* to be headed in that direction, as in this piece by Lisa Robertson, one of the more "accessible" Tsunami poets:

BOYCOTT

It is fascinating to circulate among the quietly hemmed
streets when skintight jars reinvent the idea of pressing
and I learn that ribbons are refreshingly submissive,
compared to plastic whose vocation brims

(8)

it understands that the "author" as much as the words has departed from the solacing old model. She is as problematical and unstable, and needful of readers' participation as any "skintight jars." She is words.

Derksen says that the juxtaposing of seemingly incompatible words, one of the most easily noticeable gambits of the Language poets, is done to reveal the ideologies behind the statement. Here the aging Vancouvers from the sixties are on their ground — they remember that such was both the purpose and the effect of Brion Gysin's (who did not stay to construct Edmonton) famous cut-up method of the Beat days. Allen Ginsberg's "hydrogen jukebox" did it for him; and one knows that Gertrude Stein's *Tender Buttons* continue to do it for many readers and writers.

Nowadays there are few adults who care that Dylan Thomas was once "young and easy," but the objects, food and rooms of Gertrude Stein retain their fascination — because they are other, because she is among them, intersecting with them, not emitting them, not expressing herself. The all-too-common continual presenting of self as phenomenal topic rather than subject in context is worse than borrowing A. J. M. Smith's verse forms.

There is an obvious contradiction in the city of avant-garde poetry, of the serious avant-garde art that enrols theory. This is especially true for a "movement" such as the KSW, made by poets who did not rise from the academy, who proclaim social and political structures, but who compose poetry that, due to its enigmatic nature, seems to some people to be elitist. But we remember that Eliot said that serious poetry in his time had to be difficult, and Eliot became the most often imitated poet in the English-language world.

In our time, from our city, David Bromige is a key figure. In the late fifties and early sixties he was a contemporary of the *Tish* poets and their downtown friends. At that time he was learning to shuck the British stanza he had learned in childhood, and though sometimes seen as an imperialist voice, to attend to the local as celebrated by the young Olsonites. In "Wonder Merchants" Tallman called him "one of the most appealingly human of the West Coast poets," whose poetry "is informed by something inside that doesn't flinch and won't budge, I cannot bear to tell a lie."

Bromige went from Vancouver to Berkeley, to the San Francisco of Robert Duncan and the younger poets working out the late phases of that city's alleged "renaissance." In more recent years Bromige has been publishing in the magazines frequented by the Language poets in the U.S. Here is something he has written about the relationship between enigma and the social context:

> ... we begin to glimpse what is the profound vocation of the work of art in a commodity society: not to be a commodity, not to be consumed, not to be a vacation. Isn't this the piece talking to itself, hoping to be overheard, & contradicted. Because, the interest evident in the construction, rhythm of the sentence, obviates the need for the content. (Not to deny the feelings, of course. And I, as you probably do *not* know, am a sucker for children in pain."
>
> (11)

People in other parts of Canada see the West Coast as eccentric, even while regular national bank buildings arise between us and the westering sun. Even Europeans, reaching for the marginalized exotic, reach for Vancouver. Thus has the name of the city been used in the poems of Guillaume Apollinaire and Blaise Cendrars, paid-up members of the Parisian avant-garde; they list Vancouver as a far imaginary destination. Vancouver, it would seem to people in the easts, is a place where normal authority does not quite work. That is, of course, a fable that Vancouverites like to permit. Even the less wealthy of us fill our Monday afternoon hot tubs with Perrier water.

The poets of postmodernism differ from the Modernists in this way: they question one authority without having the temerity to offer another, whether Anglicanism, fascism, history or myth. They are so much disposed against authority that they distrust any signs of it in themselves. They permit the signifiers to slip. Irony cannot, therefore, get a grip. Authors are long gone. Writers disappear among the readers. The very notion of a canon is at the best tentative. Postmodernism's notorious self-reflexivity (a tautological term if there ever was one) is in question as the concept of self gives way to a social metasensibility. Theory is now *inside* the work, not a shadow before or after. If there are "truths" they are temporarily constructed, not found out. What the Bay of Pigs and the U2 spy camera confessions did for the received truths of the U.S. citizenry in the sixties, poststructuralism has done for the denizens of postmodern Vancouver and all other eccentres. Culture is a fiction, not a tradition. Boundaries are therefore flexible, at least those between forms and genres. Literary contests that offer prizes in categories called poetry, fiction, non-fiction, children's literature, and so on, are recognizably sentimental or centrist. Difference rather than the universal is now sought: Quebec and the West are trying to show Ottawa and Toronto that it is all right to look for a postmodern federalism. Poetry is political after all.

It could be posited that Modernist poetry did not assemble an anthology in Vancouver because from 1915 to 1945 Vancouver was a hick town in which any poets were trying to be Kipling (he owned property in the neighbourhood where many of the KSW poets now live). It could be argued that Modernism could not take root in such a place anyway, even the diluted modernism of English-speaking Montreal poetry. The Modernists gathered fragments of old traditions, built deep intricate forms to urge their faith in fixed systems, order, wholeness. The postmodernists replace faith with doubt, and complex depth with complex surface. They also accept those things once thought to be failures: contingency, multiplicity, fragmentation, discontinuity. The Modernists knew those things as *method* but not as belief, not, surely, as *desiderata*.

So the ambiguous relationship everyone notices — postmodernism contradicts Modernism while extending it. Modernism's priests, Eliot, Pound, Joyce, are succeeded by secular folk. Writing is a signifying practice rather than a scribe's service. Our city is not far from a plate tectonic faultline. Destabilizing in our poetic community has been brought about gladly by an understanding of poems as (con)*texts* rather than words on the wall or in the Book, whether the latter be the Bible or the Norton.

Robert Duncan, whose visits to Vancouver were so generative, said "... those of us who are addicted to fabrication believe that the entire universe is truly a fabric, made-up, and that we are consequently in tune with it" (in Waldman and Webb, 1-12). There we are, retreating in front of the Modernists, and sneaking up behind them.

The city looking out from the poet's eyes. Robin Blaser moved from San Francisco to Vancouver in the mid-sixties, and has been a ludic figure here ever since. He has never described the scene, but he has been writing it all this time. Here is the end of part 17 of his ongoing "Image-Nation" poem:

the sacred returns with all its faces,
fiery-footed

the fiery dew of the streets, coloured
by oil-slicks and dawn, leads down
to the sea at a snail's pace   who
looks wishly upon it, unlocks the lock-hole

of the chest again   I slept,
the prose thought, and it seemed to me
   that eyelids wept

(39)

Diamond in the Rain

THE GRAND ROMANCE of Canadian history was the improbable laying of railroad track across the seemingly empty continent to the little city at the end of things. For the portion of a person that is still European, that outpost on the edge of a giant unimaginable ocean was dark, scary exoticism, with a fascinating light in the middle. Guillaume Apollinaire, the great Italian-Russian surrealist poet who wrote in French, said it this way:

Étincelant diamant
Vancouver
Où le train blanc de neige et de feux nocturnes fuit l'hiver.

Of course the railroad has been succeeded by the highway and the air lane, but the romance remains, as Canadians in the snow exaggerate the mystery of the warm rainy city at the foot of snow-headed Pacific mountains. Blaise Cendrars, the great Swiss poet, friend of Apollinaire, and ceaseless traveller, wrote a poem called "Vancouver," in which we hear: *"ces halos bleuâtres dans le vent sont les paquebots en partance pour le Klondyke le Japon et les grandes Indes."*

The names of our province, our city and our streets are still European, but on the edge of the world, as we must seem to be to easterners, we do not live in history. We live in mythology. We are consigned to nature. We do not like to eat indoors. We share the madness of California but we import our oranges. And we are less European all the time. More than a third of the people who live in Vancouver are descended from Asia.

When I walk across the street, I tread carefully, because I do not desire to be hit by that silver BMW driven by a young Chinese woman with a cellphone held to the side of her head. She is a Vancouverite as I am. I am on my way to that sushi bar over there, where I will manipulate *ohashi*, little sticks with clumps of salmon roe between them. Yum!

How can I convey our life on the rim? Toronto has more novelists than we do, but we have more poets. Montreal has more federal politicians than we do, but we have more mad people in the streets. Ottawa has more doughnut shops than we do, but we have more cups of organic tea. When we jump onto a plane, we fly to Thailand.

Rivers flow quickly from our mountains into the sea, and the salmon who came down those rivers four years ago have been to Japan and back, and now they are going back up those rivers to give birth and to die. The Native people said goodbye to them four years ago, and now they are saying hello. They have been doing that since time began here. When we Europeans and Asians came here the "Indians" showed us how to prepare and eat the salmon.

If we look down from our mountains we see blue halos in the ocean, behind the long sea canoes of the Native people, who showed us how to find the fur seals, so that the men and women of Europe could wear flamboyant hats for three hundred years. By the time that Blaise Cendrars found Vancouver the trains filled with Oriental silk were departing eastward, filled too with armed guards, dangerous mystery on steel wheels over snowy prairie.

Really, we rest protected by an inland sea, surrounded by hundreds of mountaintops protruding from the ocean, our Pacific islands covered with cedar and ferns. No wall here is as old as the stone fence around an ancient convent in downtown Montreal. But from our windows we see stones billions of years older than any human ambition, and we feel the desire to stand among them. We can see every year of human life around us — stains, wounds, expensive show homes scarring the high slopes of the mountains on the north shore of our inlet.

After the railroad tracks and the highways and the air lanes came the internet. In February the people of Vancouver like to e-mail their friends huddled under piles of snow in Ontario and Manitoba, and tell them about the flowers that are blossoming in their gardens and along their streets. In return, people in Ontario and Manitoba say very rude things to their friends in Vancouver.

The scientists say that one day, not too far in the future, there will be an enormous earthquake along the West Coast of Canada, and Vancouver's forest of high-rise apartment buildings will collapse into a tangled mountain of glass and steel. This is the dark dream that enters the minds of Vancouver's citizens while they sleep. But in the mornings they forget. They look into the rain clouds over-head and imagine that they see a patch of blue sky. If that patch is there, and if it begins to spread, and if the sun shines its light on all the wet trees and bridges of the city, the wide awake people see the most beautiful sight ever seen inside or outside a poem.

Remember Appropriation of Voice?

1. Imagining the Parthenon

A few years ago I was in the British Museum, visiting the so-called Elgin Marbles. I had looked at the Parthenon twenty-four years earlier, but this was to be my first look at those sculptures the benevolent Brits had saved from Aegean ruin.

Unfortunately there were television lights and cables and cameras and technicians all over the room that one could otherwise see had been arranged with a sense of reverence and drama. The Japanese were making a television show, and I was really disappointed and annoyed to be deprived of my moment.

Those foreign creeps are messing with our Marbles. That's a verbal translation of what was going on in my head.

Our Marbles. I was a Canadian in an English museum looking at some ruins of carved stone hijacked from Greece by agreement with the Turks two centuries ago.

Lord Elgin said that he was saving the Marbles for art and from war. He lost money doing it, and he was probably a good heart. But he lived with imperial and racist assumptions. The Greek parliamentarians who say that the sculptures should be repatriated are probably right, even though they do not represent the people who made them.

Now here is a point that is often forgotten: Lord Elgin originally asked the Ottomans only for permission to make accurate drawings of the sculptures so that English sculptors could reproduce them. The Ottomans said go ahead and strip the place.

Let's say that the stones should be in Athens, and that it is all right for the English to learn from them, even to copy them, to act like their eighteenth-century writers and try to imitate the Classics. Let their relatives in the U.S. South build parthenons on their plantations.

You see that I am writing about cultural appropriation and a little of the complexity of the subject.

In the late 1980s in Toronto, Ontario, there was a kafuffle at the Women's Press concerning a fight among editors about fiction dealing with women's lives. A lot of people in the hinterlands were puzzled by the clangour, and received perhaps only an outline of the issues. But apparently the main news was that the editorial board was split due to the fact that some stories were excluded from an anthology because the main characters were not comfortably white although the authors were.

Might and cringe prevailed, and the stories were turfed. The public, through the press, was not told that the stories were excluded because they were of inferior composition, nor that they argued the inferiority of a dark race. They were turfed because white women should not write about non-white women.

When a loony dictator a few years ago brought down a death sentence on Salman Rushdie for writing a comic novel with Mohammedans in it, writers all over the Western world started wearing lapel buttons that declared "I am Salman Rushdie." You know that Salman Rushdie is a white woman.

Some folks think that writing is a tool in the service of "the people" or their deity or a divine cause. They generally favour conservative methods for fiction or poetry. Other folks think that writing is travel of the imagination. They will allow a writer to write in the persona of a famous playwright's dog as long as the writing is cared for. They don't say you have to be a dog to do it.

To insult people, even though it may be some kind of right, to denigrate them, to make Indians talk like teepee Amos and Andy, is a kind of spiritual mugging. But simply to write about them is not theft. The imagination is a human glory that makes us believe we can be more than we have been so far. We do not rob someone else just by imagining. We invent something and offer it to the world.

As Canadians, as carbon-based entities who live in this air, we owe a living to the people who live in the lands exploited by our European or Asian forebears. Even if there were no history, we owe them a living because they need it. We owe them a living till they can make one, no matter the reasons why they are poor.

If we took away their gold and clothes and art, we have to give it back now, no matter our old stories about good intentions. If we said they could not do the sun-dance or the potlatch, we have to admit now that those were none of our business. If they want to tell stories of Coyote or Jesus, that is their true fiction.

But if the First Nations in this communal air make up, say, ten percent of the population, that doesn't mean that they have to make up ten percent of the population among the writers at a big Upper Canada literary meeting.

There was another Toronto kafuffle in the late 1980s. Some writers of whom we, out here on the margin, had never heard were protesting that a PEN meeting was not organized according to racial population.

They said that they were not widely heard of because of race. If they were quoted correctly, which is not likely, they used the term WASP and included several Catholics in that group. Their chief spokesperson was a black woman who is a lawyer and a poet. I had never heard of her, and when I read her book I was relieved to see that she is a good poet.

But look, I wanted to say, I believe what Pindar and Yeats said, that athlete and sage are one. Basketball and swimming are as holy as poetry. In the U.S.A. eighty percent of basketball players are black (and very tall), and almost all competitive swimmers are white. These athletes express both economics and culture. There are few swimming pools in black neighbourhoods in North Carolina and Brooklyn. But a lot of little short black kids want to fly like Michael Finley.

Michael Finley is a great athlete, and he is a millionaire. I will write poems about him because he has continued as many years as he could to show me his amazing beautiful moves. He has more money than I will ever have, and I don't feel ripped off at all. I literally dream of making a double-reverse slam dunk, but I wake to write in-your-face poetry and dumb semi-literary essays.

Sometimes when I used to grade some English papers at my university, I had students come and see me about their F or their D.

Some told me that they had always got an A or a B before this. I said to them sure, sure, but now you are in my class. Some others said that they worked an enormous number of hours on their papers and got F or D. I replied that English professors don't pay by the hour. But I showed by whatever means available that I wished that they could write wonderful papers.

Do you see what I am coming to? In a Toronto newspaper in the early 1990s I read a letter by a member of the jury for the Governor-General's Award in fiction. This jury member was defending her decision to vote against books by famous writers. She said that it was time to encourage those writers who had been toiling for a long time without great reward.

I heard those sentiments spoken by people in the League of Canadian Poets, and then in the Writers' Union of Canada, two large groups with a lot of clout in unwary government circles both domestic and offshore.

I like unions and I have been proud to be in a number of them, and I honour their lines. But I think that I, an ACTRA member, should be able to write a story in which the central character is a WUC member even though I am not. As an editor I did an anthology of baseball fiction. It contains nineteen stories, all by men. If I had been able to find a baseball story by a woman I would have printed it — as long as it was well written, even if the protagonist had been a male shortstop.

Spider Robinson's novel *Telempath* is told from the point of view of a young black man with a missing arm. I'll bet Spidey didn't type it with just one of his eight limbs.

We are dealing with two strange notions of the relationships between living and writing, it seems to me. One is the idea that literature is a kind of anthropological projection of a group ethos.

The other is that literature is a democracy in which effort is more to be rewarded than is talent. The other day I saw an advertisement for an essay contest that is sponsored by B.C. libraries and the CBC. It informs us that spelling, grammar and punctuation will not be factors, so that the contest may be "inclusive."

The aforementioned kafuffle-makers wanted justice and equality for people who were identifiably repressed, I think. But trying to restrict and enumerate and homogenize the imagination are not the way to achieve those things. We have had powermongers who tried it — Puritans, Stalinists, Hitlerites, imams, and recently, a U.S. president. Have you read any good North Korean novels lately? Do you remember any good Jewish composers from Vienna, 1944?

If you lay down rules for the writer, tell her she has to use Maoist principles in her verses, or imitate Robin Mathews's favourite nineteenth-century Canadian poets, you may train a good party cadre, but poetry will go down the Love Banal. Eventually you will create something like the Bulgarian writers' union of 1960. When you make exclusionary rules about artistic composition, a certain kind of artist rises to the top — the hack who can work politics better than invention.

Literature is not a method by which people should utter truths already known by politicians, whether those politicians are in or out. Neither is it a depiction of the ways of some eternal principle. The greatest art we have known has always tried to invent a new way of being, a new way for the art itself to be. In this it resembles the politics of revolution.

The work of art is not a servant of the individual who made it. Neither is it a servant of the collective. It is a third thing. Its spiritual and social purpose may be to show that the world can be lifted off the ground to show the beauty underneath.

Anyone who wants to apportion the experiences to be written about, or nominate the writers along non-literary lines, or reward anonymity above accomplishment, seems to me to be what we used to call counter-revolutionary.

Back when we figured that we could all have a revolution.

2. Huck and the older white guy on the raft

There was a time when I had never heard of a North Korean novel and I had never heard of "literary rights." Apparently they are what you violate if you write a story in which your central character is something that you are not. In Canada in recent times you are violating "literary rights" if you are of Scottish extraction but write about an immigrant from Haiti or a member of the Douglas Lake Indian band. I think that men are prohibited from writing about women, too.

I just want to say a few things about colours in this regard. Forgive me if I talk about well-known books. Some time ago I read a really good novel written by a white USAmerican man who lives in France. On the second-to-last page I found out that the narrator is black. On the last page I found out that she is a woman. I had really been enjoying the novel, and now I could enjoy it doubly, or triply, I thought. The author withheld the news on purpose, and it worked very nicely.

When I was a young wanna-be novelist I read *Giovanni's Room*. It was the first novel openly concerned with homosexual life that I had ever read. I felt as if I had learned a lot, and had read some really good prose. It did not strike me as anything but interesting that the author was black while the main characters were white. I had seen that earlier in Willard Motley's *Knock on Any Door*. When my parents were reading the swashbuckling book-of-the-month novels of Frank Yerby (who lived in Spain), I don't think they even guessed that he was black. ("Check the colour under that bodice you're ripping, fella!")

One of my favourite black writers is Ishmael Reed. In an essay called "Before the War, Poems as They Happened," (in *Shrovetide in Old New Orleans*, 1978), Reed praises the cultural gain made by the "admixture of symbols, textures, images, and rhythms arising from the poet's exposure to more than one culture." Lawson Fusuo Inada writes poems filled with black people's locutions. Lorenzo Thomas writes about Vietnamese people. Jerome Charyn's novel about the wartime incarceration of Japanese-Americans is a good read, as far as I am concerned. I don't think that he violated the literary rights of Jeanne Wakatsuki Houston.

Here is what Ishmael Reed says about people trying to exclude other people from writing about their lives: "What all this goes to show is that anyone who tries to keep his cultural experience to himself is like a miser, moribund in a rooming house, uneaten beef stew lying on a table, and lonely except for the monotonous tick tock of a drugstore clock — all that gold stashed in the closet doing no one any good."

As I said, we don't need any Amos 'n' Andy black people or Amos 'n' Frank Indian people, but here is the way to get rid of that foul stuff: let the writer or publisher know what's wrong with it. Don't ban all writing by white people about black people and vice versa. Don't throw out William Eastlake's Indians along with Tonto.

That "literary rights" business reminds me of a le Pennish-sounding phrase that came from the literary nationalists a few years ago — "birthright Canadian." It reminds me too much of the phrase Quebeckers used to hear thirty years ago — "speak white." It reminds me of Hitler's idea that Jews could not write music to be performed by "Aryan" orchestras. A lot of fascist notions come from minorities that threaten to become powerful.

I mean, come on. *The Flintstones* was written by a Japanese-American, and *Star Trek* by an African-American. Whose literary rights were they usurping?

The Grand Tour
to Gleis-Binario

IN THE EIGHTEENTH century the British writer was expected to make his Continental tour and to report on it. In the nineteenth century the British poets travelled on the Continent, and then went to live there, usually in Italy. Percy Shelley would point to the top of Mont Blanc (mandatory *topos* for the Romantics) in the very middle of Europe, and pronounce: "the power is there." Europe, north as it was of the Mediterranean, was the soil that had nurtured post-Aristotelian thought, and received its seeds into itself.

When writers in the British diaspora paid homage to the relative stability and cultural density of Europe, they included Britain, sometimes treating Britain as their forebears had treated the mainland. Typical sentiments of a traveller to the motherland may be seen in *An American Girl in London* (1891) by the Canadian novelist Sara Jeanette Duncan:

Then there is the well-settled, well-founded look of
everything, as if it had all come ages ago, and meant to stay
for ever, and just go on the way it had before. We like that
— the security and the permanence of it .... At home I am
afraid we fluctuate considerably, especially in connection
with cyclones and railway interests — we are here today,
and there is no telling where we shall be tomorrow. So the
abiding kind of city gives us a comfortable feeling of
confidence. It was not very long before even I, on the top of
the Hammersmith 'bus, felt that I was riding an Institution,
and no matter to what extent it wobbled it might be relied
upon not to come down.

Even the public conveyances, in clamorous motion, offer the assurance of an "Institution."

Observe now what Andrew Taylor, a much-travelled South
Australian poet, has to say about public conveyances in late
twentieth-century Europe travelled by a post-colonial:

"Gleis" and "Binario" are the two words used in German
and Italian respectively to designate the place in a railway
station where you board a train: "platform" or "track"
roughly translate them. I thought I saw the two words
coupled, as they undoubtedly must be in many border and
thus bilingual places, from a train window as I passed
through Lugano, Switzerland, on my way into Italy.
Obviously no physical town or country called Gleis-Binario
exists. But it is surely an Italian Switzerland of the mind:
where to arrive is to find that you've just caught a train in
several languages, which is taking you in several different

directions, and to diverse and devious ends. If the poems in the present collection [*Travelling*] don't actually inhabit this country, which surely is to be found as much in Australia as anywhere else, they are at least an attempt at travelling towards it.

Of course Europe has changed since, say, 1816, though its great ancient monuments cheat time even in the age of acid rain. But Taylor is percipient in pointing out that the visiting poet has changed a good deal more. Though he travels to Europe, perhaps hoping to find a constant source, maybe an antipodean Fountain of Age, he will find, as Taylor does, that his most prominent image is the Autobahn, or as Robert Kroetsch does, that he has got lost among the *Gleissen* of Frankfurt's train station.

These post-colonial boys are not Henry James's innocent Americans being deceived by the venal Europeans who inhabit the old stones. Ruskin's beautiful imperfect stones of Venice are not what they used to be themselves, nor where they were. Any tour of Europe now must find a place made of jet planes and freeways that roll through the mind.

There's Reality
in Your Syllable

THE NATURE OF the real is always a matter for argument, and it is a pretty good argument for the practice of fiction — probably the best possible argument for the practice of fiction.

Robert Kroetsch, our main western writing hero, said that the fiction makes us real. We go around repeating that loveable saw every chance we get, especially at meetings of writers and critics. Kroetsch wants us to start there, not to make of his remark the summing up of an argument.

People often quote what appears to be the Author's intention found early in my novel *Burning Water*: "speaking together to make up a history, a real historical fiction." That was intended to be advice as to the beginning of a project called the writing and reading of that book.

Of course any serious writing is an attempt to investigate the real. Emile Zola was trying to do that, John Dos Passos was trying to do that, and Robert Kroetsch is trying to do that. Emile Zola invented realism, based on laboratory science, to do it. Dos Passos imitated the unmediated camera eye to do it. When Kroetsch has a bunch of loony Canadian prairie men build a towering lighthouse made of ice a thousand miles from the nearest ocean, he's after the real.

Now I will tell you who is not after the real. Writers who write books or TV shows with the intention of satisfying their audiences are not interested in the real. They are acting out fantasies, their own fantasies of the Hollywood writer's Monte Carlo life, and their audience's soap opera afternoon life. The audience is there, waiting to be fooled. They name their children after the people in soap operas and drugstore titillation romance paperbacks: Tiffany and Shawn, Jessica and Chad.

Still, television and all the other information technology in the hands of the uneducated have shaken the world of the serious writer. Realism, for instance, is now an anachronism, because the world is so diffuse in our eyes that it is impossible for a mere book to imitate it. The class structure and antagonisms that gave rise to realism are still there. That world survives. But we can no longer limit a world and try to represent it, to use Henry James's verb.

So what can we do instead? We can try to make a text rather than trying to represent a world. A text is potentially unlimited. There are only twenty-six letters in the English language, and sometimes some of them are redundant. But they can be combined in what appears to any reasonable mind as an infinite number of structures.

Is this playing around, as opposed to the serious world of Emile Zola? Try to imagine any complex invention that we now seem to rely on — the airplane, the hydro-electric dam, the microwave, the kidney dialysis machine — try to imagine our making one of them without the combining of twenty-six letters.

A fiction is made in a similar way. Fiction as a word was made itself, from parts in various European languages, meaning made up, meaning built.

The most real thing in the world is an English sentence. The hand that signed the paper felled a city. Writers always notice very early in their lives the relationship between the word "sentence" as found in a written text and the word "sentence" as found in a criminal court. When I used the adjective "serious" in front of the word "writer" earlier, this is what I had in mind. When he commits his words to paper he is committing seriousness, as if he were the judge making his decision.

People should be as serious when they are naming their children. Or building their children.

Some serious people in the reading audience might wonder about my writing of potential infinity in the building of a text. They will say that we are now being forced to think of the earth as finite, of its resources as endangered by sprawling wasteful idiots. How can someone talk about potential infinity in a world such as this?

My reply is simple and careful. You need not try to represent a finite world by means of a limited literature. You can look on your twenty-six letters as the parts of a pattern that can be made in time as large and varied as the universe. It can grow in front of you like a new big bang. But you can prove your care and your seriousness during the application of every additional letter.

Every additional letter.

If you still want to think about mimesis, here it is. The care that you desire from the mortals on this earth, the steps necessary to keep this planet alive, can be imitated by the writer who knows that he is at the back edge of a potentially limitless structure made of letters. Make a sloppy syllable and it will be in the system for who knows how long. What is the half-life of a bad metaphor?

I know that poorly written fiction will disappear under the midden in time. I know that no one will be reading our drugstore books with the counter-display bosoms on the covers in a hundred years. That is not what I am thinking about. I am thinking about the relationship of fiction and the real. I am thinking this: that person who watches soap operas and reads bodice-rippers has already shown a carelessness toward the ecology of words. Can we expect that person to take the Amazonian rain forest seriously?

If you want to write about the Amazonian rain forest to make your point about reality, all right. Just be careful where you are leaving those words, will you?

V V V V V V V

I HAVE ALWAYS liked the idea of a group of poets. I disagree with
that critic who called poetry the "sullen art." Sullen means all
alone, and that may be an okay way to write a novel, but for most
of our history good poetry has been produced by poets working
with each other, or against each other. Wordsworth and Coleridge
made their great odes as arguments with one another. Keats and
Shelley fed each other's imagination. The English Romantics holed
up during storms and concocted nineteenth-century classics. A
hundred years later the Imagists slapped poems like poker cards on
the table around which they sat.

Right after the Second World War, there were two lively poetry
groups working the streets and salons in Montreal. They turned
their city for a few years into the poetry centre of English-writing
Canada. The small presses with which Louis Dudek was involved,

for example, would print the books that collectors and critics go to now when they want to understand how modern Canadian poetry got going.

I am not about to tell you that seven youngsters in Montreal in the seventies were Byrons or even John Gould Fletchers. I don't think they got tyro poets in Regina saying that they wanted to band together and become western Vehiculars. But in the history of recent English-language poetry in Montreal, the Véhicule group, Ken Norris, Stephen Morrissey, Tom Konyves, Claudia Lapp, Artie Gold, John McAuley and Endre Farkas, provided a very welcome radical chapter.

I lived in Montreal from 1967 till 1971. For me, Montreal was of course a storied site. In the forties Irving Layton and Louis Dudek had joined Torontonian Raymond Souster to create the fabled Contact Press and rescue Canadian poetry from the genteel tradition that Montrealer F. R. Scott had made fun of in his poem, "The Canadian Authors Meet." Leonard Cohen had emerged, published by Dudek, befriended by Layton, to act out the role of blessed *poète damné.* Milton Acorn met Al Purdy in Montreal, and got published by Contact Press. Soon there were dozens of whippersnapper poets, guys like Seymour Mayne and K. V. Hertz and Avi Boxer, who would start their own little poetry mags in the early Sixties.

But by the time I arrived there in Canada's centenary year, English Canadian Montreal was a poetry ghost town. The old guys were still around, at least part of the time, but they were not causing any trouble. Cohen and Mayne had moved out. Roy Kiyooka was there, but his best poetry was in the future. There were some English-language poets in their thirties, but they were staid. They resembled the academic poets in Iowa and the versemakers trying to get something together in the post-war desert that was the

English tradition. They fashioned metaphors and crafted stanzas and considered the spirituality of nature as opposed to the disappointments of contemporary city life.

They may have thought of poetry as the sullen art.

I felt a little lonely myself. Thank God I was involved with the paradox that was the Sir George Williams University reading series. Into this time-trapped world we brought the news — Victor Coleman, Michael Ondaatje, Michael McClure, John Wieners. I also taught creative writing, if you can imagine, and what a strange contradictory world we lived in. It was the late sixties, the time of great radicals and obstreperous youth. My "students" knew about Malcolm X and Frantz Fanon and the Velvet Underground. But they had not read Charles Olson.

There I was, in the middle of Montreal, holding up a poem by Charles Olson. There were the English Canadian poets, wondering whether Robert Frost might be a little too daring. These were the people who thought it was okay to use the word "whereupon" in a poem. They were conservative, I thought, largely because they were insular. They must have been aware, minimally, that there was a post-Imagist poetry out there, but they were quick to protect against it, calling it names. They favoured the conservative British arts scene, where the ability to be clever with name-calling was apparently an asset.

I left for the West Coast in the spring of 1971, having enjoyed Montreal, having talked with a few youngsters who seemed happy to hear from the outside world. Artie Gold, for example, could quote from Frank O'Hara, while downing a couple dozen latkes at Ben's.

A year and a half later a hip new arts gallery named Véhicule opened just about where Sainte Catherine Street started being west, and before anyone knew it there were Sunday afternoon poetry readings in the gallery. Those seven youngsters I mentioned began to cohere as a group, and you could be pretty certain to hear them doing their stuff on Sunday. Before too long, the gallery took its place among alternative arts spaces across Canada, and became the hip Montreal site for poetry readings by people from out of town.

Then, as these things went in those days, a poetry publisher named Véhicule was born, and three of those seven poets formed the editorial board from 1975 till 1981. Véhicule Press took its place among the little poetry presses of the country, learning its direction from, say, Talonbooks and Coach House Press, where the concerns for contemporary modes in poetry were accompanied by a desire to make interesting art of their books. Printer Simon Dardick and poets Farkas and Gold bent their heads together the way printer Stan Bevington and poets Victor Coleman and bpNichol used to do. The first book was Ken Norris' *Vegetables*. Affixed to the cover was a seed package with seeds in it. My copy featured, if I remember rightly, eggplant.

For five or six years the Véhicule collective produced nice little poetry books that quickly became book dealers' collector items. A quarter-century later, one still likes to sit and reread John McAuley's *Nothing Ever Happens in Pointe Claire* or *The Trees of Unknowing* by Stephen Morrissey. When one was in town, as one was in those days of the mid-seventies, it was nice to drop in at Véhicule and check out the art on the walls or wherever it was, scan the page proofs of Artie's new book, sprawl on the floor and listen to Claudia Lapp chant her new poems. It was nice to know that it was *there*, and that Montreal was *here*, with us.

They were a restless bunch, this collective, and the backlist from the Véhicule Press does not cover their activity in the small-press inky business. McAuley ran Maker Press (which published an anthology of the collective's poetry), Morrissey started *Montreal Journal of Poetics*, Konyves ran the peculiar item called *Hh* (he was always the one most involved in the history and course of the central European avant-garde) and Norris had an international mag/press called *CrossCountry*. There were other scraps of publications, too, the charming ragged edge of the paperback scene.

Artie Gold, for example:

Every group of young poets ought to have a Rimbaud.
  Ses strophes bondiront: Voilà! bandits!
  A hundred years after Rimbaud wrote his first poems and landed in his first jail cell, there I was teaching creative writing, as they called it, in Montreal. Naturally, quite a few of the students I sat with have gone on to publish poetry, but none of them at that time *read* as much poetry as did A. Gold, as he then signed himself, with the possible exception of his friend Dwight Gardiner. I was delighted to find that Artie had read Jack Spicer and Frank O'Hara especially, and that he thought of them when he wrote his own stuff. At that time the established Montreal poets, and the vast majority of the would-be poets, did not read Spicer and O'Hara. My fellow professors had never heard of them.

  But Artie had, and that is how I knew that he was serious about poetry. He was not interested in getting famous or expressing his uniqueness or preparing himself for a job teaching creative writing. (Artie never chased any kind of job very hard.) He wanted to know what was happening at the front end of the arts. What I noticed in 1970, and what keeps coming through his poetry, is his learning, his engaged reading of the avant-garde. Unlike too many of his peers, he really knew what surrealism was, and he also understood the history of glass art, for example. A tremendous collector, he had an apartment crammed with geodes, artdeco lamps, Arthur Rackham illustrations and insolent cats:

> you could have seen his silhouette
> leaping like a made up mind
> across balconies
> below streetlight moons

Late night Hallowe'en superhero Artiepoet. For Gold the image is what the human mind can do. Reference is not as important as utterance, or maybe we should say that when it comes to skewing one, it will be reference. In this way Artie Gold is not Arthur J. M. Smith.

Spicer and O'Hara reminded their readers that poetry is made of speech, and that speech can be exciting no matter the subject. In other words a young poet doesn't have to write about suicide or seduction to be interesting.

In fact smart-talking poetry corporal Gold was, in my opinion, just what the seventies needed. We had a lot of younger lyricists consolidating their post-language territories, solemnly dishing out free-verse stanzas on the northern experience or immigrant families toughing it on the plains. Gold is a city poet for sure, wielding lingo instead of a Canadian agenda:

> So many things remind me of you
> The birth of christ: Georges de La Tour (around 1633)
> page 126 Art news Annual/1955: The Repentant Magdalene
> a nude, Kirchner painted. A Matisse

Since his first poems Gold has always shown taste. He has sometimes given in to a weak impulse, to be another poet entirely, a
tabloid cantor or something. But withal he is an erudite collector
of history's hippest poets — in that way he was usually ahead of
his peers, reading Mayakovsky when they were reading something
from their high school textbook or *Rolling Stone*. They were likely
listening to some two-chord guitarist, while for Artie a quiet influence might be Charles Ives:

> just the gentle old man
> thinking and humming
> beside a piano river.

The point is that Artie learned good and early that he wanted to
live in a world populated by such figures. For him culture was not
that thing the vulgarizing anthropologists have made it, whatever a
society makes and does. Culture was what our artists refined. Not
that Artie went around in velvet suits, carrying a scented hand-
kerchief to his nose. "My muse must be a neighbor with/ a street
address," he wrote. That's just fine, because while he seems to be
saying that his poems will be filled with actual and motley big-city
detail, fig newtons and slippery porch steps, he is also here violating
the territory, plunking a chunky hipster beside the Pierian Spring.

All this while most of the wide-scattered Canadian poets have
never entertained the notion of asking the muses for anything.
They think that they can "express themselves" in tidy anecdotes
about spouses in bed or toddlers in the autumn leaves (I have just
glanced at a typical Canada Council L.C. Poets quarterly).

One hears that Artie Gold does not conduct a particularly safe
life, either, but I wouldn't know for sure. I know that his lines are

not something I, for instance, would dare walk across Niagara on.
He takes chances. So while he can somehow invest an accurate and
homely image with great sadness, "the tumbler lying on its side on
the darkened rug," he can also take risks that fling a kind of pleated
reality at you: "In the soft plaid mesquite/ she extends her arms
to me."

He has a daring ability to objectify his voiced poem by starting
a new one this side of it:

I have been thinking a great deal
about my bike that will be stolen.

I don't like things whose inevitability
works against me.

Why have you driven through my heart?
Make that   what.

Are we listening to him and therefore wondering about the written?
Or are we reading and suddenly seeing a second-last draught as
perfectly polished speech?

I don't know how prolific A. Gold is now, but he used to write a
tremendous number of poems, huge shaggy piles, more and more of
them, pushing for the apogee, where there might be more poetry
than life, when the impossible crashes down, and it turns out
that his life will be his major poem, the comprising of all those
fragments. He tried to shore up the world itself with his fragments,
I thought. Think.

In his most recent poems he has done what I ask of all serious
writers younger than I — he has developed a poetry I have a hard

time following. I remember David Bromige plainly stating that he had gone into poetry because it was difficult to understand. The difficulty is a gift of which I am glad.

I am also glad to have known this fridge-emptying, quarto-filling poet, irrecoverably middle-aged, I suppose. He was the first person who called me GB, now my signature.

To continue:

Here is what happens with any young arts collective worth paying attention to: the individuals that make up the group are restless and creative, and begin to pursue their varying interests while cherishing their early collaborative work in their memory, a place into which any artist will reach all his/her life. Tom Konyves, for example, became fascinated with the possibilities of videotape when that medium was new. He made something he called "videopoetry," and would become a West Coast video-arts doyen. Endre Farkas started a press and organization called the Muses' Company, and gave his attention to collaborations between poetry and dance. Claudia Lapp moved back to the U.S.A., eventually to Oregon, where she and her poetry are involved with visual artists and spiritual healers.

While the gang members were getting to be thirty, and some of them taking up teaching jobs, and most of them exploring multi-media and performance arts, the urgency of their poetry press declined. In 1982 Véhicule Press published an interesting compromise anthology called *Cross/Cut: Contemporary English Quebec Poetry*, edited by Ken Norris and Peter Van Toorn, the most interesting of the young conservatives. That anthology was a turning point: from then on the press would do a severe turn-around to publish the neo-con poets who had been the antithesis of the movement, and the Véhicule poets (they had first been called that by Wynne Francis, a professor at Concordia University) would be a name for a former collective. So goes the history of poetry, including the local history.

So we would get anthology after anthology, including a nice fat one in 2004. It was an opportunity to see the widely diverse recent poetry of seven former Vees. Tom Konyves told me that the poets are ordered according to their astrological signs or some such fortunate nonsense. The present-day Véhicule Press is not interested. They recently had a twenty-five-year anniversary party, at which there was apparently no mention of these middle-aged folks. On the internet you can find a picture book of Montreal writers as seen by Véhicule Press. None of these seven is anywhere to be seen.

The life of English language poetry in Montreal is now in the hands of two remarkable women — Erin Mouré and Anne Carson. They made it into the picture book, despite the radical contemporaneity of their work. One senses that there is some animosity being exercised to handle history.

Ken Norris' first poem in the seven poets' collection is a good introduction to that history as seen from within. It ends:

> We always
> had the freedom to create
> something out of nothing, to fill the air
> with music when there was nothing
> going on at all.

I filled a notebook full of clever insights into the verse in this volume. But I am less interested in those than in the recent directions taken by these kids I have known so many decades.

I like the new, more venturesome Norris. He used to be very strictly realistic and plain-spoken, the ideal student of Louis Dudek. Now his syntax is straight, but his images tilt: "you don't love the real; you love your mind playing across it." Morrissey has, in a way, gone in the other direction. He used to turn every poetry reading into an experiment in delivery; his poems in the anthology delve into autobiography and family history. His work resembles that of Marty Gervais, insisting without any easy moments, on recovering the events that lie under a carpet of years. Konyves is witty, terse and cynical. He chose his surrealist roots, and they, along with his years as a video artist, have led him away from exposition. Like Norris, he addresses the function of this update:

> There are poems and there are poems.
> we used to say, for we were defenders
> of the poems, the guardians of the poems,
> and our habits changed and our families grew
> until we forgot what we were defending
> and we secretly relinquished the poem

Lapp now writes hearty poems denouncing the enemies of the earth. She has become what one would hope and expect from an artist in the U.S. northwest, an environmentalist, one who lends her strength to the anti-war movement and favours the wisdom of pre-propaganda children. Gold still offers us outrageous poems that flip like intellectual fish just out of the water, not quite graspable in the bottom of the boat. You can hear his voice even if you don't know it — his lines compel companionship. McAuley has grown pleasantly weird. He translates the Roman poets with iambs and anapests, setting us up for his other poems, in which he presents such things as Virginia Woolf brushing her hair on her last day of life, imagining eating the little bits of fat under her scalp. Farkas has always been the most French of these English-language poets. Here he offers us a brave long Quebec love poem.

Any anthology that has anything to do with a moment from so many years in the past is going to make you a little sad, the kind of sad that mortality has so much to do with. In this case, of course, that sadness is bound up with the fact that the neo-cons have infiltrated the magazines and universities in the little community of English Montreal.

But here it is anyway, a reminder of those wonderful days in the early seventies, when the collective wrote and sang and danced and painted and sat on the Véhicule floor, and the world came to Ste Catherine Street. It is a book, seven living poets and the spirit that makes people grasp the means of production, still here.

Ken Norris was the last to reach the age of fifty. In his 2003 book titled *Fifty*, he offered this simple dedication: "for the Véhicules,/ all fifty now." Seven times fifty makes up a year of days. Let's spend it reading what we have so far.

God Only Knows

Earlier this year I took part on a public panel in a little theatre at the University of Winnipeg. We discussed various things about poetry and the writing of poetry, and of being a poet and so on. To close the event we had questions from the audience. One person asked us, in a friendly manner, why we had become poets.

So I could show my book to my mother, and say, "See? You were wrong!" I replied.

It *is* an interesting question, and a rest from "Where do you get your inspiration?" or "What audience do you write for?"

At this point I could fire a lot of answers at you. I could tell you what the famous poets have said about the subject. John Donne, Walt Whitman, Hilda Doolittle, bpNichol, Susan Musgrave. I might do it, too, but I have recently moved back to the West Coast, and all my poetry books are still in boxes.

I do want to say something about the subject, though, and I do want to entertain a number of possible justifications for becoming a poet. I do remember what one poet said when he was asked why he was a poet. Robert Duncan, the great San Francisco poet, said "To exercise my faculties at large."

Notice that Duncan did not single out any particular faculty. When I was in grade three, my class was told that your brain is kind of a commanding officer, that the eyes or the ears or the taste buds or the fingertips would experience something and send a message to headquarters, where the brain would consider the situation, very quickly sometimes, and tell the fingertips to get off that stove element. Duncan the poet did not see that hierarchical, that *colonial* order. When verse was there to be composed, it was sometimes the ear that would lead in the poet's response, sometimes the dancing feet with their un-iambic beat.

Ezra Pound had told us that we poets had to employ three things at once, *phanopoeia*, *melopoeia* and *logopoeia*, that is, what we see, what we hear and what we think. What Duncan wants us to be aware of is how enjoyable it is, how like an athlete we are, that person who delights like a frisky colt in his sheer physical abilities. This is not a case of flaunting it if you've got it. No, it is not about you; it is about those lovely faculties.

No, not about you. When I asked my daughter's elementary school teacher why she was doing "creative writing" instead of grammar, the teacher said it was so that the children could express themselves. I immediately went to work on that kid. If she was going to go around expressing herself she would never be anything more than an elementary school poet, I reasoned. I let her express herself, sure enough. Scream as loud as you want, Precious, I said, these walls are soundproofed. She turned out to be a pretty good poet and a better short story writer. Never would have got past elementary school if she'd been satisfied to express herself.

No one is interested in a recitation of your dreams, and other people are not curious about the patterns or deeper meanings of your vomit or other excreta. If you are so intent on getting all your internal external, it is going to be pretty well the same stuff all your life.

So, why would you become a poet, Bowering?

Well, I grew up in a small town in the Middle Ages, and there was a lot to do, but not much of it had to do with the arts. I mean, I did act in plays in school, and I did share a homemade photography darkroom with my pal Willy, and I did drawings and cartoons, and once I got to be a radio disk jockey. But really, writing was all one could do. So I decided to write. I mainly wanted to be a sports reporter somewhere where baseball is important, but I would settle for writing fiction; however, that called for sustained attention and you had college to go to and so on, and no one was asking for fiction, so I settled for poetry. You could use a ballpoint pen to write a poem on the inside back cover of the paperback novel you were reading, and later type it right, and eventually some editor at the *Canadian Forum* would relent and publish it, maybe because it fitted nicely on page five, under a story about the Commonwealth Conference.

I am a poet because not to be a poet in 1968 seemed to be tantamount to admitting that your life might as well not have been lived.

I am a poet despite the fact that a poet makes about 11 cents an hour, which is even less than I got thinning apples in Naramata, B.C. when I was fourteen. Okay, during the two years that I was Parliamentary Poet Laureate of Canada, that figure doubled, but very soon I had to go back to being an ordinary citizen poet.

Recently I went to an exhibition of works by the great Quebec painter Jean-Paul Riopelle, and as you know, the magazine reproductions of his works from the fifties can not render the thick sculpturish marvels he made. I am a poet because, just as you can tell that Riopelle loved the turmoil of gooey paint he carved with his palette knife, I love the designs and crooked things you can do with words. These are the sounds we made to drop from the treetops, the words we invented so that we could put together a world.

Ezra Pound said that poetry is news that stays news. We hear it somewhere, and after we have carved a few words or a lot of them, that somewhere is still there. There is only one survivor of the battle at Troy, and that is Homer's *Iliad*. In Troy the local politicians and preachers and chamber of commerce might have had something to say about Helen and the Greeks, but it all went in one ear and out the other. Get Homer's lines in your ear, however, and no matter what language they are in, they will bring you the news about a lot more than a giant toy horse at the front gate.

I am a poet, not because I want to *be* the news. That was fun for those aforementioned two years, but it didn't do poetry much good. I don't want to *create* the news. Unlike other people, poets don't think or talk much about creativity. I want to write poetry, because if I am good enough and fortunate enough to know where to listen, I can *remember* or *write down* the news, and deliver it.

What you see on the front page of the *Vancouver Sun* is not the news.

Sometimes people ask you why you became a poet when everyone knows that if you want to make money as a writer you have to write movies or television or paperback novels about detectives or dragons, something that people can consume without hurting their heads. Percy Bysshe Shelley's poetry books were published in editions of three hundred, and that is a number that fits pretty well with Canadian poets these days. Once in a while a book of poetry will become a big seller at the big box bookstores, but generally only when it has been written without too much effort by someone who is already famous as a singer favoured by teenagers.

Who in their right mind would write serious, difficult poetry?

You got that right.

Over the centuries there has been a lot of talk about the close relationship between poetry and madness, or maybe poets and madmen. And sure, there have been cases of poets who wound up in loony bins, or should have. Books have been written about the high incidence of suicide in the poetry business — we are right up there with dentists. In the movies the poets are usually big guys with uncombed hair who are drunk all the time. Well, poets say that they hear voices telling them what to write, and would-be poets talk about expressing their inner selves. No wonder people think they're crazy.

When I was young and getting ready to be a poet, I had sentimental notions about being crazy. But as soon as I got serious I knew that poetry was one of the few truly sane things in my life. Compare it, for example, with politics, real estate, and television. By "sane," I might mean something that will cut through the lies that fill the air we have to breathe. People are firing lies at us all the time. The president of the United States, General Motors, the Dean of Education, the chief of police, the Minister of Education, the Nike shoe company.

Poetry, when it is any good, is an antidote to all that, an inoculation, a shield. When an authoritarian regime, a colonial power

George Bowering

or a global corporation wants to use people and abuse people, it first uses and abuses language. Some SUV manufacturer calls his machine "freedom" or "a revolution." Some invader says that he is spreading freedom around the world. First the language, then the language people. Authoritarian regimes and colonial powers that feel threatened see to it that the poets are in jail or dead. If the poet is the most popular guitar-playing folksinger in the country, he might get his fingers cut off his hand, as happened to Victor Jara in Chile, when that country was crushed by an authoritarian regime with the backing of a colonial power.

Here in Canada the poets might feel a little embarrassed to answer the question "Why do you write poetry?" with the claim that we want to protect our country from oppressors. The poets get killed in Greece and Chile and El Salvador and Nigeria, but not in Canada, eh? In fact, we get a little envious of poets in other countries, because the powers that be don't care what we say and publish. But in Montreal during the 1970 invasion of Quebec, the poets' books and records were taken out of stores by guys in uniform, and some of the French-speaking poets were thrown into the calaboose. The prime minister of Canada called this an "apprehended insurrection." Once, when the crazy socialist poet Milton Acorn read from his book *I Shout Love* on the grounds of the Ontario legislature, his audience was rousted by cops on horses. If you work on it, you can get into trouble for your poetry in this country.

But there are all kinds of people who turn into poets. There are really good poets who have no home. There are really good poets who live in big houses in Toronto. There are good skinny poets and good fat poets. There have been, one is either pleased or sorry to say, really good communist poets and really good fascist poets, and probably even really good capitalist poets. There are excellent Christian poets and Islamic poets and atheist poets. I greatly admire Ezra Pound's poetry but I want fascism to disappear from the earth. I am a heterosexual Canadian who is highly displeased by the country where my grandparents grew up, but I would love to have been the homosexual U.S. poet to whom these lines were granted:

> Katie is making
> velvet roses: next
> to a green pair, she
> fastens a bunch of
> wooden spoons. How
> striking they will
> look, on the bodice
> of her dance frock!

Why become a poet? Why write poems? Because sometimes when you are writing, words and their sounds and the images come together as if you were not there, and leave something as adorable as anything you will see while walking along a hilltop in the morning at Tahiti.

17 Questions

1. *When did you realize that you were going to be a writer? Did your childhood influence your writing?*

Years ago I published a piece on that topic, in, I think *Autobiology*. First I wanted to be a policeman, having read a lot of comic books, which were mainly about bringing criminals to justice. But I read a lot of books, a lot of westerns, and then science fiction, and of course other stuff. I was always reading, carrying around a book. Friends or enemies would say why don't you live life instead of reading about it? I wish I had thought then of the obvious answer — that reading was my life. So of course if you live in a small town you read books and then the natural thing is to decide to write books. I wrote for the school annual at Southern Okanagan High

School, and more important, I wrote about baseball and basketball for the Oliver *Chronicle* and the Penticton *Herald*. For the former I was paid 15 cents an inch and for the latter I was paid 25 cents an inch. I published a piece about this in *A Magpie Life*. My childhood influenced my writing in two ways. One: I lived in the dry hills of the B.C. interior, so that the places I hiked every day resembled the landscape in western movies and novels, so I was determined to write some, and I did, and before I did, I reacquainted myself with Max Brand and Luke Short. Two: my childhood was contrary, or maybe not — I lived in a little town where you could not get most things, but I listened to radio stations from San Francisco and San Diego. I read magazines from New York and Chicago. I wanted to be a major American writer.

2. *What kinds of life experiences, if any, have exerted a profound influence on your work?*

That is a vexing question for a person who has been battling realism for so many years. I mean, when I was 20 my favourite fiction writer was James T. Farrell, a champion of naturalism. I loved his books, Studs Lonigan, of course, but mainly the other kid, the one with the glasses, who wants to be a writer, eventually. So naturally, my first novel, unpublished, 550 pages long, entitled *Delsing*, is autobiographical, takes this guy George Delsing from really early childhood, till he is 21 years old, I think. Some of my stories make use of the Okanagan Valley as I knew it in the forties and fifties. Especially the setting, orchards. But the most profound experience that has had an influence on my writing has been reading, books, fiction, things novelists say about fiction. I may have taken Farrell as a model at one time, but in later years I have looked for ideas from Borges and Stein and Sorrentino. Rather than starting with the question "what was it like?" I start with the question "I wonder if a person could — ?"

3. *Do you keep a journal or diary? Is memory important to you as a writer?*

When I was a young writer/poet in the sixties, all the other young writers in my crowd were hot on keeping journals. I was, I think, the only one that did not keep a journal. I tried. In the summer of 1963, for the famous poetry month at UBC, with Olson and Ginsberg and all those people, I went to the UBC bookstore, for the purpose of starting a good journal; I mean here it was going to be, the chance of a lifetime. I bought a kind of artist's sketchbook, a thing with heavy paper and no lines, and started keeping a journal of the events. I was still putting the odd entry into that journal twenty years later. But I have been keeping a diary since 1958. A couple years ago I made a book out of some of that. It is a dull diary, though; it is a lot different from a writer's journal. No ruminations about the writing art. No philosophical or political thinking. It has, for example, my bowling scores. Once in a while I will list 26 cities I have been to, their names starting with A, then, B, etc. There will be a list of people I saw at a party the night before. Dull stuff. On one page there is an acrostic announcing an erotic achievement. Most of the time it doesn't amount to much. In 1958 and in 1968 I was pretty good at filling a page (that is the standard) every day. Nowadays two weeks can go by without an entry. Sometimes I don't fill a page. What I like to see is the city I was in, say, on July

30, 1981. Often you will find reviews of my books taped in, or newspaper photos of my friends. Memory? When I wrote *Delsing* I made use of the perfect memory I had till my early twenties. After I wrote that my memory began to disappear. But poor memory is good in that it, like deafness, promotes postmodernism.

4. *Who are some of the writers you admire and why?*

Oh, there are so many. Percy Bysshe Shelley, H.D., Robert Creeley, Margaret Avison, Gilbert Sorrentino, Sheila Watson, George Stanley, Erin Mouré, Jerome Charyn, Samuel Beckett, Ethel Wilson, Thomas Hardy, Gertrude Stein, Claude Simon, Georges Perec, Paul Verlaine, Ezra Pound, William Carlos Williams, Fred Wah — well, as you can see, it goes on and on, Italo Calvino, Dorothy Richardson, Suzette Mayr, on and on. I am so damned happy that there are so many great writers to read, and that you can always find an author you didn't know about or hadn't bothered reading, and just enjoy the fact that she published 30 books and you have 29 more to go. I have many reasons for admiring writers. You might not have expected me to list Thomas Hardy, but there are lots of good reasons for digging him: he was an accurate champion of women's rights, especially of the right to happiness; and he gave his heart to his concerns (teachers usually say that Conrad was the superior artist, but Hardy gives you heart, and not a clumsy heart, either); and Hardy has a terrific sense of humour, especially when he is making fun of people who think that they are more important than they are. On the other hand, I love Erin Mouré, because she wins an audience, and then strives to exceed its tolerance.

5. *Do you have a regular schedule? What is a normal day for you?*

Some writers, such as Allen Ginsberg, can write while sitting in the passenger seat of a car, in airports, in the lower branches of a catalpa tree, maybe. They write prodigiously in their journals, and when a book of poems is needed, there it is, for the extracting and polishing. Not me. Occasionally I still dash off a few lines on a napkin in a greasy spoon, but really, I work best with a routine. It does not matter where I am, as long as I am there for a while. I have written novels and long poems while in Italy or Denmark or Germany or Costa Rica. I have written books by hand in scribblers, by typewriter lugged through airports, on big computers and laptops (always Apples). But I love a routine. I like to get up in the morning and do my fooling around and delaying tactics — sports pages and crossword, etc. — knowing that I have a thousand words to get down. I like to write in the afternoon. But most important is that it happen every day, and that a set number of words gets done. For my last history book I let myself go with 750 words a day. When I was in Trieste and Vancouver and then Costa Rica and San Francisco, writing my novel *Burning Water*, I wrote a thousand words a day, by hand in these wonderful little Chinese notebooks I got in Chinatown after Robin Blaser showed me one. At first I could get my thousand words in less than two hours. By the time I was approaching the end it was taking me ten hours to get the thousand words. There was so much to keep track of, so many strands to remember.

6. *Do you need inspiration to work? Or a special environment?*

Regarding a special environment, see above. I do like to have a nice boring work room. For most of my early years I worked on the kitchen table, and I am often drawn there these days. But I also like to have a computer room and my own chair, and a window that I can cover with a blind or curtains, or cardboard. I have always done that. I remember that when Gladys Hindmarch and I were both living in Kitsilano, she had to have a room upstairs with a window through which she could see a lot of Vancouver. I was around the corner, working on a round table that I later gave Gladys, downstairs, with the curtains drawn. I did write one book, *At War with the U.S.*, her way, looking out an upstairs window in another part of Kitsilano. A lot of stuff down on the street got into that book. As to inspiration: my poetry should be inspired, let's say "dictated," to use Jack Spicer's term. There are a lot of techniques you can devise to keep your will out of the procedure. It is especially interesting when you are writing a longer poem, especially a serial poem, in Spicer's sense. When I am writing prose, though, the entry of the surprising can be accompanied by the freedom to make things up. I firmly believe that the fiction writer, for example, does not capture or represent (to use James's term) the world, but rather puts something new into the world. At least a new arrangement.

7. What do you do when the work is not going well?

All my life I have heard about "writer's block," about the terrible suffering that must be something like insomnia, I don't know. I don't ever recall having such a problem. I guess there have been times during which I was not as pleased with what I was writing as I might have liked to have been. But here is what you can do: if your poem is not coming, you can either say okay the poem is finished, or you can say okay I will now get to that article I have been meaning to write. There is always something to write, isn't there?

8. *Do you talk about work in progress? If yes, what are you working on now? If not, what are your reasons?*

I know the superstition. If you talk about what you are writing, the muse will quit on you. I know that there are even writers who will claim that they are not writing anything at all, including Sharon Thesen and Michael Ondaatje. When I was younger I thought it was a kind of neat romantic superstition, so I would never talk about the book I was writing. But now I do. I just don't go into detail. Save the juice, I guess. At this moment I am, if I ever get through this interview, embarking on a new book, which I have decided to write by hand — or rather, circumstances suggested that I write it by hand, in notebooks with spines but no lines. I was sitting in a bar with Jean and my agent Denise, talking about what I should write during this winter in Ontario. There was the novel I have been waiting for years to do, but there was also, more and more, the book about baseball and me. Denise asked what I would be happier doing. I said, well, I have been complaining for years that I couldn't get at this novel because Penguin had me doing all these history books. Denise said, yes, but what would you be happier writing? The baseball book, I guess, I said. So you see. I have hand-written the first chapter. I have begun the second chapter, barely. This month I have been researching, if that is not too ambitious a word, a later chapter. That's all I am saying. Of course, I might get back to the YA novel I got halfway through a couple years ago ...

9. *Do you work with an editor?*

Yes and no, and sort of. Of course with Penguin I have always worked with an editor and a copy editor and a fact checker. My association with Penguin started with Cynthia Good as my editor, for the novel *Caprice*, and then she was my editor, but she was climbing in Penguin, to become publisher, and then president. All this time she was feeding me ideas that I "would be perfect for." Apparently I tended to bring the history books in somewhat fatter than she had in mind. For the last one, *Stone Country*, she had it written into the contract that the maximum girth would be 100,000 words, and when I came in at 135,000 they made me cut it. I think I managed to keep about 110,000. Here's my favourite story about that. When Susan Renouf was editing my novel *Shoot!* for Key Porter, she said that I had to cut a hundred pages. I cannot do that to my darling book, I said. I will help you, she rejoined. And so we sat in the cafeteria of Eaton's or Simpson's or something, and started throwing out pages. There were two sources of extra pressure here. The place was closing, and they let us know that we were out of there in a half hour. But worse, David McFadden was with us, kibitzing in the usual McFadden way. Oh, my heart was broken when I saw the pile of pages we had yanked from the body of my darling book. But when it came out I was pleased with it. Actually, I think my editors will tell you that I am easy to get along with. I also play that little game in which I am an innocent lad from the west and these hardened women from Toronto can push me around or trick me or bend me to their desire.

10. What is your opinion of critics, and have they influenced your work?

Northrop Frye wrote a good essay in which he argued that there should be such a career as literary critic. What a dream. The normal thing in this country is that a veteran poet's new book is reviewed by a tyro poet. Maybe that's okay; maybe the old guy has to be kept in line. But I have also noted that the reviewer is almost always a poet of the status quo, conservative, anecdotal, lyric. Well. Reviewers are not the same thing as critics. Here is the way I look at reviews and critical essays: I will listen and take advice if the critic or reviewer is a writer that I think knows what is going on. If Ondaatje or Kroetsch says something, I listen. The question of influence is something else. I suppose that in some way I have, from time to time, been influenced by what a critic says, whether about my work or someone else's. But I could not, or can not right now, bring an example to mind. Certainly, though, if you said that Charles Olson was a critic when he wrote "Projective Verse," or that Ezra Pound was a critic when he wrote "A Few Don'ts for Imagists," then I have been greatly influenced by critics. See what I mean? I have usually told young'uns that if they want to learn something about poetry, go to the poets. Read Shelley's essays or W. C. Williams's autobiography.

11. Do you feel any obligation towards your readers and do you communicate with them?

Of course, one enjoys the fantasy that a reader somewhere in Saskatchewan is holding his book open and shaking his head in wonderment and respect at the sheer brilliance of the writing. And though it makes me all shy, I am happy when I am told by someone I don't know that he really likes my poetry, let us say. But the only reader I have in mind while working is yours truly. I am so busy trying to hear the line or the sentence that all else fades into the near distance. Here is where I really admire Erin Mouré. Her first couple of poetry books were really well-written, and you could

tell that this person was going to win prizes and be important. But
the nature of the poetry was not all that much different from other
really good descriptive poetry in Canada. It was, for example, easy
to read, with enjoyable images. She developed a good fan base, as
they say in the entertainment business. But then her poems started
getting hard to read. You had to work to grasp even a bit of them.
They were "experimental," and "post-modern," and "avant-garde."
Her early fans, who wanted more of the same, were unhappy. Oh,
Erin, she was so good, and now she has been kidnapped by all those
far out crazies. As to audience: I would be disappointed in myself
if all my readers understood everything I was doing; but contrarily,
it gives me great pleasure when some ill-dressed twenty-year-old
toting a heavy book bag tells me that he caught the reverse
reference to Mrs. Louis Zukofsky in a short story I wrote. As to com-
munication: I usually write anyone who writes me. It may take me
a while to get back to him. With e-mail, the situation is simplified.
I mean other than the messages you get from distant highschool
kids who have to write an assignment on you and they want you to
give them some "ideas."

12. How do you relate to fame and recognition?

I like it if it is in print, like the flood of newspaper and magazine
pieces that were generated when I was made the poet laureate. I get
all embarrassed and don't know what to say when it gets personal,
when a couple of people are telling me how wonderful I am. In
between are those moments when you are getting an award in front
of an audience. Well, that's okay. I was really amused when I went
this summer [2003] to my home town, Oliver, wine capital of
Canada, to be fêted, given the keys to the city, presented with a

barrel of wine, bottles with my picture on the label, etc. All over town, at the supermarket, at the holy roller church, at the town hall, etc., there were big signs welcoming me home. I even got a handful of free tickets for Jean and me to go tubing down the Okanagan River. Wonderful. But I was still bashful when someone came up to get a book or a bottle signed. I never know what to write. If you stick a microphone in front of my face, I can talk fast for hours. But all I can say to ordinary people is gee, thanks, uh.

13. Do you think the writer has social responsibilities? If so, what are they?

I admire some writing done by writers who claim no political adherence, and who are then seen to go into back rooms with right wing thugs — as for example Borges. I can even read with some pleasure Stalinist assassins such as Neruda. I admire Roque Dalton, the revolutionary soldier murdered by the Maoists in his own army. I can agree with a Wildean notion that your responsibility is to write well. Personally, I subscribe to the romantic tolerant left, and in my books you will not find good things said about the U.S. government or the government by developers, as seen recently in British Columbia. I think that the reader has great responsibility socially, that people who shun the news because it is so "depressing" are a waste as human beings. Writers, in the world I would like to reside in, are not obliged by their talent to try to form opinion, but they will decide to do it. I admire Margaret Atwood for a number of things, and one of them is her willingness to speak out and to lend her influential name to causes.

14. Have you worked or do you think within a political or religious framework?

I have politics and I have religion, but I do not look to their standards when I come to write something. This is a hard question. I think that I would get out of the difficulty by addressing the word "framework." Let us say that the traces of Christianity left in me will be noticed in my displeasure with U.S. foreign policy, as seen in my history books. The U.S., I believe, is the greatest enemy that Christianity has ever had, whether we are talking about the attack on the spirituality of the Bible by those moronic preachers who can only read it literally, or the violation of the Ten Commandments by the U.S. military in small countries all over the world. Am I now talking about religion or politics? I can remember that in grade six my teacher Rudy Guidi was explaining socialism to us, and I thought, well of course that is a logical and emotional extension of Christianity. I still think that. That is why the great socialists of the Canadian prairies were preachers.

15. What is your greatest fear?

Death, eh?

16. Your greatest joy?

That's over with now. It involved being a second-baseman and, therefore, the middle person in a double play. There are other joys, publishing, assurances of love, seeing the Canadians beat the USAmericans in some sport. But if you have never been involved in turning a double play, I am afraid I can't tell you how absolutely joyful that is. Charlie Parker must have had a sense of that when he did his solo in "Scrapple on the Apple."

17. How would you like to be remembered?

I've said this before. I would like to be the writer whose name will not come first to people's lips, but whose name you can't quite leave off in your hurry to get to the next topic. I want to be the necessary example of the opposite when people are characterizing our era.

Atwood's Hook

MARGARET ATWOOD SPEAKS her poems in a monotone, and fills them with severities. Just about every poem, then, is ironic.

Atwood's writing, the poetry and the fiction especially, is often violent, or presents violent anatomical images. But more often than not, that violence is married to wit. There is another irony laid on the first one.

I guess I should be relieved, said Rennie. That you didn't hack off the whole thing.

We don't do that any more unless there's massive involvement, said Daniel.

Massive involvement, said Rennie. It's never been my thing.

(*Bodily Harm*, 34)

Bodily harm and bitter humour — Atwood's theme and method. The poem that comes first in Atwood's public canon is a jest about drowning.

When a poet has been around as long as Margaret Atwood has, she becomes identified with a bunch of anthology poems. Perhaps they are not her best poems, but they are the ones most often read, the main supports of a reputation. "The Animals in That Country," "Death of a Young Son by Drowning," "Marrying the Hangman," "Notes Towards a Poem That Can Never Be Written" — Atwood has a solid album of greatest (and hardest) hits.

But there is one poem that is, while often cited, something apart. It appears not so much *in* a book as *on* it. It has no proper title, no real page number, and not even a formal beginning or end:

you fit into me
like a hook into an eye

a fish hook
an open eye

It appeared first in *New*, a USAmerican magazine hospitable to Canadian poets. Then it showed up as the page one poem in *Power Politics* (1971), where it is one of three very short pieces, each with a pair of two-line stanzas, that are placed in the bottom-right corner of the page. It is thus signalled that these three poems are different, perhaps apposite to the text. The one which we are considering is further differentiated by the fact that it has no upper case letters.

It became even further differentiated when it was reprinted in Atwood's various volumes of selected poems. Now it is moved from page one to the title page as a kind of emblem or epigram, and now it is printed in italic letters. It looks, that is, like a quotation, perhaps a quotation from Margaret Atwood.

William Carlos Williams is stuck with his red wheelbarrow, titled or not. Gertrude Stein is associated with various aphorisms, such as her definition of Rose. But the most famous short poem of the twentieth century must be Ezra Pound's "In a Station of the Metro":

The apparition   of these faces   in the crowd   :
Petals   on a wet, black   bough   .

It has occurred to one that Atwood's poem sounds like Pound's, not only rhythmically, but with its complete-sounding first part and its tacked-on surprise ending. Then one has noticed that either poem is made of nineteen syllables, and that in either case the units are made of twelve syllables and then seven syllables.

Then, as if that weren't enough of a resemblance, one hears that in both poems the second part end-rimes with the first. One can look further, of course. In her second part Atwood does what Pound did — juxtaposes two clear nouns. Pound wanted, he said, to paint a quick image, something to see intensely; Atwood's reader shuts his eyes quickly, in order to keep on seeing.

But Ezra Pound's poem, oft-quoted as it is, was not hoisted to a title page, not turned to face the rest of his *oeuvre*. Its punctuation and line-shape have been altered by conservative editors, but it is still in Roman type. It is also a Modernist painterly Imagist poem: it contains no subject pronoun and no verb. Its syntax is spatial, instantaneous.

Atwood's poem, on the other hand, is a grammarian's model, at least at first (leaving aside the matter of inaugural and final punctuation). It has a pronoun subject, a pronoun object, and an active verb-preposition combination in between. Further, it differs markedly from the Pound poem by using the mechanics of a simile, the excursion through the manipulating mind that was bypassed in Pound's quickness. Pound's effort is pictorial. Atwood's is political. It is the introduction to a book of poems called *Power Politics*:

you fit into me
like a hook into an eye

a fish hook
an open eye

The book appeared in 1971, a year before *Surfacing* did. Atwood usually writes a book of poems about something, usually a political issue, followed by a novel to make that something clear to the mass audience. In this case the topic is imperialistic power. Let's guess that "you" is the same U.S. addressed in the poem "Backdrop Addresses Cowboy": ("you are innocent as a bathtub/ full of bullets"). The endangered "me" is a vulnerable nearby country.

But the imperialism explored in both poems and novel is male sex-role power. This is the reader's trope: U.S. male lover-statue, addressed for 58 pages by Canadian female lover-victim. Politics makes strange beds.

hooker
and
looker

During an episode of fancy in the book, the she called "I" plunges a dinner fork into the heart of the him called "you." He reaches for her subcutaneous microfilm. She becomes a stone that he throws repeatedly to the ground. She ingests him like a drug. Bodies and fists make themselves hard. It is a violent book full of love poems. Its first four lines are ambiguous as any foreign affair.

you fit into me. From what angle is the speaker saying this? In other words, what is the tense? Is the masochism still happening, or has the speaker become a "creative non-victim"? In some dialects the past tense would be "fitted," so a further indeterminacy is provided for a line that seems to sound quite sure.

Even without that uncertainty the poem begins with the means to make its reader uncertain. Perhaps this is the ambiguity that attends all sex, in which penetration may be invasion. The poem does not say "you fit me," or "you fit in me," and it is a long way from "I fit around you." Grammatically the first line presages the violence seen later.

But still, "fit" is a nice word. It suggests order, the way things ought to be, a good condition; it suggests the reconciliation at the end of a drama, a happy or merciful closure.

Unless someone is saying "why then Ile fit you."

The word "fit" has its source in clothes-making, one of Atwood's favourite tropes. She often portrays her speaker as an Ontario granny, knitting, darning, making masks and dolls.

So the first part of the simile: the lovers come together as if they were fashioned to, and in doing so they offer comfort. The parts they resemble have always been called male and female, as are similar connections made by carpenters and electricians and plumbers. If such things fit well, they are called "true," as are stories sometimes.

Clothes-makers decided to call that loop or hole that catches the hook an eye (and one might think of the alternatives available), thus making a simile that Atwood would eventually unmake. So when we read the poem for the first time we say to ourselves: oh, *that* kind of eye, as on a cape. We are saved from pain and mutilation. At last we are going to see an Atwood text in which there is no beheading, dismemberment or impaling.

But the simile about a simile is defigured, and we are in familiar Atwood country after all, where the human body, especially the female human body, is likely to be taken apart. In Atwood's world you cannot have your cake and eat it too.

Power Politics has a lot of pronouns in it, and you and I may be certain that that is an important fact for this sequence of poems. One of the figures that occurs often in it is the alternation between the closed flesh and the open I:

Get me out of this trap, this
body, let me be
like you, closed and useful
                    (*PP* 19)

your closed eyes beat
against my fingers
I slip my hand down
your neck, rest on the pulse

you pull away

there is something in your throat that wants
to get out and you won't let it.
                    (*PP* 34)

If a hook and eye are big enough and fancy enough, and on a military tunic, they together are called a frog. As one might expect in a novel called *Surfacing*, the little amphibian is an important image. For one thing, it has no neck, so its body and head are one, a condition the book's narrator envies. Still, she fits a fish hook into it, and will "hook it on securely while it squeaks" (p. 64). A pickerel swallows the frog, which seems fitting, because it is a leopard frog, also called a pickerel frog. And the pickerel swallows the hook, and is killed by the knife of the fisherwoman, who says that "one of its eyes is bulging out and I feel a little sick, it's because I've killed something, made it dead" (p. 65). An open hook, a fish eye.

That is something like coincidence, but perhaps more properly something like what Jessie Weston called "ensemble."

Sherrill Grace (who calls the piece a "poemlet," perhaps thinking of an eyelet) says that Atwood achieves her effect by shifting from metaphor to metonymy, from "like a hook" to hook. Fish hook, eye: open eye. But such an observation is possible and likely only if one takes the sartorial meaning as primary. "Hook and eye fasteners are ordinary domestic objects; fish hooks in open eyes are another matter" (Davidson, 61).

But go back — suppose she had written a two-line poem:

you fit into me
like a hook into an eye

Here a reader, cued only by the word "fit," might have to reflect: oh, she means a hook and eye fastener. Then familiarity with Atwood the scary domestic scissors-wielding mask-maker will tell one that this poem is really flipping back and forth from metaphor to metaphor. A fly-fisherman reading the first two lines might not, as a seamstress would, think of clothing first.

Sherrill Grace is on the right track. She says that Atwood's "poems are characterized by a cool, literal language that functions syntagmatically" (Davidson, 61), and that the metaphor here is unusual in her work. I would amend that to seeing the cool, literal language, but to say that it usually operates in metaphor, here using a rare simile.

In other words, Atwood uses a kind of prosy assertiveness in unfamiliar country. Her speaker does not say that the affair is like a bad movie, nor that it reminds her of a bad movie. She says,

You take my hand and
I'm suddenly in a bad movie
(PP 3)

Then the metaphor is extended to the ends of the poem:

The smell of popcorn and worn plush
lingers for weeks

Atwood's use of metaphor is clean and readable. It is a perfecting of the first meaning our schoolteachers gave us for the word. Metaphor, we were told, is simile with the "like" removed.

Linda Wagner understands Atwood's usage well, and says perceptively of *Power Politics*, "the fun in the book comes through Atwood's myriad inventive descriptions of the power struggle — as politics, war, physical waste, innuendo, sly attack." Of our epigram she says that it alerts us that "reversing the cliché toward unexpected bitterness is a common tactic in these poems" (Davidson, 89).

Clichés are fossilized metaphors. In her reversing, Atwood returns us to the literal. Here the literal is seen to be unpleasant to say the least. Hence the new metaphor, at once cruel and sexual.

you fit into me
like a hook into an eye

a fish hook
an open eye

Yet what an odd phallic image, the hook. A hook hangs on. So do hookers, till they throw the fish back. But traditional sex-role narratives have women trying to hold their men, and men trying to get loose. Mothers tell their children: look out, you'll get your eye poked out. Or, don't be blinded by love.

In the writings of Freud and Lacan there are probably some interesting discussions of sexual imagery that would be useful here. But I am interested in Atwood's title, *Power Politics*. The open eye is traditionally emblematic of consciousness. Freud reminded his readers that the eye is an erotogenic zone, perhaps the most remote. Most remote from the genitals but closest to the brain, let us say.

In dreams, one remembers Freud having said, the loss of an eye or two represents castration, as it is supposed by him to do in the story of Oedipus. That is to say, a threat to the eye is a threat to power, in the Cyclops' cave or the sexual arena.

There are, of course, occult powers. Certain spooky animals can see in the dark. Ancient systems pose the watery depths as the unconscious, and the eye of the fish as perception there. Famous seers such as Teiresias had to sacrifice normal eyesight in order to gain secret wisdom or spiritual insight. If the verb in Atwood's poem is in the past tense, perhaps it claims the painful occurrence as a muse's cruel activity. If that seems far-fetched, consider this:

> we collide sightlessly and
> fall, the pieces of us
> mixed as disaster
> and hit the pavement of this room
> in a blur of silver fragments
>
> (PP 11)

The power one fears the most is the power that can take away one's soul. Some people say that the soul can get out of the body by way of the mouth, and perhaps it does, in a poem or a death rattle. Some people have always said that the eyes are the windows of the soul. Break and entry is particularly fearsome there.

In *The Golden Bough* Sir J. G. Frazer tells us that all over the world the fish hook has also been long associated with the soul. In rites concerning aging and sickness and death, various peoples use hooks to keep the soul in its body. But foes use hooks too, to fish the victim's soul out. Often these anglers will commemorate their sport or work, perhaps learning to be "fishers of men."

Sheila Watson was certainly thinking of souls when she wrote *The Double Hook*. Without those rituals and needs that make the communal human soul, she said in a famous spoken preface to the book, people can be "driven in one of two ways, either towards violence or towards insensibility" (*Sheila Watson: A Collection*, 183).

There is a lot of soul-chasing in Watson's story. Her character Ara, who sees and hears most important things, sees God as the Hound of Heaven:

Sometimes I think of God like that, she said. The glory of
his face shaded by his hat. Not coaxing with pans of oats,
but coming after you with a whip until you stand and face
himin the end.

I don't know about God, William said. Your God
sounds only a step from the Indian's Coyote. Though that
one would jump on a man while his back was turned.

(DH, 71)

Watson's vision of doubleness is a lot like Atwood's, I think.
Atwood's hook is, as we see, doubled, both repeated and revisioned.
Remember Ara's image of God's face while you read a passage from
Watson's narrative that has always been used also as an epigraph to
her novel:

He doesn't know you can't catch the glory on a hook and
hold on to it. That when you fish for the glory you catch
the darkness too. That if you hook twice the glory you hook
twice the fear.

Hooks and eyes. Watson's novel is more about eyes than
anything else. One character is always telling us what he has seen.
Others, for various reasons, can see what is not there. One is
blinded for what he saw.

On the first page of the book we are told that the *mise en scène*
is "under Coyote's eye." The French edition of the book is titled
Sous l'oeil de coyote.

In her famous thematic guide *Survival* Margaret Atwood does
not have much to say about *The Double Hook*, perhaps because it
does not fit into her thesis very snugly. But *Survival* was published

in 1972, a year after *Power Politics*. Atwood notices this about the transformation of Ma Potter's soul, her appearance as a poolside tree: "The vision, of course, is in the eye of the beholder" (*Survival*, 203).

There is a lot of intertextuality in Canadian literature. In one of his novels Robert Kroetsch has his "narrator" find a copy of *The Double Hook*. In one of his poems, some time after a passage about whether the shoe fits, he writes: "if the hook fits the eye, madam, whoop-de-doo" (*SP*, 53). One does not suspect that Kroetsch is talking about souls, though.

Is Atwood talking about souls? When someone says "you fit into me," we tend to think of bodies, conjoined. The appositive of "me" is at the end of the second line, "eye," or I, we suspect. So "you" becomes hook, a maimed pirate, maybe. We are suddenly in a bad movie, and probably we should back out, stop looking at all the boats we've noticed in the poems.

The worst thing that can happen to a fish is not the hook but the surfacing. This "you" is not a fisherman, but a hook, or he becomes a hook in the sport of "you" and eye. But this hooking and eyeing is only a moment, isn't it? There is no capital letter at the beginning of the poem, and no period at the end. So it is the middle of something longer.

Here we get another contradiction, or another part of the system of contradictions. Look at that verb again. Yes, it can be in the past tense, and it can be in the present tense, but what present tense? It is the ongoing, continuous, habitual present tense. It goes on happening, as in "I wear a size seventeen collar." You fit into me.

So here is the contradiction. The four little lines look as if they are a moment, a fragment from the middle of something longer, but the verb may say that this is happening all the time. In the *Selected Poems*, the poem is printed in italics, to prolong the contradiction. The italics say that these four lines are thus separate from the rest of the text. Yet, putting them in italics makes them sur-textual. They colour and include whatever is to follow.

What follows is no more ambiguous, in terms of tense, than any other poetry these days. *Power Politics* is written in the preterite, the future, and the ongoing present. Until the last verb of the sequence. The final poem is called "He is last seen," but contains the pronouns "you," "me" and "I." "You" brings "me" a "new death." It is figured as a glass paperweight:

Inside it, snow and lethal
flakes of gold fall endlessly
over an ornamental scene,
a man and woman, hands joined and running

That is an interesting alteration of the image "on" Keats' Grecian urn. The poet's speaker, in his or her observation then nearly parallels Keats':

Nothing I can do will slow you
down, nothing
will make you arrive any sooner

Then the poem and the book end:

You are serious, a gift-bearer,
you set one foot
in front of the other

through the weeks and months, across
the rocks, up from
the pits and starless
deep nights of the sea

towards firm ground and safety.

That last verb, "set," is like the first verb, "fit," in that it can be read as over and done with. In any case, as the last verb has that power, to remind us of the first verb, we should be reminded to consider the first ambiguity.

We might consider the notion that the speaker of the epigram is *desirous* of getting that action into the past.

He, called "you," has set his feet, one after the other, towards safe ground. Perhaps she can say, goodbye, I'll keep an eye out for you.

George Woodcock has written some of the best words on Atwood's ambiguity here. He says that the epigram we are reading takes us "to the very heart of Atwood's kind of poetry" (Woodcock, 313). The eye, he says, "sees, and is hurt, and so perception and feeling merge into each other." He then calls Atwood an objective poet and praises the complexity she can provoke with "that limpidity of tone which tempts one to adapt a phrase of Orwell and talk, in relation to Atwood, of verse like a window pane." (If we are still thinking of souls, that last is a neat pun.)

Woodcock does not say so, but he reminds one that no matter what the poem says, the hook is Atwood's. She made it, set it and fit it. Perception and feeling should, she hopes, merge into each other for the reader too. Hook and eye may be any number of figures but they are first very clear and sharp images. They draw a reader's active response. Any teacher who has read the poem to a new class knows that.

So we can not ever forget the eye of the beholder. One hopes that when a reader opens a book and sees that the first word is "you," she will feel for at least a while that she is being addressed. Certainly, when a poem is put into italics and lifted onto the title page, and starts with "*you*," it seems at least to flirt with the convention of the prefatory address to the reader.

Creative-writing teachers used to tell their charges to start their stories with a "hook." Who but the reader was to be the fish? Whose eye but hers was to be captured? Woodcock reminds us that Atwood, with her clear concrete nouns and the "tortuosity" that follows them, is the complete angler.

But this poem does not say "I fit into you." So if the reader is represented by a pronoun, she must be the hooked (the speaker, the writer) or the hookster (the real writer). The smart reader here looks for another designation of that "you" — and finds him. But the temporary advertence has been worth it: the reader will keep her eyes open, and protected, all through the reading of the book. She will be as alert as the poet wants her to be.

She will enter this book quickly *because* she is alert, in this way proving to be an advance on Atwood's progressively insane (because imperialistic, wilful) pioneer:

> For many years
> he fished for a great vision,
> dangling the hooks of sown
> roots under the surface
> of the shallow earth.

It was like
enticing whales with a bent
pin.

(SP 1966-1984, 49)

In power politics an open eye will take you further than will a great vision.

When you recite out loud, "you fit into me ... ," the people around you, unless you are at the doughnut shop, in which case you do not recite it, will first smile, and then try to complete the koan.

That is to say, this is a famous poem. It has worked itself free from the book it first began, then decorated. If it gets more famous it will work itself free from its author, as quotations from the Bible, Shakespeare and Pope have done. It will become part of our folklore, at least among those people educated to a level above folk tastes.

Thus the "you" in the poem and the "me" herself and eye will work free too, and come to refer in general, or momentarily, to any speaker and mock tormentor. Like all literary words that pass into the regular world, this little poem will take on meanings that might puzzle its author of a couple decades ago. Hugh MacLennan's "two solitudes," borrowed from Rilke's lovers and applied to Quebec populaces, was supposed to suggest a basis for cohesion, but the phrase is generally now used to suggest the opposite.

In the public world Margaret Atwood is perceived as a heroine and a fury. She wears her ambiguity well, a symmetrical fearfulness. So her poem, no matter how independent it becomes, will retain the grimly funny and suitably political ambiguity it begins with: "you fit." You belong. You hurt like hell.

Once Upon a Time
in the South

Ondaatje and Genre

MICHAEL ONDAATJE IS the plainest of men. He never has a decent haircut. He wears jeans that look like two blue bags. His favourite movie is a spaghetti western.

It takes him years and years of painstaking assembly to write one of his elegant novels. His lyric poems are the envy of lazier poets for their meticulous wonder. He writes as if the fragile balance of our universe depends on every sentence he accomplishes.

Between his early lyric poems and the recent semi-historical novels, he produced a sequence of books that were characterized by confusion and transgression — of literary forms, and most notably of genres. In conversations and interviews and in his restless works, Ondaatje has always shown a fascination with genre fiction and especially with genre cinema. His most famous crush has been on the western movie. One of his books features an author's photograph of the Ceylonese boy dressed in cowboy gunfighter gear, a picture that like many in the endpapers of his books was designed to mislead readers into realization.

In the 1970s and 1980s Ondaatje was notorious for producing books that confused his readers and the critics about their modes. In 1970 he won the Governor-General's Award for *The Collected Works of Billy the Kid* in the poetry category, but critics then and more recently have suggested that the book is really a short novel. The fact that it is assembled of prose dialogues and photographs and interior monologues leads one to think that Ondaatje was deliberately blurring the boundaries between forms. He has gone on record as saying that it was a scenario for a movie. The book is also ambivalent about genre. The troublesome title promises a whole literary career for a gunfighter sometimes thought to be illiterate. The discontinuities visible on the pages suggest a historical ana. But there is good reason to see the book as an incursion into the field of "penny dreadfuls" or "dime novels," those cheap narratives about the Wild West in the nineteenth century, most of which promised an authentic story while practising extravagance for the dream-besotted eastern (or South Asian) readership.

That was the book that preceded *Coming Through Slaughter*, and its "narrator" will make a disguised appearance in the later book, as will its author, presumably Ondaatje. The book then to follow was the equally puzzling *Running in the Family*. It shares more than a title's present participle with its predecessor. Reviewers did not know what to call it. Was it biography, autobiography, memoir, family saga, travel journal, photo album, poetry, short stories, social history, tall tale, satire, oral history, sociology, or portraiture? Was it a novel?

2.

I am not going to talk about genre in the sense that Plato and Northrop Frye did. Plato maintained that there were two modes of writing poetry — the descriptive and the mimetic. They had an ideal existence, and separated narrative and theatrical verse. He relented after a while, and said that there was a third, mixed mode that resulted in the epic. When neo-platonists were asked about the obvious existence of lyric poetry, they said that it was mimetic of the self. This is the sort of thing that caused trouble in genre studies. It was not long till champions of the idyll and the epithalamion claimed genreship for their favourite interests. No wonder that Italians such as Bruno and Croce said that it would not be long till every poet had his own genre. The notion of ideal modes had disappeared by the time of the Renaissance.

But still, critics do want to classify. If there are not ideal divisions, there can still be earthly, maybe psychological divisions. Northrop Frye goes further, replacing the ideal with something between heaven and earth: "The true father or shaping spirit of the poem is the form of the poem itself, and this form is a manifestation of the universal spirit of poetry" (Frye, 98).

I do not quite understand the difference between human beings made in the image of God, and human beings having universal characteristics. Frye's analogy between the individual human and the individual literary work must now meet a world full of experiments in reproduction, as well as miscegenation, mongrelization, organ transplants, mass migration and cloning.

There are those who say that the greatest works have always been those that violated the boundaries of genre. Not so Alan Tate the New Critic, who liked some of the poetry in *Finnegans Wake* but dismissed the book as a misdirected hybrid.

It is nice to have the idea of genre, though. It gives us a diachronic measure to lay athwart the synchronic measures that engage us — literary groups, best-seller lists, fads, technological adjustments.

Here are two more ways in which I will not use the word "genre." A lot of my professor friends just use the term to separate prose and verse, and maybe drama and non-fiction. That seems to me a waste of a nice foreign word. In the art world a "genre painting" is a depiction of ordinary people going about their humble tasks. The term has occasionally been used for poetry or novels about the lower classes.

There is a trace of that class snobbery in the way that I will use the term. In the publishing world "genre fiction" means those kinds of popular prose that are easily separated into categories of books sold by the millions to non-literary readers. These will include, in the Western world, detective stories, spy thrillers, westerns, romance novels, science fiction, and several sub-categories of each. One of the most interesting things about these books is that though their readers are not presumed to be intellectually discriminating, they will seldom deign to try reading a book from a genre that is not their favourite, not even if it is written by one of their favourite authors. Science fiction readers do not read Harlequin Romances. Many science fiction readers will not even read non-scientific fantasies involving other worlds.

3.

In North America, and probably elsewhere, there has long been a popular genre of romance fiction involving a nurse in an exotic setting and situation. She usually encounters a dashing and seductive exotic male — often an aviator. He is never a patient swain.

4.

Question: why do people like to read genre fiction?

Question: why does Michael Ondaatje like to write books that resemble genre fiction?

There are many people, who like to call themselves "big readers," who gobble up mass-market genre fiction wholesale. They look at fiction as recreation, as rest, as escape from a frustrating world into order. They are rewarded by the familiar, whether in the chosen mode or in a single author's writings. Remember, they do not like the book that their author produces outside his usual series or genre, even if it is in another popular genre — spy novel rather than police procedural, for example.

As for the writer of genre fiction — let us say the western — he is adding his particular voice to a kind of collaboration. The western has a vocabulary and a set of conventions, and thus a community. The book that its author produces will be part of a community lore, pulling together intertextuality woven by other books and the pleasure of the readers who like to find themselves in their landscape.

Everyone who reads difficult books remembers a golden youth when he received great pleasure in simply reading. When he was young he consumed lots of books of a certain genre. People argue that "children's literature" is a genre in itself. I read hundreds of westerns and then hundreds of science fictions. When I began more and more to add literary books (Hemingway) and near-literary books (Maugham), I continued as best I could my habits of sinking bodily into the world of the book. It helped to read a literary book that seemed to belong to the genre I was experienced in — Orwell's *1984*, for example. When I did a book report on *1984* my grade eleven English teacher gave me heck for just reading science fiction.

In other words, genre-reading seems to preserve the innocence of childhood. Here we could be talking about comic books, movies, radio programmes, baseball novels. Genre reading is nostalgic. When a literary writer flirts with genre writing, he is often described as a parodist. Perhaps he is — we can easily find examples — but he is not making fun of the books he read as a youth — he is not advising his readers to grow up. He is not trying to head off a reader's escape or his own. Maturity does not entail moving on. It allows one to declare that the pleasure of reading a generic fictive world can be incorporated with artistic intent into serious contemporary text production, whether in the avant-garde, at the political barricade, or in the heartland of a country's canon.

5.

As a poet Michael Ondaatje did not look for marketing by a "professional" publisher; he *joined* Coach House Press, the fervid alternative in the 1960s. Where the commercial presses look for efficiency in production and attractiveness in packaging for the market, the poet is a kind of contract worker hired and paid by the season. At Coach House Press, the activity was collaboration. Artists and writers and printers tried ideas on each other and came up with works that will always remind us that the author was there, figuring out how to make a book. This kind of collaboration is probably the realization of a dream that the young writer had when he was fervently reading himself into a world different from the marketing model called high school and after school.

When Ondaatje's first book *Dainty Monsters* (1967) was being built, he picked out the Ceylonese batik for the design of the wrapper. When House of Anansi published *The Collected Works of Billy the Kid*, it was designed at Coach House, and signed with that photograph of little Asian boy Ondaatje in full western movie regalia. The "Acknowledgements" page in *Running in the Family* (1982) supports collaboration as necessary to composition: "A literary work is a communal act. And this book could not have been *imagined*, let alone conceived, without the help of many people." Sort of like a movie.

6.

Ondaatje's only piece of extended criticism is his series pony on Leonard Cohen, published when Ondaatje was twenty-seven. Of all Ondaatje's Canadian predecessors, Cohen is probably the best known mixer of forms. Some of his books of poetry contain the lyrics of his most famous early songs. His last book of poems is a collection of Buddhist-Jewish-Christian prose meditations and prayers. He wrote a sequential dramatic poem that was produced as a television documentary extravaganza, and on that occasion the poet declared that he was a hotel. After the age of sixty Cohen brings his poetry to a television channel that specializes in three-minute advertisements for record companies. Cohen lives in the DMZ where genres meet.

Ondaatje, in his chapter on Cohen's first published novel, introduces it as an incursion by a poet into the field of the *kunstlerroman*:

> the novel was rewritten at least five times, with the result
> that its descriptions, dialogue, and portraits are shaved down
> to an almost poetic form. The book has the effectiveness of
> a long prose poem, with each scene emerging as a potent and
> enigmatic sketch rather than a full blown, detailed narrative.
> As in a poem, the silences and spaces, what is left unsaid, are
> essential to the mood of the book.
>
> (Ondaatje, 1970, 23)

This is not mature critical writing, but it shows an interest that may be itself interesting to those who want to read Ondaatje's books written after 1970.

Introducing Cohen's second novel, Ondaatje transcribes a radio interview with Phyllis Webb, in which Cohen announces that he was trying for one genre while, like the Black Romantic he had been called, rifling the storehouse of what would appear to be its opposite:

> I was writing a liturgy ... a great mad confessional prayer,
> but using all the techniques of the modern novel which was
> the discipline in which I was trained — so there's this huge
> prayer using the conventional techniques of pornographic
> suspense, of humour, of plot, of character development and
> conventional intrigue ... *Beautiful Losers* was everything I
> could give at the time.
>
> (Ondaatje, 1970, 44-45)

Everything he could give. Cohen's image of the writer as a person who pours out all the modes rather than stitching a text together is worth remembering when we encounter a book such as *The Collected Works of Billy the Kid* or *Running in the Family*.

Billy won that Governor-General's Award for poetry in the year that Ondaatje's little book on the collected works of Leonard Cohen came out. During this time the Canada Council often recruited writers for help, asking them what category certain texts should be entered in for the GG competition, especially when they were texts from Coach House Press. Some of us told the CC that they were almost getting the point. Trendy Canadian Literature commentators said, remember, that *Billy* was Michael's first novel. A few years later, remember, Ondaatje told Sam Solecki that "with *Billy the Kid* I was trying to make the film I couldn't afford to shoot" (Solecki, 20). In that book the piece on page 90 starts: "Sound up."

But poems and novels and movies are art forms, not properly genres. There was a real genre, popular from the last quarter of the nineteenth century into the second quarter of the twentieth. This was the true revealed authentic adventurous life story of someone famous and western, often an outlaw, quite often Billy the Kid. It is interesting to note that Ondaatje shared the Governor-General's stage with his friend bpNichol, who was receiving the poetry award for *The True Eventual Story of Billy the Kid*.

You had to be ironical to enter your title in this list, of course. But Ondaatje was also trying to write Billy Bonney's autobiography. He called these pieces "Left Handed Poems." I think that he was aware that Billy was left-handed only in the fancy of those yellowback authors who wanted to present him as diabolic and glamorous.

Of course everyone remembers his first impression of the book — it is a hodgepodge, an olio, a collage, a very obvious compilation of forms. The appearance of the pages, turned or flipped, speaks against continuity and decodedness. If these are his collected works, Billy worked as a lyric poet, a documentarist, one of Ondaatje's many photographers, and a pop novelist.

7.

The question of genre has, from the first reviews onward, been the first question that critics and readers ask about *Running in the Family*. On the ISBN page it is called biography. In the list of Ondaatje's books appended to *The English Patient, Running in the Family* is called a memoir. The first page, in italics, is written in the third person, and appears to be the beginning of a fiction.

But this book, too, is *assembled*. It combines autobiography, travel journal, photographs, and all those approaches mentioned earlier. To make matters more interesting, it is sometimes written in the "present tense," and sometimes in the preterite, depending on which genre is being imitated — or parodied. Further instability is produced as the book (Ondaatje's third book in a row to have a present participle in the title) is delivered sometimes in the third person, sometimes in the first, sometimes singular, sometimes plural.

Linda Hutcheon, of course, calls the book an "historiographic metafiction." She says that all Ondaatje's books are "texts and meant to be read as such, that is, with suspicion" (Hutcheon, 303). Smaro Kamboureli, in "The Alphabet of Self" writes of it: "... it whimsically insists on inhabiting the terrain of autobiography while at the same time displaying its energy as a text that wants to be the 'other' of what it declares to be." So, she says, "autobiography in relation to *Running in the Family* is not a genre but a rhetorical trope" (Stitch, 83). She is right, and I believe that we can say that of all Ondaatje's entertainment of genres — western, nurse novel, detective novel, etc.

When we run into a little chapter made of verse, or a photograph, we cannot help asking ourselves: now, how did this get here? And we know that the writer, not some kind of inevitable god of narration did it.

In his 1984 interview with Sam Solecki, Ondaatje said, probably without teasing, "You know, I wanted to call my new book of poems, *Secular Love*, 'a novel.'"

First the writer pushes textuality into our faces. Then he tries to disappear. Or is he trying to make the *author* disappear, as he did with Billy and Buddy?

"Left-handed poems," he said, as if poems were a gun. But only in legend was Billy left-handed, only when he had slipped from life into genre. Ondaatje is right-handed. If he wants to write left-handed, he will have to wait till they make dime novels and horse operas about *him*.

Billy died in 1881. As often happens with pop heroes, rumours of his continued life abounded. Stories and movies in which an aged Billy talks to youngsters make up a sub-genre themselves. Ondaatje finds an odd fate for him in *Coming Through Slaughter*. Under one of Billy's numerous names, Antrim, he appears as a patient in Buddy Bolden's loony bin. Antrim, who gets a shot of some drug every week, insists on getting this week's shot in his left arm, though the doctor insists on the right. The dispute triggers an escape from the prison, and almost from the text.

8.

We have come, thank heaven, to understand that any kind of writing, from office memo to epic poem, is action, not just imitation of the world. Writers are doing something, not copying what they see. Writing is part of a dialogue with the world. So a writer writing anticipates the responses of his readers. Nowadays, the theorists of language-composition use the word "genre" to talk about the writer's decisions in addressing the situation in which his rhetoric will find its way.

So the detective novel is not just a book that shares certain formal characteristics with its predecessors. A detective novel is a book that addresses the expected expectations of the detective-book reader. Everybody knows this. But does everybody know why Michael Ondaatje makes serious books out of nurse novels, westerns and family chronicles?

Does anyone know why Ondaatje begins his novel about various artists as if it were a journalist's magazine travel piece about New Orleans? A travel journalist uses the second person because he is promoting travel to reader-customers: "Circle and wind back and forth in your car and at First and Liberty is a corner house with an overhang roof above the wooden pavement, barber stripes on the posts that hold up the overhang. This is N. Joseph's Shaving Parlor, the barber shop where Buddy Bolden worked."

When the author begins his writing in the second person, the reader knows that she has been induced to take up a subject position in her own narrative of reading. It is actually easier to travel in space than in time, so the writer here offers at the beginning not history, but "His geography." But he then offers, in that context, lots of well-researched detail about the city during the era of barber and trumpeter Buddy Bolden. "History was slow here," we are told, and Buddy's various homes still exist "away from recorded history." But if we are going to chase a central character whose main activity is disappearance, at least we are going to be offered a lot of detail about the streets of gambling, music, alcohol and prostitution. We will "circle and wind back and forth" in a place during a time before there were cars to get us there. There is a novel to get us there, a historical novel. We get a setting in which time and space are already mingling, including our own time. On first mention, the central character leaves us where we have arrived: "Bolden walks off and talks with someone."

Henry James told us that the serious novelist takes history as his model. James was hoping to establish the novel as a high art, like painting, which had taken nature for a model. He wanted to escape the social implications of genre. Writers like Michael Ondaatje are trying to escape Henry James. *Coming Through Slaughter* is an extremely un-Jamesian book: it is a wild proliferation of genres. The front cover of the first edition bears a time-battered photograph of Buddy Bolden's jazz band, promising documentary; but the title page reprints a less-cropped version of the photograph, showing that the band is assembled in front of a big white sheet that does not quite hide the real world in front of which it is hung. Ondaatje does this sort of thing with all the genres he introduces. They will be handled fondly, but they will be exposed to irony.

To give the name Webb to the detective who spends most of the book's time trailing Buddy, is to mock one's own trope. To use the name of the self-parodying cop of *Dragnet*, the most famous camp-detective television show, is almost unforgivable. So what are we to think about such comic deflation when we come to know that Webb, like the photographer and the trumpet player, will be revealed as a mask for the author: "Webb circled, trying to understand ... taking almost two years, entering the character of Bolden through every voice he spoke to."

Speaking to a voice is a pretty good way of acting out the dialogic nature of any job in literature. That is what theorists in composition mean by "writing tasks as defined by rhetorical situations (classically stated as purpose, audience, and occasion)."[1]

Ondaatje is playing with genres (forms made by others) to invent something his own. He leaves his signature everywhere. We almost begin to suspect that there is a genre called the Ondaatje. Does anyone, Bakhtin or you, believe that you can invent a genre? If there is an Ondaatje, it features this response to the author's Canadian critics, who complained that he set his books in Australia, the United States, Asia, Europe: in *Billy* the riders mention riding into Canada; in *Slaughter* there is an early reference to "Miss Jessie Orloff's famous incident in a Canadian hotel during her last vacation." Canadian content is that easily taken care of. It happens as quickly as Billy's dropping in on Buddy's book.

As if it were a movie, the Ondaatje allows the author's friends to drop in, too. One of these is bpNichol, the famous Canadian experimental poet. He appears as Crawley, who tells Webb about fasting in order to expel "the tail of shit," a regimen that Nichol at least once described to Ondaatje. Much later, the Canadian academics and anthologists Geddes and Moss are listed as the undertakers and embalmers of Buddy's corpse. Of course Ondaatje will swear that the names are accurately historical, but in *Billy* there is a cat named Ferns, an unlikely name for a cat, but the actual name of a Canadian academic poet.

It is almost as if Michael Ondaatje were finding genres in life and comically mixing them with genres in fiction, isn't it?

9.

I know why Ondaatje toys with the genres. I've written a literary western, a Heraclitan spy novel, a young adult science fiction, and a literary historical sea adventure. When Gertrude Stein was asked why she read a detective novel every day, she said that she did so because the central character was dead before page one, so one did not have to get bogged down in the Jamesian symbiosis between character and plot.

The writer writing literary resumptions of genres remembers the fun of reading, his experience, the satisfaction of re-encountering vocabulary and gesture. This writer is self-absorbed, all right, as hostile critics say, but he is also handing the memory to his reader, and his reader, noticing the play, is highly aware of the textuality of the book, and therefore of her contribution, finally of her life. If this is what is meant by the pleasure of the text, the reader may not be surprised to notice herself coming through laughter.

In his next book, Ondaatje will take a run through his family, turning an occasion for auto-bio-graphy into fiction, making sure that we notice a wide gap between the I that is written and the I that is writing. In Billy's story and Buddy's story he takes the time to inform us wary readers of the relationship between pronouns.

Someone without a pronoun says of Buddy: "Did not want to pose in your accent but think in your brain and body ..."

Billy (?) says: "Not a story about me through their eyes then. Find the beginning, the slight silver key to unlock it, to dig it out. Here then is a maze to begin, to be in."

I am amazed that after all these years I have not figured out the meaning of that letter "g" that one is shown how to erase, though I have just been told that it is the silver key. Ondaatje's favourite novel by John Berger would not be published till two years later. If I dropped my personal initial I might be allowed into Billy's I. One does not yet know, but one does know that the book is not *about* the gunslinger through the I's of others, not those numerous first persons.

Not the visiting single first person, either, not that simple egoist shove so popular among Canadian poets who find some historical figure and fashion a long poem by a written "I" who died long before all this started. No, not that pose for anyone in Ondaatje's book. The problem for those Canadian poets and their long poems is that they are so busy pretending to be a personage that they do not give their attention to the art — of writing. What is the occasion, I always ask — how did this writing get into my hands?

If the writer is so conscious as to write right on top of the usual lull-inducing genre, you the reader know where he is and what you are both doing. You can see that such a thing would not be as clearly done on top of a mainstream bourgeois literary form. It could not be so joyful. Parody of the ordinary is ordinary.

10.

bpNichol's term for operating on the overlapping margins of form or genre was "borderblur." In another essay years ago I said that Ondaatje's poem addressed to Victor Coleman marked a significant turn in Ondaatje's poetry career. "The gate in his head" was written while Billy's works were being collected, and it is usually seen as a declaration for process over closure. It notices a West Coast letter from Coleman:

with a blurred
photograph of a gull.
Caught vision. The stunning white bird
an unclear stir.

And this is all this writing should be then.

In *Coming Through Slaughter* there are lots of people circling
and trying to find Buddy Bolden — a photographer, a detective, an
archivist, a woman. And Buddy is always just leaving, a blur. He is
out the door while everyone's gaze is diverted. He can vanish from
a room, or disappear in a crowd. When he does, the writer *replaces*
Bolden. It is almost as if the writer has caused Buddy to leave the
scene. One is reminded that Clark Kent is never around when
Superman shows up.

When Buddy departs, or is spirited away, we are made aware that
the writer is present, to be accounted for. Sometimes we know this
because we can see his obvious hands on the linguistic furniture.
Sometimes his signature is on the sentence. Sometimes we are just
plain invited to look and listen.

We saw the photographer Bellocq scratching at the pictures that
appeared out of nowhere on white paper in his tray, trying to get
into them. We saw young Buddy and Webb "paste their characters
onto each other." Now we see the writer taking the place vacated
by the vanished trumpet player. He is trying to be fast enough to
be in the same place at the same time, fast on the draw. At the end
of the book we see that he thinks that he has succeeded. After
the earlier experience of white room and black room, and like a
disappointed spider:

I sit with this room. With the grey walls that darken into
corner. And one window with teeth in it. Sit so still you can
hear your hair rustle in your shirt. Look away from the
window when clouds and other things go by. Thirty-one
years old. There areno prizes.

How else might we do this conjunction save with genre, with the
confusion of genres? The fiction artist, who is obsessed with making,
desires to make a life. At the frontward edge of this desire is the
desire to make his life rather than merely live or endure it. To make
his life a fiction and therefore real, as Mr. Kroetsch said. The
producer of stable genre works is aiming at making a career. If he
has a character, a cowboy, a cop, he will exploit his exploits, against
one backdrop, range or mean street. His reader will be safe in bed,
reading by lamplight, a glass of milk to hand. She won't have to ask
herself, what is this, and who is writing it?

Ethel Wilson's Maggie

ETHEL WILSON LIVED in a posh neighbourhood of Vancouver. She was the wife of a very prominent doctor, and employed immigrant servants. Her first book was published in her sixtieth year, her last book fourteen years later, though its author would live to be almost ninety-three. Her few public remarks about writing appear quite unassuming. In her 1959 essay, "A Cat among the Falcons," she referred to literary critics as high-flying falcons and herself as a "country cat" sitting and looking out a window.

Her early critics took her at her word. They did not know, perhaps, that she was an expert fly fisherwoman as is her Maggie Lloyd, protagonist of *Swamp Angel*. Even her supporters, most of them men who matured in the school of modern realism, tended to patronize her, presenting her as an unambitious chronicler, innocent of intellectual and moral matters but somehow gifted in limning character.

Most of these commentators regretted certain faults in Wilson's writing style. These included inconsistency, irritating changes of pace, and above all "authorial intrusion." None explained how an author can be said to intrude upon her own invention. They saw her direct remarks to her reader as slips into Victorianism. They should have reread her feline essay, noticing that the fiction writers she cites are the innovators, what light critics call the "stylists." They might have noticed that she praises the "incandescence in a lighted mind" to be found in Sheila Watson's newly-published *The Double Hook*.

A remarkable exception among the early critics was Helen Sonthoff, who found treasure just where the fellows were finding lapses. Hers is one of our great essays ("The Novels of Ethel Wilson," *Canadian Literature*, 1965). It locates Ethel Wilson among those writers who make their readers experience the writing, and Sonthoff quotes Gertrude Stein, who said that the sentence should "make you know yourself knowing it." Ethel Wilson, whenever she was asked to say what it was that the young writer had to learn, suggested the sentence.

Once in a while you will find a Wilson sentence that strikes you as odd. It might have a crack in it; it might have forgotten which way it was going. When you find a little oddity in a Wilson sentence, you should question the seeming simplicity that has gone before. You could be afforded a glimpse of the moral, philosophical world of which Wilson was supposed to be unmindful. In the midst of the world the author has made familiar, you might suffer some defamiliarizing. At that moment you might get irritated and fault the narrative's professionalism — or you might sense the presence of a cat, and feel the hairs on the back of your neck rise.

Wilson's purpose is not cheery. When you are least expecting it she lets you see a moment of something dark, something Joseph Conrad's river-travelling Marlow might have seen between the wide leaves. Consider the idyllic scene of Maggie's fishing the bright Similkameen River:

> Maggie continued to cast. In the pleasure of casting over this lively stream she forgot — as always when she was fishing — her own existence. Suddenly came a strike, and the line ran out, there was a quick radiance and splashing above the water downstream. At the moment of the strike, Maggie became a co-ordinating creature of wrists and fingers and reel and rod and line and tension and the small trout, leaping, darting, leaping. She landed the fish, took out the hook, slipped in her thumb, broke back the small neck, and the leaping rainbow thing was dead. A thought as thin and cruel as a pipe fish cut through her mind. The pipe fish slid through and away. It would return.

In less than a page the cruel thought does return, and it brings Edward Vardoe with it. For the second time in the novel we are brushed with the thought of the "humiliation" that drove Maggie to leave him, the guilt in deciding to cease her "outraged endurance of the nights' hateful assaults and the days' wakings in a passing of time where daily and nightly repetition marked no passing of time." As in our reading of Conrad, we do not know with certainty, yet we think we've seen the edge of a universal darkness. When Nell

Severance suggests to Edward Vardoe that in his own darkest vengeful mind "murder would be a pleasure," he does not contradict her. Neither he nor his estranged wife is an innocent traveller, nor is their creator. More and more as Wilson composed her fictions, her characters were compelled to consider unexplainable death and the fear that wreathes it like vapour around the fragments of a train wreck.

Wilson's travelling protagonists leave the seeming unity and comfort of family to discover disappointing and frightening chaos, and set about creating an uncloistered order. Remember the Ancient Mariner, that returned traveller: with thoughtless murderous skill he brings down the albatross; when he blesses the watersnakes *unaware*, the stinking bird falls from his neck and the narrative wind arises. You will remember that Maggie *forgets* her own existence just before she despatches the little trout and feels the darkness "cut through her mind." Now recall that verb in this "authorial intrusion":

There is a beautiful action. It has an operative grace.
It is when one, seeing some uneasy sleeper cold and
without cover, goes away, finds and brings a blanket, bends
down, and covers the sleeper because the sleeper is a living
being and is cold. He then returns to his work, forgetting
that he has performed this small act of compassion. He will
receive neither praise nor thanks. It does not matter who
the sleeper may be. That is a beautiful action which is divine
and human in posture and intention and self-forget-fulness.
Maggie was compassionate and perhaps she would be able
to serve Vera Gunnarsen in this way, forgetting that she

did so, and expecting neither praise nor thanks — or perhaps she would not.

The last five words epitomize Ethel Wilson's noted "tone," and serve to attract the reader who wants to feel, paradoxically, closer to the seemingly detached writer. Wilson knew that she was producing that paradox, and she employed it as well in the telling she had to do about her subjects: "all fly-fishermen are bound closely together by the strong desire to be apart, solitary upon the lake, the stream."

Paradox, or at least contradiction, in any case metaphor, is signalled in the novel's title. Observing that range from primordial slime to divine flight, one might expect a story of triumphant emergence, but I do not think that the angel emerges. I think that no matter how compassionately Maggie acts, even in the Christian terms that the book clearly suggests, the pipe fish still swims in her mind. A swamp angel is not necessarily a gun. The dictionary that Wilson alerts us to on her first page tells us that the swamp angel can be an eremite in the bog, or another name for the hermit thrush, that feathery song.

Birds are important to Wilson's fictions. They fly in formations, break their necks against windows, and carry messages quicker than the symbols Mrs. Severance complains of. Fifty brown birds fly in this book's first sentence, and Mrs. Vardoe (or the narrator) asks what they are. Perhaps they are swamp angels; certainly they are "birds returning in migration," probably ironic precursors of this still earth-held Vardoe woman. They are recalled in the fish that return to the water above the ooze into which the gun settles in the penultimate paragraph. "Things are falling into place," one reads a page earlier.

Maggie Lloyd's place is somewhere between the birds and the fish. She will never fly further than her flight from Vardoe, and she will never live full time among the seals or in Three Loon Lake, no matter what her avatars say. The fish do not reside in a swamp and the birds are not angels. Take that delimiting a step further: birds such as eagles eat fish and take them flying; people such as Maggie Lloyd make flies out of feathers and feed trout to their death.

Look at those birds and fish again. For Maggie the birds are seen and the fish are imagined. For Ethel Wilson they are all imagined, and so what are they for the reader?

Ethel Wilson the writer wanted two things that are opposite and necessary to one another. She genuinely loved the physicality of British Columbia, and used her great sentences to make it brightly visible. If the rivers and lakes are to become allegorical landscape, that will be permitted, but they will live before the imagining eye first. There is also a dark universe, however, that turns and looms outside the range of the human eye. As dogs and other animals sense oncoming earthquakes, Wilson's protagonist and reader, easing into the pre-visual world of nature, enter the dream of Eddie Vardoe, whose face becomes the face of a child and then a sharp-toothed mink screaming in the forest.

"Going fishing?" everyone asks Maggie. "Yes, I am," she replies pleasantly. Like any novelist, a fisherwoman can tie a practiced fly, search the best rainbow shoal, and still be in the dark as to what she may, with her single hook, hook.

But in fishing she offers a faith in order, in a not-quite-predictable order. About the plots in her earlier books, especially *Hetty Dorval*, Wilson was sometimes upbraided for her use of coincidences, especially coincidental meetings. In *Swamp Angel*, an often recurvate text, she responds to that criticism through the words of the never-shy Mrs. Severance, who tells Albert Cousins that she believes in two things: coincidence and faith. That sounds a little like the paradoxical reality that Maggie the questor comes to learn. Is a coincidence an island of random order in a sea of chaos, or is coincidence chaotic itself? To the realist non-Jungian critic it is a cheat or a failure of vision. To a person to any degree religious it can look like evidence of supernal regard for the mortal world.

In any case critics have always held *Swamp Angel* to be superior to its predecessors in terms of authorial control. This is so partly because despite her probable opinion on the matter, Wilson cut back on coincidence. This novel's plot is articulated by illnesses, accidents and injuries. Plot is developed and characters are constructed by these reminders of human frailty and fallibility. They start with the battlefield death of Tom Lloyd, and include, among others, the fall of Nell Severance in the street, Haldar Gunnarsen's car wreck, and the sudden storm that brings an end to Mr. Cunningham's strength. Each event has a part in bringing Maggie to her place in the boat on the lake, on the way to the lodge where the smoke is rising from the chimneys. Of the accidents and the tangles of emotion that have got her there, Maggie has told herself simply, "life is like that — if it's not one thing it's another." Wilson gave her that common language to keep her normal, to show us that all her compassion and personal strength are simply human possibility, not the attributes of a literary hero. The epigraph for *Mrs. Golightly* quotes Edwin Muir on the world we have to inhabit: "a difficult country, and our home."

Most of Wilson's stories are about the problem of home, and most of these are about a girl or woman looking for the meaning of the term. For Maggie, the house in which she had lived with Eddie Vardoe was "home" with quotation marks. It had been a fake haven for the younger woman who had become widow, orphan and childless all at once. So like a fish, she goes upstream to something she seems in the darkness to recognize. In the short Chapter 5, Maggie Vardoe is reborn as Maggie Lloyd, and in her snug cabin finds her first comfort as this new child. The word "home" comes from a root meaning to lie down. In Vardoe's bed she lay in anguish every night. Here, on the other hand,

> [t]he cabin was a safe small world enclosing her. She put out a hand, groped on the stand beside her bed, took up the small yellow bowl, ran her thumb round its smooth glaze like a drowsy child feeling its toy. How lovely the sound of the wind in the fir trees. She fell asleep.

The next day she rides through the town of Hope.

But the lodge on Three Loon Lake is surrounded by dark forest, and as the people who live there know, unpleasant things can happen any time. The reader should be on guard as well. If you were ever in a mind to swallow the fish story about the author's self-image, the country cat far from the nearest pigeons, look again at the end to the scene of the fawn and the kitten:

> The kitten awoke, completely aware of the birds in the woods. She jumped down and trotted along the verandah and onto the ground. Then, flattening her-self, extending herself paw by predatory paw, she passed crouching into the forest.

Swamp Angel is a short novel and a highly complex one. On rereading it we are rewarded with the assurance that we will never be able to tell anyone what it is all about. Wilson's feigned simplicity is the most complicated trick of all. For a careful reader the text is as difficult as this world our home.

The Autobiographings
of Mourning Dove

WHY DO WE visit graves?

Why would we travel to a place we have never been to before, and stand at the foot of a grave in which lie the remains of someone we have never seen in the flesh?

In the summer of 1992 I drove to Omak, Washington, to visit the grave of Mourning Dove, the first Native American woman ever to write a novel. At the tourist bureau they had never heard of her, but they told me that the graveyard I had mentioned was in Okanogan, the next town.

The graveyard, white and dry under the hot familiar sun, was deserted. I parked my car and got out and stood where I could see the whole place. Then I walked to the area that looked 1930s-ish. The first grave I looked at was hers.

She had bought this plot out of her minimal wages from hard

orchard work, a grave in a white people's cemetery. In Jay Miller's introduction to her autobiography, I had read that the words on her marker were only "Mrs. Fred Galler" (xxvi). But now I saw that someone had cut a rectangle out of the old stone and put a new marker in its place. It depicts a white dove flying over an opened book upon which appear the words:

MOURNING DOVE

COLVILLE AUTHOR

1884-1936

There I was, a still living white male, standing, and eventually kneeling at the last narrow home of a great woman I had not heard of while I was being educated there in that Okanagan Valley.[1] She died when I was seven months old. I did not read her books until I was the age that she had attained at her death. What did I think I was doing there? I was reading.

Why do we read autobiographies?

Reading is a cultural act, and our habits of reading will accumulate into a description of our culture. As Janet Varner Gunn puts it, "The truth of autobiography is to be found, not in the 'facts' of the story itself, but in the relational space *between* the story and its reader" (Gunn, 143).

Traditionally we have read male autobiography as a version of history, as the story told by those statesmen and militarists who have exercised power. Traditionally we have read female autobiography as *alternative*, the occluded life, domestic, personal and perhaps solipsistic. Perhaps concerned with the permission to write such a thing at all, with an identity. Estelle Jelinek writes:

"In contrast to the self-confident, one-dimensional self-image that men usually project, women often depict a multidimensional, fragmented self-image colored by a sense of inadequacy and alienation, of being outsiders or 'other'; they feel the need for authentication, to prove their self-worth" (Jelinek, xiii). Of course many of the most successful female autobiographies have narratized the overcoming of obstacles, and the attainment of an identity that is quite satisfactory, thank you.

Of course if you were a woman, and if you were from the interior plateau country, and if you were aboriginal, you were triply marginalized. You might be exotic, but if you wanted to be a writer, you had to do your writing with whatever skills you had managed to develop, in a tent or a shack, after ten hours of working in an orchard and after cooking the meals for your husband and yourself at least. That is why a still living white male will think more than twice before trying to apply normal academic, theoretical or ethnographic methods to your autobiography.

There have been several versions of the main facts assigned to Mourning Dove's life, the disagreements caused by her fictionalizing and through the errors made by white academics coming from their various angles to use her story. She was most likely born in 1885 in Idaho, the first daughter of Lucy and Joseph Quintasket (Dark Cloud). Lucy was the daughter of a woman from the Colvile Tribe, one of the tribes who share the enormous Colville[2] Reservation in northeastern Washington, and of a man who came from the Lakes people of eastern British Columbia. Mourning Dove's other grandmother was from the Nicola, a somewhat mysterious people who lived among the Okanagans near Merritt, B.C. Her other grandfather was probably an Okanagan, though for literary and political reasons Mourning Dove suggested that he was a white man named Haynes. There were white people named Haynes in the area. My mother used to work in Haynes's packing house in Testalinda, a mile from the Indian school at which Mourning Dove taught in 1917.

The Quintaskets usually lived on or near the Colville Reservation, among people of several Salish tribes[3] who had been reduced to poverty and the meanest of jobs in agriculture by the policies of the powerful whites in the eastern States. Christine Quintasket managed to get some schooling. First she went to a boarding school, and was introduced to the English language by French-Canadian nuns. Later she went to the Colville Mission school in Fort Spokane. When her widowed father married a young woman, Christine went to Montana, to trade menial work for a chance to go to an Indian school there.

But she spent more time at home than she did at schools. At home she learned a love for narrative from her two most important teachers, an adopted grandmother and an adopted white brother.

These two instilled in the Indian girl a desire to be a storyteller and a writer. For her last formal schooling she went to a business college in Calgary, where she endured the typical racism of that city, and learned things such as shorthand and typing, skills that would prove handy later while she was gathering traditional stories or writing her life by coal oil light in the night cabin. The school in Calgary did not make her spelling and grammar perfect.

But Mourning Dove wrote three important books that are in print now: *Cogewea: The Half-Blood*, a novel that has been aptly called a "protest romance" (Larson, 177), *Coyote Stories*, her versions of tales she collected from elders on both sides of the International Boundary, and *Mourning Dove: A Salishan Autobiography*, which was not to be published until a half-century after her death. The three books are equally autobiographical, and they are all about something other than Mourning Dove's life.

Mourning Dove worked herself to death. She died at the age of about fifty-one, though by her own construction she would have been forty-eight. She left no children. In the grave she was for decades Mrs. Fred Galler. Now the name on the stone is Mourning Dove, and the occupation is author rather than Mrs. For any reader standing over that stone she has no age.

Sometimes I used to ask students what their first and last names mean. Hardly any of them knew. So this is what a name means in non-aboriginal society: a few words on an ID card. But in a Salishan world, a name means a great deal more, whether the name of a place or the name of a person, and everyone knows this. A name is a gift, or it is family property. It is bestowed or it is earned. It is an act of honour.

When she was a little girl her parents called her Kee-ten. When an old neighbour woman named Ka-at-qhu died without passing her name to a grandchild, Kee-ten became Ka-at-qhu. A few years later a shaman woman who was pleased with the girl's help gave her her name to carry on, so now Kee-ten was also Ha-ah-pecha. Mourning Dove said that people on the reservation still used those names when speaking to her decades later.

But by this time in history Indian girls were also carrying Christian names. In the white world she was known by equivalents of her name Kee-ten. She was Christine and Christal and Cristal and Catherine Quintasket. At the convent school she was enrolled as Christine Joseph, because her father's name was Joseph. When she was first married she signed her letters Cristal MacLeod. During her second marriage she was Christine or Catherine Galler. But Christine Quintasket wanted to be a writer, and she wanted to be an Indian writer who would be read by white readers. She decided that as a storyteller she would take the name Hum-ishu-ma. Then she decided that the English version of her writer's name would be Morning Dove, because that bird is, in Colvile legend, the faithful wife of Salmon, and welcomes him upstream every year. Salmon-fishing is the sustenance of life for the peoples of the great Interior Plateau. In a museum in Spokane, Christine saw that the proper spelling was Mourning Dove, and though she said that it was because of that connotation not the same bird known to the Indian people, she settled on Mourning Dove as her writing name. That is the story of Mourning Dove's name.

The name Haynes does not figure at all. But these names do: Lucullus Virgil McWhorter, Heister Dean Guie, and Jay Miller. They are the names of three white men who had, in their various ways, faith in Mourning Dove's importance, and helped in the preparation of her three books, the last of course unknown to her.

When an Indian person authored a book in early twentieth-century America, she was met with two challenging responses. One: is this person really an Indian or another Grey Owl? Isn't D'Arcy McNickle really three-quarters European stock? What about Thomas King? Two: did this person really write that book, or was it done by a white anthropologist with an ear? Did Black Elk speak much?

Anyone reading *Cogewea*, especially in these latter days, notices that the language is folksy and out-westish when the spirited "half-blood" heroine is joshing with the ranch hands: "I'm a thinkin' yo' all'd make a good preacher woman. Them there kind what wants ter be made perlice wimin an' jedges an' th' main push. Wantin' to wear breeches an' boss th' hull shebang" (42). But often the reader will find a lecture about the conditions imposed on Native Americans by the U.S. governments, and find that these passages are rendered in the language one expects from a schoolteacher who once had to read Cato: "They lacked the perceptive sagacity of a certain great reformer of nearly two thousand years ago; who, when carrying the Message to the benighted Athenians, 'stood in the midst of Mars hill' and declared that it was of their 'Unknown God' to whom he had noticed an altar erected, that he spake" (133). This is Cogewea in conversation with the opportunist easterner she resists and then unhappily falls for.

The novel is, as it says on the title page, "Given through Sho-pow-tan," the Indian name that she and others gave to McWhorter. It is pretty clear that it was McWhorter who added the didactic diatribes against white exploitation that delay the narrative. One wonders whether the undoubtedly good-hearted McWhorter thought that the stilted language was normal enough to be used by Mourning Dove the author or by her characters. Was McWhorter's grasp of fiction so poor? Of course he had a somewhat different agenda than that of his co-author. In later years, when Mourning Dove sent new manuscripts to McWhorter she asked him to stay away from the arch rhetoric, from what she called white people's big words.

It is a sad fact of life that when white anthropologists who are genuinely sympathetic with the cause of indigenous peoples become interested in their stories, they are interested in them for anthropological reasons and thus marginalize their literary qualities, hence exhibiting what could be called a subtle racism. Jay Miller says that Mourning Dove's letters show that while she was working on the Coyote stories, "McWhorter was concerned

that *Indian* themes and concerns be highlighted, whereas Mourning
Dove wanted to express her knowledge and literary talents" (*Autobiography*, xxiii). Intelligent people on both sides of the text
understand that problem and work together to make the best of an
imperfect situation. There are several such problems in the area
of ethnobiography. Mourning Dove's Coyote stories and autobiography would have been, perhaps, more interesting to read in
scripted Interior Salish.

Mourning Dove was an Indian woman writing in the language
of her white readers. Just about any of her readers was going to be
more interested in her as a representative of her people than as a
novelist. The same was likely to be true of her editors. Mourning
Dove was also a politician. In addition to the long hours she
spent on ladders in orchards, at laundry sinks in rooming houses
and at her ill-lit typewriter, she spent a lot of time working for
Native people who were caught in the hard machinery of liberal
democracy. She rescued families from border police. She wrote
illuminating letters to newspapers and the State house. She became
the first woman on the Colville Reservation Tribal Council.

In all her books one can discern her two principal social purposes — to make certain that her people's stories and the story of
their life will be preserved in print while their way of life is being
threatened by officially-induced poverty, and to make a bridge
between the Indians and the whites on their land. It is easy to
assume that these two ambitions are at odds with one another.
But Mourning Dove, whose view must be taken as better qualified
than ours, did not think so. She was aware of the dangers one
must inevitably pass through. One of the most amusing scenes in
Cogewea concerns the heroine's anger at a white woman's fanciful
book about Indian life. Some of the ranch hands joke about the

misinformation they have handed to an eager female tenderfoot scribe: "Why, them there writin' folks is dead easy pickin' for the cowpunchers" (94). Finally "Cogewea found solace in consigning the maligning volumn [sic] to the kitchen stove" (96). Writing this novel during the second decade of the twentieth century, Mourning Dove seems to anticipate most of the arguments heard more recently about paternalism and misappropriation of voice.

In *Cogewea*, with its melodramatic plot and editorializing, the most interesting and accomplished passages are those in which Cogewea's grandmother, sometimes in her sweat lodge, tells the stories and traditions of pre-contact Salishan life. They are interesting not only because of their ethnographic information but also because of their narrative skill. They are clearly Mourning Dove's purest contribution to the novel.

And they are most clearly the nearly perfect conjoining of tradition and the individual talent. That conjunction is what Jay Miller has tried his best to produce in the autobiography. I like to notice the nice title: *Mourning Dove: A Salishan Autobiography*. Everyone has treated of that word "autobiography," and its constituent parts. James Olney has shown the way in which twentieth-century reading has shifted attention from *bios* to *autos*, from life to self (Olney, 19). Miller's title tells us that in our approach here we have to look for something else, something created by the concepts of person and people among the aboriginals of the Interior Plateau, and by the dynamic of Mourning Dove's doubled ambition. It is after all *a* Salishan autobiography, and thus promising of a singular life. It is also a *Salishan* autobiography, not just that of Christine Quintasket.

It is assembled from boxes of mismatched writings that Mourning Dove left to Dean Guie's attic. In the frantic and illness-filled years before her death she thought that she was writing two books —

one an ethnographic description of Salishan life, and the other a narrative of her own upbringing and education. The book that Miller assembled from her papers is an admirable conflation of these intentions. Curiously, in this "autobiography" of America's first Indian woman novelist, there is no recounting of her writing *Cogewea*, nor of the tiresome twelve-year wait to see it published.

Miller arranges the papers in three main sections: "A Woman's World," "Seasonal Activities," and "Okanogan History." The first chapter is called "My Life," and is the most clearly anecdotal autobiography as well as the longest chapter in the book. Yet it is filled with seemingly impersonal lore, and the later chapters on such things as salmon-fishing, are narratized with memoirs of the Quintasket family and others. Miller admits his own anthropological bias, and allows that he helped to "create" the text. Perhaps the academic professionalizing of his trade has saved us from McWhorter's stentorian rhetoric. And maybe we could say that all three editors "milled" Mourning Dove's texts, somehow extending her process when she developed the Indian tales she gathered from elders. Miller says of the compromise he has fashioned: "the autobiography does represent a personal ethnography of lasting value" (*Autobiography*, xxxiv).

Mourning Dove said that she wrote to prove to her white audience that Indian people were not the savage stoics that had been created in the white romances, that Indian people felt strong emotions, just as strong as those felt by the recently arrived aliens. She said that the Coyote stories were "set down by me for the children of another race to read" (*Coyote Stories*, 12). It was not only Indian education that she was interested in. Though any text can offer only a momentary joining of understandings, she hoped that each of these joinings would contribute toward a world in which tolerance and familiarity would replace the systemic racism that characterized official life in her part of the country.

What about the danger of appropriation that seems now to accompany more interracial knowledge? It is obvious that any autobiography invites appropriation: here is my life for your dollar. Appropriation, if it is a problem, is not the big problem. For the First Nations of America, the problem has been misappropriation, and expropriation. Autobiographies and autobiographical fictions are going to be read, one hopes. If the reader somehow then becomes a writer, his writing will be about his experience. His experience here will be reading the book.

Do you remember when we were kids and we wondered whether what other people called "green" might be what we would see as "red"? As kids we learned that we had to accept the fact that we joined in our understanding only through words, through the text. Reading Indian stories, having good Indian friends, putting headbands around our heads, will not make us Indians. If we try to write or rewrite Indian narratives we will not do it. Autobiography is a narrative of mortality, and we all have our own deaths to do. Yet the pleasant thing about autobiography is that old-fashioned closure is impossible. Perhaps the author is dead, in Roland Barthes's sense, but she is also never dead. At the "end" of her book one is left hanging, alive, expecting the truth to be revealed eventually but perhaps by another. A Salishan autobiography, then, should imply that the Salishan peoples are alive, that no one has written their epitaph.

Remember what Barthes wrote at the beginning of his essay "The Death of the Author": "in ethnographic societies the responsibility for a narrative is never assumed by a person but by a mediator, shaman or relator whose 'performance' — the mastery of the narrative code — may possibly be admired but never his 'genius'" (Barthes, 142). That is what we have to understand about Mourning Dove's doubleness: when she wants us to appreciate her writing ability as well as the ethnographic information she is imparting, it is not originality she wants us to scrutinize, but performance. She is not trying to get us to know that she has deep feelings, but that Indian people, the Okanagans and the Colviles, have deep feelings.

Mourning Dove knew how important it was to the very lives of her family and tribe that she understand the function of the reader. She knew the principle that Barthes invokes near the end of his essay: "a text is made of multiple writings, drawn from many cultures and entering into mutual relations of dialogue, parody, contestation, but there is one place where this multiplicity is focused and that place is the reader, not, as was hitherto said, the author ... a text's unity lies not in its origin but in its destination" (148).

So how do we North American white men read Mourning Dove without looking for Pocahontas?

Pocahontas has always haunted American literature. And there has always been a kind of ethno-pornography in the response of white poets and other writers. First she was wild, savage, naked, lewd. Then she was romanticized, penny-dreadfulled, tom-tommed till her feet ached. In this century she was "redeemed" by poets such as Hart Crane and William Carlos Williams, becoming the essential Native spirit still alive in the Europeanized American continent. But always she was the image of desire, the exotic removed from her society to become the object of a male gaze. She was the literary equivalent of the naked model.

Certainly Pocahontas never wrote anything. One might as well permit women to become painters rather than the painted. In American publishing there was one kind of book about Indians that was always popular. This was the captivity narrative. It was especially successful when the captured and then rescued and then autobiographical person was a woman. The stories were usually religious in denouement, and filled with anti-Indian sentiments, filled with descriptions of cruelty, paganism and savagery. Reading them was not just a cultural act — it was a pornographic act as well.

There were no captivity narratives written by Indian women forced to live among the Christians. Not until recently.

Remember that there was in the nineteenth century (and still is in some quarters) a sentiment at large that says that all writing by women is autobiographical. Women, commonly regarded as properly the object of the male gaze, would remain so in the reading of their writing. One would think that Gertrude Stein took care of that problem.

Early in the *Autobiography* Mourning Dove offers a story of her grandmother Pah-tah-heet-sa, a Nicola medicine woman. No one could make a Pocahontas of her. Once when the people were travelling over the high Nicola trail to visit in the Okanagan, Pah-tah-heet-sa went well ahead of them, gathering huckleberries.

When this brave woman drew near the berry patch, she saw a grizzly feeding. This did not stop her. She took her digging stick of dogwood and prepared to fight if the bear meant to charge at her, which the bear did not hesitate to do. With a howl that would have frozen the blood of any coward, it charged. She threw off her pack and held her stick to challenge the brute, saying "You are a mean animal and I am a mean woman. Let us fight this out to see who will get the berry patch."

The bear did not answer her but opened its mouth wide and came at a leap. She watched for her chance and drove the sharp stick into the animal's mouth. The bear fell back in pain, then jumped at her, even more angry. The fight went on long enough that the warriors approached, not expecting to see such a sight. When they drew their arrows to shoot, she commanded them, "Don't shoot. Wait! We are fighting this to the finish. He is a mean animal and I am a mean woman. We will see who is the strongest and conqueror in this battle."

The woman roared in imitation of the angry bear and drove her stick again into the wide, wide mouth. Every time it charged, this would drive it back. The people watched the fight until the sun lay low in the western sky. Only then did the grizzly walk away, broken and bleeding. The old woman had only a few scratches.

She picked up her basket and gathered the berries she had won, while the people stood in wonderment. She died very old when she and her buckskin horse rolled down a steep embankment near Oroville. She and the horse drowned and were both buried on the bank of the Similkameen River in an unmarked grave. Thus ended a brave, mean woman. (5-6)

Anyone of a comparative-literature mind will note the resemblance to European stories of the confrontations and deaths of noble knights. But I believe the story of Mourning Dove's grandmother.

I also think I know, as much as a white male reader in this latter time can know, what the story is for. I know that Pah-tah-heet-sa lives on in Mourning Dove herself, and that she continues to live in Okanagan stories. I think of Maeg, the rooted and political woman who appears toward the end of Jeanette Armstrong's novel *Slash*. Maeg is from the U.S. part of the valley, but has parents from the Canadian side. I think that she is seen to be Pah-tah-heet-sa, and Christine Quintasket and Mourning Dove and Jeanette Armstrong. I think that she may have had something to do with the transformation of that gravestone in Okanogan, Washington.

Beth Cuthand, a First Nations writer from the Prairies, put the question of autobiography this way: "Often when we are writing, it's not our words that are coming. The grandmothers, the grandfathers come and write through us" (Dybikowski, 53). No need for a muse when there is a family around. And you do not need to be a writer to take part in the making of the family story, the tribal story, a story of the Okanagan land. Among the Okanagans and other peoples of the Interior Salishan, response was expected from the listeners, encouraging voices to keep the narrative going. Among the people of the Plateau, invisible property is more valuable and more lasting than visible property. Autobiography (if we post-Hellenic people can use that term here) is a care that would be failed if it were to fall simply to an individual with a unique story to tell.

But Mourning Dove's *Autobiography* is also directed toward a non-Indian audience. What can we do to respond properly, to keep these stories alive among us too? Why do we bother visiting the banks of the Similkameen near Oroville?

Mourning Dove learned her double narrative task right at home in her Indian father's house. Teequalt, the new grandmother she brought home, taught her Salishan stories and taught her to pay attention to her own gift as a storyteller. Jimmy Ryan, the white boy her father brought into the family, was fond of yellowback novels, and taught his little sister to read the English found in them. Once her mother papered the walls with pages from a new one. Jimmy and Christine read the walls.

Mourning Dove decided that she would try to trust the white world. She knew that she was turning tales into text, the people's property into information. Janet Gunn says: "What is made present is not merely a past that is past. What is presenced is a reality, always new, to which the past has contributed but which stands, as it were, in front of the autobiographer" (Gunn, 17).

In front of the reader, too.

Man with Pencil

YOU REMEMBER ALL that Canadian nationalism that was going on in
the arts and in the universities in the 1970s? You remember those
national sociologists who were saying that a 1921 poem by Bliss
Carman:

> Back to the world with quickening start
> I looked and longed for any part
> In making saving Beauty be —
> And from that kindling ecstasy
> I knew God dwelt within my heart.

was more important to Canadian readers and writers than a 1921
poem by Ezra Pound:

There died a myriad
And of the best, among them,
For an old bitch gone in the teeth,
For a botched civilization,

Charm, smiling at the good mouth,
Quick eyes gone under earth's lid,

For two gross of broken statues,
For a few thousand battered books.

According to the national sociologists, the Ezra Pound poem, a virulent attack on contending empires that killed art and human life, was dangerous because if a Canadian were to read it, the Canadian would be cooperating in the USAmerican imperial designs on his own country. Charles Olson, whose insistence was upon the artist's diligent investigation of his own geography, would also come under attack for U.S. expansionist hegemony.

Greg Curnoe was a famous nationalist, or perhaps a famous anti-USAmerican, which is another way of putting it. He was smart enough to know that when Clement Greenberg praised work of "international" quality, he was talking about the standards upheld in New York City. He was a one-man border commissioner who drew the undefended Mexican-Canadian international boundary. He went to the Venice Biennale but he did not show in Detroit. He got incensed when his work was called Pop Art, because Pop Art was a USAmerican fashion trend.

Here is what separated Greg Curnoe's anti-USAmericanism from that of the national sociologists: he did not think that Ornette Coleman and Charles Olson were part of the U.S. takeover grab.

The loudest voice in the national sociologist camp came from a bad poet and scholar who went to university in the U.S. Middle West. I always wondered whether he might be a deep mole, charged with the task of discrediting Canadian nationalism. Greg Curnoe was one of those guys you know who met serious reading as a responsibility. Roy Kiyooka was another. These guys are often painters who cannot get through a life without writing a lot. In one of the films in a 2001 Curnoe exhibition, Greg says that you should remember that he is not just living a painter's life: he also writes, he says, and plays in a band.

You know these guys. Isn't it interesting that they often do not enter college, or even finish high school? I was the person who introduced Kiyooka and Curnoe. They were both highly interested in Stanley Spencer, and I thought that it would be fun to listen to them talk about painting. I can't remember anything they said. But I remember their bookshelves. They had the same books in their bookshelves. These included Ezra Pound's *Cantos* and the selected poems of William Carlos Williams and this and that by Gertrude Stein. I was always ready to tell them what I thought about these things. But Greg also had a lot of stuff about early twentieth-century European painting and poetry. Thank goodness he was always willing to tell me stuff about that. He also told me why it was a good idea to listen to Albert Ayler, the amazing open heart of the tenor saxophone. Albert was found dead at age thirty-five in the East River. Listening to him, according to some fiery academics, is collaborating in U.S. triumphalism.

What kind of writer was Greg Curnoe? When you think of Greg and words, you probably think first of his lettrist stuff, the rubber-stamp pieces, the painted words. I tend to think of that pencil behind Greg's ear. As you know, he could not keep that pencil off his paintings. For years and years he would not put his signature on a painting (although he would have it stamped "Original" on the back), but more and more, he would write stuff on a bicycle painting or a self-portrait. What you find there might be a document of something his son ate that day.

Document. As a writer, Greg was a collector. In his studio there is that collection of unfamiliar pop bottles with the pop inside them, that collection of old toys, those bookshelf rows of tapes made from short-wave broadcasts during the war between Britain and Argentina. There are the journals, thirty years worth of them. Outside the house he was digging into the ground, looking for signs of early habitation. Inside the studio he was writing those journals. What was the purpose of the journals? Not, despite times of depression and need, not self-expression. Investigation. A hundred notebooks of trying to understand things. Not things ranked from family spat to life after death. Stuff.

Document is to writing as the regional is to painting. Neither a documentary nor a regionalist painting is ever going to be anything like objective. But neither are they going to be expressions of self. One of the writers who wrote about this subject was Charles Olson. When Greg Curnoe made a record of something he found interesting (his favourite word) about his region, he was not trying to describe the local or express his feelings about the local or interpret the local. He was trying to *be* the local.

Hence those big ink stamp letters. He had to push really hard to make them take. What he was making was something for you to stand beside, not something to make you shake your head and cluck your tongue and say to: "How true, how true."

If he gives you a list of the addresses of houses that members of his family and friends of his youth lived in, you will probably get pretty bored in time, but you'll realize that Curnoe is *insisting*, that he is demonstrating the principle of his method — he is collecting and presenting, not subduing and arraying. If he were a poet he would not use a simile. If he were a novelist you might think that you were reading Robbe-Grillet.

Let us take this to an extreme. Nowadays when I look at a big Curnoe painting made up of words made up of upper case letters, I usually do not read the words. I try to read the painting, as a painting. I imagine standing as I did all those years ago, with Greg Curnoe, remember a man standing by his words.

Milton Acorn

IF YOU WILL agree that Milton Acorn was a socialist poet, you will know that he would not want to appear mysterious. Yet when his poems began to appear in magazines such as *Canadian Forum* in the late fifties, readers were cautious, or at least puzzled. There was that name, that surname and that first name. And there was that address. For a while at the beginning of his writing career Milton Acorn had the same address as Alfred W. Purdy. Earle Birney was one among many people who suspected that Milton Acorn was a pen name for Al Purdy. As it turned out, such suspicion could be seen as a compliment to both poets, though they might each balk at that notion.

No, Milton Acorn was not mysterious, and had no desire to be mysterious. He was convinced of his role as a public poet, as a bard-like figure to be identified with his land and his people, with his native Prince Edward Island first and last, with an independent and progressive Canada, and with the workers and unemployed. In his first poem he called P.E.I. "a red tongue," and in his most famous poem he told us that he had tasted his blood.

Public he was. He was poor and he was handicapped. He was unemployed as far as the corporations were concerned. But he was public. He was always in the newspapers, so much so that when he died *The Globe and Mail* printed two obituaries in the same edition and put his picture on the front page. In Toronto the police broke up his reading with Al Purdy in a back lane behind posh shops on Bloor Street. Earlier cops on horseback dispersed a crowd listening to him in Queen's Park. On the West Coast the U.S. customs officials prevented his visiting a woman in Seattle. The paparazzi flashed at him in public safety buildings and at a famous Toronto bar. When he went to the Governor-General's house to pick up his award he did not appear in a dull grey suit.

"I shout love," he shouted in the sixties, in the noisiest year of the Vietnam decade and the most public period of his career. Yet in his early poems and in his last books he showed one of the most delicate ears in our poetry, a tuning-in not only to all our speech rhythms, but to the latest poetics in New World literature. His sources and attentions were not only literary. He responded to many voices. He dedicated his books to Max Ferguson, LeRoi Jones and Dorothy Livesay.

Acorn was at his best when his great ear was connected to his socially committed heart, as in "Detail of a Cityscape," a poem in which the opening question is not just a matter of rhetoric:

Have you noticed
how the cripple

struggles
onto the bus?

From where I sit
a hand,
white-knuckled
on the rail
is all I see;

and then the parts,
a head, an aimless
cane flopping,
hooked to a wrist,
levering elbows,
the poor twist
of a torso,
finally those disobedient
feet.

Once on, he lurches
onto the unrailed bench
next to the driver
. . . the most uncomfortable seat;

because if he tried for another
the surge of the bus starting
would upend him.

Raymond Souster and Margaret Avison have written in their
compassionate ways about such passengers in this lifetime, in that

cityscape. Acorn managed to join such select company with an eye for the necessary detail of the love he rightly ascribed to his attention, and with an ear that knew how much invention was just enough.

I have been praising Acorn's verses in review after review since 1961, trying to bring a balance to the usual response that has concentrated on his image and his politics and ignored the fact of his fine craftsmanship. Al and Eurithe Purdy have attested to the inferiority of Acorn's skills as a carpenter, but when the Maritime carpenter sold his tools in order to survive as a poet, he embarked on a career in which he would make unfaltering objects of great beauty and use. Apprentices who try to get by with subjective smudges of words might do well to listen to the man's words: "Remember that poetry, like carpentry, is a craft. Learn every technical thing about it you can."

That does not mean to write without social intent. Acorn said that he wanted every poem to have at least one line that would arouse the ire of some oppressor. Too often shallow readers assume that a poet has to drop his art in order to make his political message stronger, or the opposite, that a political poem should not stop to consider matters of form. That is a pitiable error of our time. Milton Acorn may sometimes have shouted his love, but he did so in lines that followed one another with no danger of embarrassing themselves. Decades after "I Shout Love" was written it can be read with admiration for its sureness, which is a quality you are not likely to find in most of the furniture you bought that long ago.

Milton Acorn is dead, they say. He died in Charlottetown, the small city he was born in during the first decade of the Russian Revolution and the first year of Mussolini's regime. He will not be writing any more poems for people, but he left instructions for anyone else who wants to do so. I am glad that I finally dedicated a book of poems to him and sent them to him there on his island, in the last year of his life. He will not be reading any more poems for people; I am sure that he knew that.

But everywhere in his country he is still here, as they say. Milton, thou art living at this hour. Here is the end of a poem written in June, 1971:

I'll be a statue to myself. While I live let that suffice.
But if I die (for which I have no plans)
You can raise one more if you like
Of bronze, granite, carborundum, diamond or ice.
Don't forget the cigar. Keep it burning
Preferably as a beacon for mariners:
As for that number two statue — make it hollow.
Put a little doll inside, gyrating thru motions, poses,
    shapes like every version of the question mark
    in every script.
That'll be me at my real age ... Nine years.

Purdy's Purple

WHEN I WAS a poetry aspirant in Vancouver in the very early sixties, I sometimes stood around on the dark rugs at Hannah Kaye's bookstore. It was the literary connector in downtown Vancouver, where the second-hand book you wanted might have been in a cardboard carton still packed because of a lack of time and shelf space. Any young person who wants to be a writer has to have this kind of place. Kids come down out of the hills for such bookstores.

One time I happened to be in Hannah Kaye's when the mail arrived. It included a rectangular carton labelled BOOKS, but Doug Kaye opened it with a non-literary gleam in his eye. Out slid a Canadian whiskey bottle with a whiskey label on it. But the substance inside the glass was a brooding evil darkness.

This comes from distant eastern Ontario, said Mr. Kaye. It is a fluid which its maker refers to as wine. It is made by Al Purdy, who also claims to be a friend of ours. Have a taste.

In those days I drank porch-climber that retailed at eighty-nine cents a twenty-sixer, so my first hit on Al Purdy's vintage was not as great a shock as it would have been, for instance, to P. K. Page. But two days later my teeth were still purple, and I don't want to tell you about my morning urination. You might look up porphyria.

I cannot remember which came first, that wild grape wine or *Poems for All the Annettes* (1962), but I can say that I was to be affected by both for years to come. I do know that I ingested the chemical before I met the poet (1963).

The Greeks retrieved the word *porphura* from their successful adventures in Asia Minor. It designated a certain Aegean shellfish and the dye that was extracted from its corpse. The Greeks and then the Romans applied the name to a precious stone we call porphyry. That is how people in royal families came to be "born to the purple." Sometimes the stone can be dark red, and in Europe kings sometimes wore dark red trimming that was called purple.

Now that is a fair introduction to Al Purdy's poetry. Purdy's poetry is characterized by its sudden veering back and forth between classical references and domestic appetites.

When I first went to Toronto as a youngish would-be poet in the very early sixties, I was lucky enough to spend an evening at the flat of the even younger Victor Coleman. I don't remember whether there was an occasion, but the book-lined room was full of poets I had written to, and some of the names that had got me going.

Al Purdy was there with a crate of his homemade wine. Bottles of the teeth-staining stuff were passing quite quickly around the room. I quaffed it like the veteran I would appear to be.

Raymond Souster, my main Canadian male poetry hero, was there with Mrs. Souster. They lived nearby. Souster used to chuck out poetry books from time to time, and young V. A. Coleman used to creep along the lane and snaffle them before the garbage collectors could.

Souster did not wait for Purdy's wine to make its way around to him. He got up from his seat by the unusable fireplace and disappeared from the room. A few minutes later he was back with a bottle of Canadian whiskey, which he and Mrs. Souster proceeded to employ. Most of the rest of us spent the evening casting envious sensible eyes toward Souster's bottle, but we drank the *Chateau de Purdy*. Mrs. Bowering and Mrs. Purdy didn't seem to be drinking much.

In Toronto the poets' tongues were purple for a week.

⌐

"**Murex**, any of the marine snails comprising the family *Muricidae* (subclass Prosobranchia of the class Gastropoda). Typically the elongated or heavy shell is elaborately spined or frilled. The family occurs worldwide, but mainly in the tropics. The many muricids that live in rocky shallows are called rock shells or rock whelks.

"The animal feeds by drilling a hole in the shell of another mollusk and inserting its long proboscis. Most species exude a yellow fluid that, when exposed to sunlight, becomes a purple dye.

"An example of the most important genus is the 15-centimetre (6-inch) Venus comb (*Murex pecten*), a white, long-spined species of the Indo-Pacific region. The dye murex (M. *brandaris*) of the Mediterranean was once a source of royal Tyrian purple."

— *Encyclopedia Britannica*, Fifteenth edition.

⌒

The first book in Montreal small press First Statement's New Writers Series was *Here and Now* (1945), by Irving Layton. My copy has words written by three hands on the half-title page.

The first inscription just says "K. E. Grieve."

The second neatly proceeds "To Al Purdy — with the hope that a line or two of Layton's work contained here may provide inspiration for some bloody thing. Ken Grieve — August /56."

The third reads "George Bowering — poet to poet, Feb. 9, 2:30 a.m. When he and Angie were in love. Al Purdy."

The thinnish volume has a paper wrapper in a grey-mauve colour. But this copy is unique. Its cover bears (somewhat faded now) a splashy pattern of wild grape wine from eastern Ontario.

⌒

Purple is a monarch's colour, and also, one might think, a poet's colour. H. D., immersed as she was in the world of the classical Mediterranean, used it constantly, the way a dyer does, lifting it from the earth and the sea, applying it to her fabric. In her poem "To Bryher," she begins by maintaining that "Stars wheel in purple," and later that "stars turn in purple." In other poems "We bring deep-purple/ bird-foot violets," or the king Kaspar has a vision of Aphrodite-Mary with a headband of jewels that "were blue yet verging on purple,/ yet very blue." She was the queen of Heaven, out of the sea.

H. D.'s three-part novel *Palimpsest* has a middle part called "Murex." At its beginning there is a phrase in quotation marks and italics: *"who fished the murex up?"* The question occurs over and over in the stream-of-consciousness that composes the prose running through eighty pages. It is the second-to-last line of Robert Browning's poem "Popularity," an appreciation of John Keats, in which Keats is imaged as a Tyrian fisherman bringing in the shells full of precious colour.

Keats, the poet of nature, of inspiration, who expressed his yearning for "a draught of vintage":

> With beaded bubbles winking at the brim,
>   And purple-stained mouth

Some poets use colour a lot, and others seldom. I hardly ever mention a colour, for example. Al Purdy mentions them in every poem. He says the names of colours more often than any poet I know. Some poems are just spattered with colours. Some poems name colours in nearly every line. Some poems are catalogues of colours, sample books of shades.

Any reader might reread Purdy as I have, and be amazed by the continuous rainbows. Here in a minor poem called "William Lyon MacKenzie," one is bidden to see two parking lots a century apart:

> with the silver glitter of frost
> on exposed brown leather
> as there is on the red blue green pink black and yellow metal
> roofs of cars parked in the street outside Maple Leaf Gardens

In some poems the colours are not only casual effects but the very subjects of lyric regard. "Pre-School" tells of a child's education in colours. Coming from black, he finds yellow in buttercups and dandelions, red in willow roots, blue in the sky, of course, and then the darker colours. He apparently does not learn anything from crocuses or lady's slippers. The poem ends with the child searching for "one more colour/ . . . beyond the death-black forest."

Purdy's memoir of childhood, *Morning and It's Summer* (1983), is filled with memories of a boy's life surrounded by colours — of horses, fields, beards, tombstones. It too tells of a boy's education by colours: "Even the colours of things, that later became so familiar, gave rise to questions in my mind. Aware of it for the first time, red was a phenomenon. Also green, blue, yellow and orange. I wondered: are black and white things dead? And only coloured things alive?"

When we were children learning pigments we were instructed on the three primary colours and the hues that result when you mix any two. In Purdy's list here he mentions five of the six possibilities.

⸺

Purple is peculiar. It is not rare but it is treated as if it were rare, or should be. On the one hand it can be forbidden to those who are not royal. On the other hand it is abjured by those who equate modesty with good taste. Kings do not, in Shakespeare's plays, descend to prose. We congratulate ourselves when we dissociate ourselves from purple prose. I have never, though, heard the phrase "purple verse."

Poets, in fact, have normally been associated with the colour. In fact "purple" looks like a word made up of a meld of "poet" and "colour." Well. The Greek poets loved it; the poems of Sappho and

Alkman, for examples, are nearly as purple as nature. In his translation, Ezra Pound has Sextus Propertius say: "I had never seen her looking so beautiful/ No, not when she was tunicked in purple."

The most poetic person I have ever known is Phyllis Webb. There is no question about the rare beauty and exactness of her work. When I first saw her she was wearing purple clothing of extravagant cut. That was in 1957. The most recent time I saw her she was wearing purple, uncompromisingly.

Phyllis Webb is a poet's poet. The book that her poet-admirers love best is *Naked Poems* (1965). It has a shameless totally purple cover. There are not many colours mentioned in its minimalist verses, but "plum" light occurs more than any other. One will find other shades of purple light in her later works.

Remember H. D.'s "deep-purple/ bird-foot violets." The poet Fred Wah played trumpet in a high school dance band, which performed standards such as "Deep Purple." That song's first verse ends: "Breathin' my name with a sigh," which became the title of Wah's 1981 "book of remembering."

⌒

Just after Purdy had reached a high plateau of fame, when his name was affixed to the canon, he published a big book of poems with purple boards and end-papers, called *Wild Grape Wine* (1968). Its opening poem is "The Winemaker's Beat-Étude," the title picking up its pun from the then-notorious Beat Generation poets.

It is a bacchanalian (or what some people will call drunken) poem. It begins with images of the obstreperous poet harvesting the energetic vines. He then claims to share consciousness with the grapes:

I am thinking what the grapes are thinking
become part of their purple mentality

Then he finds himself surrounded by black and white cows that
gaze at him. First he takes their wish to be for entertainment, so he
capers and makes noises proper to animals, men and gods. But he
looks again and reinterprets their stare:

Then I get logical thinking if there was ever a
feminine principle cows are it and why not but
what would so many females want?
I address them like Brigham Young hastily
    "No, that's out! I won't do it!
        Absolutely not!"

However, he somehow realizes that these Holsteins are not his
maenads. First he imagines that they are all Sapphic. Then his
purple mentality is transformed: "I become the whole damn
feminine principle," and the inebriate poem spins like a roisterer's
ceiling, until he has to nail it with the conclusion of a catalogue
he had begun earlier:

O my sisters
I give purple milk!

It is a prominent poem and an extravagance that stays in the
reader's memory. So one may be forgiven for thinking that the
colour purple is typical in Purdy's work.

But I've never seen a purple cow again.

Remember Fred Wah's title. Much of his book is about breathing, the activity basic to living, poetry and the trumpet. Fred Wah can breathe his surname with a sigh.

John Donne said in an apothegmic hymn addressed to his giver of breath:

> Swear by thy self, that at my death thy Son
>> Shall shine as he shines now and heretofore;
>>> And, having done that, thou hast done,
>>>> I fear no more.

(Two years earlier, on the same subject, he said "So, in his purple wrapped, receive me, Lord.")

Ben Jonson's memorial to William Shakespeare praises that poet's lines, "In each of which he seems to shake a lance."

In our century an American poet said:

> Something there is that doesn't love a wall,
> That sends the frozen-ground-spell under it
> And spills the upper boulders in the sun,
> And makes gaps even two can pass abreast.

That something is of course [F]rost, the poet's shared silver mentality, let us say.

So one might think that a poet named Purdy, and a poet who organizes poems according to colours, and a poet whose subjectivity pervades his lines, might fall into the habit of naming the colour [P]urple.

George Bowering

Silver is a colour Purdy likes. You will notice its periodic gleam if you read through *The Collected Poems* (1986). He likes other jewellery metals too, especially gold and copper. Things are often "coppery," especially given the right conditions of light. Sometimes ebony and ivory show up, but not as often as the metals.

Silver is, I suppose, a poet's colour. More so than gold. That may be because of the interpenetration of image and sound. "Silver" sounds interesting with other words. "Purple," by comparison, sounds a little exaggerated, or even funny. There was never a silly song called "Silver People Eaters."

"Orange," on the other hand, is famous for not riming with anything. (But can you think of a rime for "purple"?) It is, I think, as extreme a colour as purple. But Purdy uses it quite a bit more. Yet I would bet that purple shows up in nature more than orange does.

Around my place it does, anyway.

⁓

Al Purdy does not say "purple" very often. In *The Collected Poems* (the McClelland & Stewart version) there are four hundred pages, filled with close type. It could have been seven hundred pages thick. In all those pages Purdy allows purple things to appear six times, and he does not always utter the word.

Purlieu, purpose, purchase, purge, Purgatory, purview, purity. These words do not show up much in his work, either. In fact, when the " — ur" sound does show up, it can only be striking, reminding us of its rarity, as in a poem about the driver with an open case of beer in the back seat and a cop on his tail:

and I signal a left turn
and he signals a left turn
I signal a right turn
and he signals a right turn

Purdy's having fun, of course, the line-endings signalling verse, which means turn. But he says " — ur" as seldom as he uses end-rime.

⁓

While driving to Duthie's bookstore to buy Purdy's *The Woman on the Shore* (1990), I saw purple flowers in nearly all the rain-glint yards of Point Grey. When I got home I washed my hands at the kitchen sink, and looked out the window at three kinds of purple flowers in the side yard.

In western Canada our mountains are often purple, especially when the heather is blooming. But in "Some Mountains Near Banff," Purdy makes do with "red alpine heather" and "yellow/ cinquefoil," and "grey oatmeal porridge" for a simile.

Mountains are often purple. Sunsets are too. So are baboons' asses, farmers' gasoline, Elizabeth Taylor's eyes, sagebrush, plums, some minerals, cabbage, oil, newborn babies, eggplants, and a large percentage of Earth's flowers. Mother Nature is not afraid of purple patches.

⁓

There has always been a special relationship between flowers and poets, at least from the poets' point of view. Any Purdy book is a garden of verses, filled with flowers of enumerated colours, with an obvious bare patch. He makes conventional use of green and grey, what anyone would expect, and then scatters blossoms as signs, either normative or profligate.

In a lyric from *Poems for All the Annettes* (1962), Purdy announces his purpose in employing flowers as images. The poem is called "One of His Mistresses Is Found Missing":

> I can't say what I know
> in my body of you;
> I can only "write poetry",
> and it is not the same,
> is not what I feel —
> is a record of failure
> in life and verse.
> Christ, there's no saying it,
> no talking directly
> about anything deeply felt:
> so I describe a flower I saw once
> with blue-black petals
> and slender torso,
> whose meaning was a colour —
> It's dead and dust underfoot now
> for many years of rain, many of shining;
> except for these lines it's gone,
> having been witnessed once only,
> which is perhaps enough.
> Now I remember it for you,
> who do not greatly care —

It is not difficult to make a Freudian reading of such a poem, of course. A penis is one of nature's purple things, often, though a wishful poet may call it blue-black. In any case, one might have expected such a phallic poet as Al Purdy to make full use of his resources.

Purdy strews flowers on every pond's shore and hillside, sees them hanging on Mexican walls, watches them with pre-human eyes as they evolve to cover the earth. In Mexico one will see more purple petals than anywhere this side of the equator, but Purdy takes no note of them. (But then he does not notice purple in the paintings of D. H. Lawrence and A. Y. Jackson.)

"In the Early Cretaceous" is a late poem. In its seventy-five lines it tells of the arrival of flowers and therefore colours on our planet. It is one of the six poems in the *Collected* to permit the royal hue, in this case a niggardly "blue-purple."

When Purdy made his famous Arctic trip in the summer of 1965, he naturally looked for any signs of colour (life) in the great white expanse. So in "Arctic Rhododendrons" he says "They are small purple surprises/ in the river's white racket." In reading this short poem one might remember my earlier words about colour and sound. Purdy calls love "the sound of a colour," and uses the " — ur" sound three times, as well as the delicate riming of "number" with "thunder" and then "lovers." Those sounds are accompanied by a nice network of other subtle rimes.

So you see and hear: when Purdy is surprised (another word with sexual connotations) by purple, he is led by tones into verse that sings more than usual for him.

When we think about the wine we will have with dinner we think red or white. We are grown up. Purple wine, we know, is that awful cheap hootch we drank when we were kids. Maybe that is a reason to avoid the colour, or go easy on it.

Often when we see the colour purple we speak in primary colours. We call it red or blue. If we are covered with purple bruises we are "black and blue." In grocery stores plum-coloured grapes and plum-coloured plums are "red."

The poet is not the only one who avoids saying purple.

⁓

The Collected Poems covers the years 1949-1986. That works out to less than one purple reference each six years.

The first occurs as an implied simile in "Old Alex," a poem first published in the sixties, and often revised and republished. It ends:

Well, who remembers a small purple and yellow bruise long?
But when he was here he was a sunset!

The second is in the aforementioned "Arctic Rhododendrons." I give a half-reference to the "violet toilet tissue" of the notorious Arctic poem "When I Sat Down to Play the Piano." In fact I am not persuaded that the historical paper was that hue — I think that the poet grabbed it for the felicitous sounds of the phrase. Note too that the possible purple in this instance as in the Alex-bruise is comic in intent.

The famous Bacchic wine amounts to a whole reference, and so does another drunken poem from the same book, a piece called "Dark Landscape." It mixes giant houseflies, mushroom clouds, and homemade wine:

drink a glass of wine and knock the bottle over
[presumably onto a book by Irving Layton]

down the dregs and stain my guts with purple
think about a girl who couldn't love me

(Remember the teacher who told you that a noun was the name of
a person, place or thing?) A few lines later the unsteady voice cites
"the afterbirth of youth." Afterbirth is, if I remember correctly, a
kind of purple, and if so a nice continuation of the gut image.

A decade later Purdy was writing prolix poems about travel inside
and outside Canada. A lot of the travel was through millennia of
time. In "The Beavers of Renfrew" we are offered a picture of prehis-
toric man:

And he shinnied down with hairless
purple behind pointed east for heat,
tail between hind legs

Once again the colour is used with comic intent.

Finally, I mark a half-reference for the "blue-purple" flowers of
"In the Early Cretaceous." If you were to push me I might allow full
points for that and for the violet toilet tissue. Then you would have
seven references in four decades.

Well, he does mention lilacs in one poem from 1980. But he just
says twice: "the whole world smells of lilacs." They could be white
ones.

A spectroscoping of Purdy's many books will show that there are
a half-dozen occurrences of the colour purple that did not make
it into The Collected Poems. These tend to be non-comic usages.
Certainly poems such as "Iguana" and "Canadian Spring" are good

enough to be retained.

There are exceptions. One of the collected purples is non-comic, and one of the excluded ones is comic, a reference to "old kings with purple carbuncles."

So why doesn't Purdy, who mentions the other colours in hundreds of poems, and who enumerates the flowers as any romantic is called on to do, give its due to the colour that appears most often in our garden?

Given the feeling against purple passages in serious writing, I can see that a restrained poet might stick to shades of the primary colours. But one does not think of Purdy as a particularly restrained poet. In self-mockery he often characterizes his own vocalization as "yodelling." In the relationship between sound and image we might equate purple with yodel.

Why does Purdy seldom allow himself to mention purple things, even though the adjective rimes with his name, and why is it ten times out of twelve used for comic purposes?

Put the question another way. Why do you seldom see Al Purdy and other men wearing that colour (except as Bacchic wine stains)?

I think I have found a clue in an early poem excluded from the *Collected*. It is "House Guest" from *Pressed on Sand* (1955). In it the speaker tells of his discomfort before having a homosexual artist (and his friends) in his house. He has to admit the artist's "stigmata of greatness," and is primarily concerned with what appears one inevitable relationship between "the effeminate child" and the success of paintings:

Is there a difference basically
Underlying mine like a Byzantine plinth,
And growing into another world — a gossamer one?

he asks at the end.

> Does the homosexual artist have an advantage over me —
> does he know something I don't know? If I am going to be any
> good as an artist, does that mean I have to be a little gay? (1955)

Purdy mentions D. H. Lawrence often, DHL the phallic poet who lived contemporary with Sigmund Freud, and who imagined naked men wrestling in companionship. Lawrence took being a poet very seriously. His countryside was a herbal cathedral. The passages in Lawrence that are wildly funny are laughed at by everyone except Lawrence. Every reader notices that Purdy's poems address serious issues but that Purdy will do anything not to be seen as self-absorbed or overly sombre.

So while Lawrence has perpetual passion licking at people's loins, and purple-stained prose, Purdy will have a needle ready to burst his own over-inflated balloons.

In "House Guest" the speaker-host says "I expect pastels on the floor ... / And mincing swear words." It is a poem among others concerned with the speaker's questions about entering the world of the artist. Do I have to pick up those pastels, he is asking himself, and sketch lightly as they ask?

Purdy returns to that image a decade and a half later in a poem called "Interruption." It is about his new homemade house built on his own plinth, and the new house guests: "When the new house was built/ callers came." These were squirrels, chipmunks, mice, and especially birds: "Orioles, robins and red-winged blackbirds/ are crayons that colour the air." In the poem, of course, the poet wields the crayons. The pastels are not on the floor — the crayons are in the sky, and the colours are shades of red.

⁓

Purdy thinks of colour as the poet's way of interfacing with the world. In the preface to *The Collected Poems* he speaks of the poet's travelling that has "evoked excitement in me that is like a small stain of colour derived from some original event." Speaking of the Arctic sea, he says "I could feel that blue seep into me, and all my innards changed colour."

Colour in, colour out. In *The Woman on the Shore* (a book with a plum-coloured cover) there is a poem called "Red Leaves," in which we are privy to the poet's search for a yellow image:

> some yellow leaves too
> buttercup and dandelion yellow
> dancing across the hillside
> I say to my wife
> "What's the yellowest thing there is?"
> "School buses"
> — a thousand school buses are double-
> parked on 401 all at once

So the world as seen in a Purdy poem will be a result of chromatic selection. We know that (a) the poet internalizes some colours, the ones that succeed in "impressing" him, and that (b) the referential and metaphorical poem will paint a picture in tones "expressed" by the artist. The primary pigments, we see, are the ones most often squeezed out — or in.

An old way of saying this is that Purdy is subjective when it comes to colours (if he is not colour-blind). He will make preposterous (and etymologically obtuse) gestures from his palette: "the sun's yellow menstrual blood." Dennis Lee says that Purdy's work is a "kaleidoscope." But Purdy says it is emotionally wrong and dangerous to "[t]ear a rainbow's spectrum apart."

Yet he will flail about to make a point regarding the awful prismatic pain of human love. How the lover must suffer, pay his dues, receive his blessed wounds, earn his purple heart.

Now I would like to wind up with an inconclusive remarking of what seems a paradox, at least to my subjective reading or misreading of Purdy's paint-job.

On the one hand we have seen that Purdy avoids using and collecting a colour by which he is surrounded while pacing nature for inspiration. He probably omits the colour because of its traditional associations with royalty, overwrought composition, and the swish lifestyle. Remember that where Purdy comes from it is pretty suspect to be a poet at all. So he desired to be a masculine, plain-speaking democrat.

On the other hand at the first full flush of his renown, when he was first becoming a public figure, he published a collection called *Wild Grape Wine*. The book is filled with images of the hairy crook-legged public figure fully inhabiting his country from coast to coast to coast. The introductory poem finishes with an image of poet as sister to cows, weird transexual minotaur giving purple milk.

What places this extravagance, this transgression fully on the other hand is the fact that I cannot help but take this "Beat-Étude" as a major Purdy work, as the central poem, at least when it comes to the poet's creation of an image or myth for himself. I think that it must be a key poem, in the sense that it will open or close Purdy's work to any reader.

So purple must be Purdy's colour. Could it be that just as in the post-Mediterranean world the colour was reserved for rulers, so in this poet's *oeuvre* it is stinted so that it will stand out on the occasion of his major poem?

If the poet as Bacchic cow-person gives purple milk do we look backward on a week of stained teeth, or into the text where we calm down and see that what was written in purple is easy to mistake for blue-black ink?

Robin Blaser At
Lake Paradox

The dying Charles Olson told Robin Blaser, I would trust you on
the image, but you have no syntax, or something like that. Here is
a famous Blaser image:

> Supper guest
>
> leaning over the white
> linen which casts
>
> a pale light
> over his face

— which seems to present no problems in reading its syntax. But
the rest of this single-sentence poem without a period at the end

carries us as a moth might fly, on a path better glimpsed than followed, to rest in a corner. The image is part of *The Moth Poem*, written "for H. D." It often favours the carefully advancing well-lit stanzas that H. D. liked in her later days, but it does not adhere to classic sentences the way that H. D.'s *Trilogy*, for instance, does.

Do we know what Olson meant by "syntax," and do we know why Blaser called his 1983 book *Syntax*? Was Blaser taking up Olson's challenge, or was he proving that he had another meaning for "syntax" in mind? There is a clue, one knows, in the "Preface" to the book:

> I read, walk, listen, dream, and write among companions.
> These poems do not belong to me.

Note that he begins the way a grammar teacher's examples do: I (verb) *etc.*

Syntax means the way things are gathered, tactics for getting language together. Words, specifically, listen among fellows. A grammar of something is a set of principles showing the way it works. The rules, a strict grandma might say, a program for letters. But syntax: I guess that as synthesis is to thesis, so syntax is to tactics.

Now the thing about tactics is that they are thought out in advance, not as far in advance as is strategy, but practised and planned toward expectations and an end. They are the practical science of deployment. We can hardly be talking about a typical Blaser poem here, not that zigging moth.

Once I got a letter from a faithful reader of Blaser: "... really, there's only one question about Blaser that needs to be answered: what's the effect on his thought of having no cognitive syntax? (i.e. the question behind that is about parataxis, and how effective it really is.)

Blaser, for instance, is a much better poet than an essayist. When he gets into trouble (i.e. becomes inscrutable) in the poetry, it's because he starts looping ideas and images together, making a marvel."

Parataxis is Blaser's poetic and his politics. In his book *Syntax* it serves his purpose well as conveyor and indicator of any message we might want to coax from a poetry. For one thing, parataxis usually shows up more in speech (formal or street-level) than it does in writing, and "companions" use the occasion of bread-breaking to depart from their lone studies and share words with one another. For another thing, parataxis makes conjugation rather than subjugation. So in his "Great Companions" series, Blaser will not use the old meditative play that would treat the great dead poets as masters; and in *Syntax* he will not treat the radio, overheard transit talk, graffiti or tombstone inscriptions as vulgarity to be "lifted" into poetic order by a bard's quotation. If Blaser is looping idea and image, he is not converting one into material for the other.

The difficulties presented by Blaser's essays I will leave unremarked. But it seems to me that for a lot of readers (i.e. people used to buying poetry books as unselfconsciously as they buy snow tires) the difficulty in reading Blaser's poetry is not the zigging of the sentences, but the learned referentiality. I am also persuaded that this is the reason for the ignoring of Blaser by the regular Canadian literature critics who like the untroubled sentences and straight-ahead similes they can purchase in the lyrics of autobiographical Canadian poets. They want to find out about an individual's exemplary pain at the loss of a father to cancer, or the ways in which killer whales and the rest of nature can be compared to human beings, to the shame of the latter. They do not want difficulty, either of allusion or lexical presentation — how often have you heard, for instance, from reviewers and others that they used to like

Erin Mouré's poetry before she got all caught up in deconstruction and reflexivity?

After a few volumes of *Image-Nations* — hard to find, expensive to buy, and filled with erudition — readers were greeted in 1983 with *Syntax*, published by Talonbooks, and full of jokes. Lots of short poems and found poems. Lots of quotations from philosophers and poets, too, but plainly attributed: "phrases from Valéry and Geoffrey Hartman, March 24, 1981."

Through it all one hears Blaser's mind (or brain, is it?) *reading* (or listening) and all at once writing, a word-compiler among a compilation of words.

How hard can it be, then, to come to the table and understand a poem like "*lake of souls* (reading notes"? When Blaser wrote "these poems do not belong to me," could he have meant that they belong to the reader? Or could he have been saying that they are not in the business of belonging?

In *Syntax* there is no table of contents, but nearly all the poems' titles are indicated by upper case letters — for instance the often used "THE TRUTH IS LAUGHTER." There are two titles that are in lower case italics. One, "*alerte d'or*," is made out of "phrases from Valéry and Geoffrey Hartman." The other is the poem under consideration. There are also two poems whose titles are presented in lower case Roman type, a one-liner called "graffito," and the last page of the book, which could be thought title-less. In the table of contents of the collected books, *The Holy Forest* (1993), this last one would be called "'further,'" indicating that it has no title but is marked off by its first word as something more than an ending to the stuff on the previous page.

In *The Holy Forest* the titles do not have upper case letters, and the title "lake of souls (reading notes" has no italics, though like "alerte d'or" and "graffito," it is differentiated by its having a lower case first letter.

Well, so what? Robin Blaser's system is a lot like Robert Duncan's, and Jack Spicer's (and bpNichol's): the various parts of "*lake of souls* (reading notes" are marked differently, but they come together, even the enclosed 1947 Blaser*kind* poem "Song in Four Parts for Christ the Son," to form this eleven-page poem called notes. And "*lake of souls* (reading notes" joins a lot of pieces called "The Truth Is Laughter" and others to form a book called *Syntax*. But then "lake of souls (reading notes" enters as part of *Syntax* into a much larger book called *The Holy Forest*. It is not difficult to imagine that *The Holy Forest* is part of a large book being written by Blaser and his companions. You are not out of the woods just because you happen upon the opening of a field. The poems, said Blaser in his 1968 essay "The Fire," are "a continuous song in which the fragmented subject matter is only apparently disconnected."

Does that mean that the reader is "free" or "bound" to connect? Or to find possible connections? Or to read like a person who knows little about this and less about that? I, for instance, have liked Blaser's poems since I first saw them in the early sixties, but have always been intimidated by them, believing as I always did in graduate school that everyone else knew more about the subject than I did. So I usually take a tack that is supposed to disarm other sailors. I approach a poem as if one can believe everything one reads, and then register my surprise when that proves not to be so. Sorry for the personal note — I won't let it happen again.

So, "lake of souls" one reads in lower case, and already one is lost, hopeful of being found, because that sounds so nearly familiar — is this lake to be found somewhere in Dante, or an Egyptian story about Osiris, or somewhere in Blaser's favoured Gnostics or Sufis? There is a lake of souls somewhere in Chinese stories, but Blaser is not calling these "reading tones," and we will not get any Chinese reading here. Of course we do not know, the syntax being adumbrated, whether that word "reading," so lately a verb, is some other part of speech. Are these notes made while reading, or notes being read, or notes doing some reading? Surely not what a lake of souls is doing? Adumbration of syntax can make one feel so *rich*. So rich, and lamenting a want of confidence.

Then the poem begins so beautifully, as a person without theoretical training might say. It opens with traditional timing, a summer dawn full of birdsong — and the poem will seem to end eleven pages later, returning not to dawn's light or the eve's onset, but mixing dark with light and (in this longest piece followed only by an "envoi" and a "further") getting us back to the aurora borealis that started *Syntax*.

The poem begins with beautiful sound, even while talking in the vulgate ("things move about quickly"), a simple response to the familiar calls of birdsong. Yet we know that this will be a longish poem about the poet's place in the relationship between belief and lone practice, because we can't help hearing it as a reply to Robert Duncan's poem on the way poesis gets going. "The light foot hears you and the brightness begins," Duncan said, puzzling us somewhat. Now "the period dissolves and becomes a curve of notes." Duncan's poet seems to be writing the whole night long, stopping when dawn is rumoured. Blaser's noting of sources will begin when day wakes, probably telling Duncan and us that he is not so much spooky as Eosic in his invitation of muse and mind.

The only two published poems in Blaser's "Great Companions" series are the ones for Duncan and Pindar, the poet that Duncan credits with the first line of his poem.

Here the birds rather than the bards seem to start this poem about reading. But does one "read" birdsong? There is a bird song at the end of every sentence this morning, but we don't know who is forming the sentences; and bird songs go up and/or down their scale. The period dissolves from a little dot to become, presumably, an undetected part of a solution, and if there is no end to syntax, there is no syntax. Otherwise reading, the only "period" we yet know of is "dawn," when things that move about quickly are likely birds, those light-foots that in poetry bring messages from heaven to earth.

If the subject is grammar, this is demonstrative, and indefinite is a pronoun. Or the spiritual condition signalled by the birds is a doubly negated (in-, de-) finite. Yes, says the bird's line-ending, it is. As if syntax has a secret the poet is challenged by. But it is morning: the condition is not a dream, not the message enjoyed by a Romantic poet or a Duncan. Wide awake at dawn, this poet is making a thematic statement, as few are wont these days to do. Flirting or arguing with Jung, he declares that we all share this condition not in a collective reverie, but in the day's light. Poetry, furthermore, is not passed from master to younger savant, but available to all, produced by earthly graffitists. Hence parataxis rather than authors. If there is such a thing as the sullen art, it is a solitude we join among us to reach. In becoming civilized we learn —

Oh no. Solitude comes from sole. Solution comes from lose. The reader is always in danger of getting things backward when he gets cute.

⟍⟋

Having fallen upon the word "civilization," Blaser thinks of the civilized seeking refuge from the barbarians. Their lesson, learned by them or not, will be that there is no such thing as privilege if the unprivileged are not in sight, that the barbarians are already inside us, where they belong. The bird's song curves — it does not merely rise or fall like a civilization.

Cavafy's poem is marked by plenty of punctuation and subordination, italicized, quoted syntax. It is the outside of Blaser's poem's inside. *Those people* (the purported, demonstrated others) *were some sort of solution*, in which a whole period might be dissolved. But they did not arrive as they were supposed to, on the dot. There never was a fall of Constantinople. It was everybody's language.

⟍⟋

Birds are not the most intelligent of earth's creatures. If their chattering gets written down, it is done by human writers, the same people that copy words out of the library at Alexandria or off the windows of a city bus. When that happens the song becomes "everybody's language," and poets rightly address skylarks and cuckoos.

Here I will have to admit that I can get my little feet more securely on Blaser's image than on his syntax:

the spiritual condition which is everybody's language
of the world is not finally as small as my own solitaire

Of course "finally" echoes "indefinite." Of course "solitaire" echoes "solitude." But is "solitaire" a game or a jewel? I would like to say that Blaser is tying up the argument of his whole (page and) book — the declaration that the experienced poet now values the ensemble world of language above any gem-like singularity — silver knobs (hmm), single jewels, shining verses. Casement windows.

On the first page of this eleven-page poem there are many v's and l's, the work of love. But there are also five words with "sol" in them. Is this working on a reader earlier than syntax, signifying a kind of sun's dawn? How many ways can Blaser make his point at once?

⁓

The second page is autobiographical prose, the prose writer the poet Blaser. He tells of his learning early the Nicene Creed, issued in Constantinople, home of Cavafy's family. Blaser says that he learned it in Latin, French and English, but we know that it was first written in Greek. It is a wonderful foil for the poet's demotic argument, because (1) it declares a belief in pure patriarchal order: *Credo in unum Deum, Patrem omnipotentem, factorem caeli et terrae, visibilium omnium et invisibilium*, and (2) it reaches for the "universal," being the only creed that was to be accepted by Christian churches East and West, Catholic and Protestant.

Yet Blaser introduces it with an image of "pouring over the crazy-quilt." I like to think that he is remembering a literal family comforter. The crazy-quilt is made of and for family memories, and made without an originary design, caught-as-caught-could. Neither does it declare anything like the universal of the cosmic Maker. It is all image, no syntax. Things go side by side, literally composition. It is homely. Blaser inscribes his own public Idaho when he twists some sagebrush into this patch of the poem. Yet sage is ancient and

Mediterranean (from earth's centre before frontier America); it was supposed to promote memory and wisdom, Blaser's two topics here.

But before he can bring his thought to a completion, the old grammar teacher's definition of the sentence, he is led at the end of his line not to birdsong this time, but to bee's sound, murmuring, beyond the Greeks to Sanskrit. Then to nowhere. And then to Berkeley in 1945. The Nicene Creed was not really a profession of belief but a submission to discipline. Blaser will seem to be a kind of musical apostate.

⟶

In the next patch or square, which like all the notes abjures upper case letters to begin sentences because there is no more beginning than ending, Jack Spicer is both "beloved friend" and new acquaintance. Quilt-makers make new covers out of old clothes; lyric autobiography happens at dawn. Crazy Spicer is in 1945 even more ecumenical than the Council of Constantinople, being both "Presbyterian and a Buddhist." He makes a campy remark about young Idaho's Catholicism. On Easter Sunday of the next year Robert Duncan, an even stranger mixture of religions, does likewise. Remembering the effect of this shock, the poet nearly lets his thread ravel, as the words loosen their connections to one another, gaps in the lines.

Finally, in the year after the poet became a legal adult, he published a poem about a kind of Apocrypha Jesus, in the campus magazine. It was praised, we are told, by one Keith Jones. Blaser holds his needle and tells us that now, or rather at the time of the poem's composition, Jones is a "labour leader among the grapes." A nice touch, this praise from a man who would be surrounded by both lowly work and the fruit of sacrament. Prose and poetry. Hesiod and Dionysus.

Blaser's reading notes now reprint the four stanzas (with Yeatsian Roman numerals) of that student's poem. It is titled "Song in Four Parts for Christ the Son." Each line begins with a capital letter, and so do these words: Your, He, God, Him, Love and Our Lady. There is lots of end-rime, and periods at the tail ends of its short sentences. It is redolent of roses and dancing. It alternates iambs with anapests, like a child walking and skipping. It is a love song that affirms a Christian relation while challenging, or at least modifying it. It is sort of like a Yeats poem stripped by H. D. Finally, it affirms a Christ lover dancing instead of sticking to a tree. It is so well finished that it ends with a couplet, both of whose lines end with periods. There is not a bird within earshot, except the unheard peacocks.

Blaser must be copying all those satisfied periods to join his two young friends in making fun of the young poet. Certainly that is the function of Anna Russell, the great singer who makes fun of opera's egos. If singers have a resonance where their brains ought to be, they have echoing empty heads. They may be ecstatic but unquestioning, satisfied with their echoing achievement, convinced that they know the score.

We are going to learn that Blaser is hearing Anna Russell on the radio, another composer of these notes, of this book of poems.

Then, "I think of," says the poem for a second time, this time of Oscar Wilde, who is the necessary satirical contemporary of Yeats, and the fifth homosexual writer mentioned so far, the peacock model for Anna Russell's wit. Mr. Wilde made a deathbed conversion to Catholicism, and upon hearing about it, James Joyce said that he hoped that it was insincere. When Oscar Wilde gets into a poem, the temptation is to say that all bets are off. In any case, Blaser avers that he thinks about Wilde's poem "nonsensically." But that's a problem, too: maybe nonsensically is a synonym for asyntactically. That would make sense, then, and our troubles have only begun. If I were gathering this poem, I would stop listening for echoes, and find something to read.

René Girard has been here almost from the beginning, or he has almost been here from the beginning. The "indefinite spiritual condition" we share, like syntax, said the dawn poet, "is a violence/ or a love." The twenty-one-year-old poet said "Love" while addressing the Sacred. Girard's book is called *La violence et le sacré*.

(Here is a simple fact. This poem is made of various prose and verse. It is aimed at coming to a form, as words come to be, there. In this way it is not unlike a credo.)

It has to be getting later in the morning or the day. The piece is getting to be more like reading notes, or affirmative quotations drawn not from autobiographical memories become writing, but remembered reading, others' writing, brought to the light of this day. Thoughtful bricolage. This Girard says to us that theorists in our spiritual condition relegate sacrifice not to the earthly body but to the imagination. We eat not our god but our co-composers' imagination. In the last years of the twentieth century, Blaser wrote the libretto for Sir Harrison Birtwistle's (!) opera *The Last Supper*. The feast allows us not into high heaven but into speech.

So now Blaser does not write "I think," but rather "speaking." And even though he gets to William Blake not by subordination but by association, he breaks into plain speech to pretend that we have syntax, the orderly coming: "let's get our principles straight —" Oh, sure! Don't we have a suspicion that Blake may have got here because a few pages and some decades back the young poets were in "Blake's Restaurant on Telegraph Avenue"? Thus was the poem wired from the beginning. Let *us* get *our* principles via twisted threads.

The Blake passages tell us of further ecumenicity, which means the occupied world. Human beings are themselves occupied by Blake's famous Poetic Genius, angel or spirit or demon, those agents whose job it is to interrupt the natural order in mortal provinces. Blaser's paradox is Blake's orthodox — the interruption of human ways is the work of all humans treading them. Thank God the radio is still on, the radio that Jack Spicer compared poets to. Anna Russell "interrupts" again, messing with a traditional song, turning its ancient soothing measures into a rackelly-backelly refuse heap, comic disorder, proving that the truth is laughter. She's got a bad attitude. Hey, we discover over and over, she can really *sing*!

Girard's interesting argument about the place of the sacred in a world bereft of the transcendent has inescapable implications for poetry, as long as we do not lose the notion that poetry has agency in the world, as long as poetry is not simply descriptive of the world or little autobiographical bits of it. All those mundane lyrics you see in all those magazines, all those little things that are pumped out in a belief that their job is to deliver pictures of the world to you, are manufactured in a desultory faith in a simple kind of transcendence. The world transcends the poem, they say — here's a little path into the world. No, don't thank me. I'm only doing my job. It goes on my c.v.

Some people probably say who was Charles Olson to make judgement on Blaser's syntax anyway? Look at Olson's poems and prose,
this for instance:

> the Mountain of no difference which I
> have climbed as other men and other men will
> have no other choice than: there is no other
> choice, you do have to listen to that Angel and
> 'write' down what he says (you don't your
> other Angel does and you obey him
> to the degree that it is impossible to
> keep doing, that's for sure!

But you might see that Olson's poem works its info exactly by way
of its subtly turning phrases with their instant new decisions. If
there are to be images, they will be by-products of the syntax. Olson
is interested in the way everything goes together. In 1963 he told
me that he was hoping to find out that Chinese is an Indo-
European language!

But violence is his, as the Lord sayeth, and then there is no Lord,
so much for the Ten Commandments and all other writing handed
down from a mountain or a congress. The sacred is that which we
are scared of. Before a one-god was made, each peril had its own
holy overseer. Before *that* system was set up, the source of the terror
had no name at all. All religions are one, indeed.

   In the young Blaser's nimble poem the day belonged to the
dancers. But Girard, writing a quarter-century later, said "Violence
is the heart and soul of the sacred." It has become as othered, as

superhuman as natural disasters. I think that Blaser is lamenting the loss of responsibility in human behaviour, and that it started to go when angels and demons no longer awed men. I also think that I am on the edge of losing the poem here, losing its argument. Or maybe the poem is in danger of losing its way. It happens. But anyone who grew up reading T. S. Eliot can see how this poet has been making this poem called reading notes, not with a clausal syntax but with an assemblage of voices. I think I remember that Eliot, or an Eliotist, mentioned a "syntax of images." Critics of Eliot were fond of saying that he and his like did violence to poetic order to achieve effects consonant (or dissonant) with the twentieth century. Call it politics.

So the crude graffito that Blaser brings from the toilet. In what has no likelihood of veracity, the anonymous writer (perhaps a puny freshman) claims to have been born on one of the geographical symbols loved by Romantic poets such as Shelley, and raised in another. But then he claims to be some sort of unlovely and isolate satyr, a brainless lout with a predilection for simple bangs.

The word barbarian was invented echoically to indicate foreign people who do not speak "our" language, who have no more idea than songbirds do of our grammar. It is becoming necessary to figure out Blaser's attitude here, how much irony we are getting, because if some people make only babbling noises, even if the barbarians ride within the gates of each reader's soul, how does that square with poetry that belongs to no one sophisticate who makes notes on erudite reading early in the morning when some poor sods are getting ready to go to work or the welfare office? Are we really looking at the dark side of the asyntactical? Are some of those birds saying "caw"?

Bernard-Henri Lévy tells us in Blaser's note that in our time totalitarianism was invented (though he must be leaving out the great religions), and that it leads to the barbarian state, and that this state of affairs is a result of atheism. The violence of politics had to become an independent entity in order to replace external gods. Lévy will not give it the status of the divine, saying rather that it takes residence in the space unoccupied by divinity, by authority. A syntax starts with an authoritative beginning: see *Genesis* I and *John* I, the beginnings of long poems in which the authors both claim order and assign it to a higher authority.

Geoffrey Hartman takes up the argument of Girard and Lévy and specifically relates the ejection of the old gods to the sprawling victory of free verse. He regrets the artifice of traditional verse that offered insight and beauty that were great because the poet's language transcended the noise of the barbarians. He presumably allows a community of poets, but will not welcome into that community the composers of gravestone wit and unambitious graffiti. Geoffrey Hartman is not a purveyor of laughter, and he would certainly not ascribe truth to it. He sees poetic diction as a gatherer — in other words as a selector of the most desirable in language.

What is Blaser's purpose here? Does he support a priestly cult, as he has in earlier times been accused of doing? Is he giving the elitists their voice in a kind of dialectic? Is he making a potential critic write in interrogative sentences? Is he changing his position as the poem grows longer, or moving from side to side in the space he has found to be his own? We remember that a poet writing "reading notes" has no obligation or reason to go back and revise a first page, where he might have written that the depths of our *indefinite* spiritual condition, like syntax, "are not a/ privilege but everybody's." Potentially everybody's, maybe.

Among the Okanagan people, there is a principle called *en'owkin*, which spirit visits people who come together to formulate civic, political and educational plans. In council, anyone from any social position can express feelings and ideas. They do not debate. When everyone who wants to speak has spoken, and everyone has heard all questions and suggestions, the best possible solutions are agreed upon and the others are not forgotten.

One supposes that a poem can work that way. An answer does not have to be traceable to an origin. Graffiti ≠ gravity.

Percy Shelley may not have loved living in the middle of paradox, but it would be hard to find a poet more paradoxical. He was an atheist whose poems, including *The Triumph of Life*, are hung on religious imagery. He was both a Platonist and a believer in historical perfectibility. In fact *The Triumph of Life* may have been unfinishable because in it he made his last effort to reconcile his amazing idealism with his equally committed empiricism. He was the most intellectual of English poets, but we remember his emotional outbursts, his ecstasies and mournings. He was loved and condemned for his advanced ideas, but he systematically set out to write poems in every form known to classical traditions, and to make them otherwise even more complex.

The Triumph of Life is written in Dante's *terza rima*, as if in contemporary answer to the trinitarian. "The deep truth is imageless," said Shelley, and the mortal's only way toward it is via images that must be expunged because of their delightfully flawed nature. If Charles Olson were somehow tuned to the source of Shelley's imagination (well, it *was* in *Queen Mab* that we first found the term "human universe") he may have been speaking of limitation when he told Blaser that he trusted him on image but not on syntax. If the truth is laughter, the surviving Blaser might say, it could be laughter that is to be heard in the depths beneath images. But whose laughter? What skeptic's? Well, Shelley, in *The Triumph of Life*, called reality "the realm without a name." It is the place in which men's linked thought is without error. Even the greatest of mortal thinkers, Shelley's championed "sacred few," can only touch the word with "living flame" before disappearing.

The depths of our "spiritual condition," said Blaser this morning, are not privileged but shared by all, and are likely the well of syntax. Shelley was the master of syntax, and custodian of its origin and diverse complexity. That is one of the reasons for Blaser's quoting of Shelley's lines about dawn here. Of the two sentences he quotes, the second takes up thirty-one five-beat lines. Even portions of that sentence work wonders: consider the meaning tempered by the turns that start "But I, whom thoughts which must remain untold," and end "Was at my feet, and Heaven above my head, —."

The deep truth is imageless. The truth is laughter. If there is a mini-essay hidden in the sprawl of these reading notations, that's it.

"A violence/ or a love," said Blaser at dawn. When William Hazlitt reviewed Shelley's poem in 1824, he remarked a "violence of contrast," complaining that the poet never succeeded in getting out of his paradox. Shelley did not signal his surrender to Life by abandoning the poem; he knew that he was acknowledging it by writing as much as he did. All poets who attempt great things get the joke eventually.

In *The Triumph of Life* Shelley uses light as his main image, the energy that usually makes images visible. He is not simple, but here is a simple diagram of the light: the distant stars, especially the most faint, stand in for the potential Imagination. But the sun, standing in for Nature, obliterates the light of the stars. Then Life, figured as a fiery chariot, replaces the sun's light. What is Life, the poem asks at its end, where traditional readers have seen its stopping as premature. Might as well ask metaphysical questions of a tiger. Shelley went out and gave up his spark to those other elements, wind and water. ❧

Here we should pay attention to the most obvious gesture: Shelley's morning is cast as noted reading by Blaser in his morning's verses, another bright bird heard from, morning's sweetest minion. Shelley knows where he is going, you say. He is using *terza rima*. He implies a paradiso. But he is no nineteenth-century Catholic — he ends with a question, and it is not the *meaning* of life that he is after. Thus Blaser's "notes" effect the shape of his poetic.

Shelley's lines are beautiful — we can thank both poets for bringing us that, even while we remember admonishments regarding beauty from Baudelaire, Pound and Spicer. But in Shelley's conscious beauty trap the volcanoes are "smokeless altars" — the revolution (see Shelley's late iconography) is dormant or at best potential. The birds are obedient and end in a period, something that the poet is reluctant to do, either for the next ten stanzas or at the end of the poem. All nature follows the patriarchal Sun. Only the poet offers a "But," and because of it acquires a trance and then a vision, which in these notes we are not vouchsafed. What Shelley shows us is an admixture of Nature and something else. It will not bring about worship. Worship is obeisance to a source of syntax not readily available to the worshiper, who normally goes to the end of his own. The Metaphysicals made a trope out of that: their syntax failed and that failure led them to visionary and paradoxical images they could report while insisting that truth lies beyond even them.

⸺

Herakleitos, Modernism's favourite Greek because he proposed paradox and parataxis, did not like Hesiod, the systematical and confident chronicler of order. Hesiod was mundane, Herakleitos incendiary. Hesiod built bridges, Herakleitos burned them behind him. He was never going to cross that river again anyway.

Ecumenical Blaser is reading a Herakleitos translated by a Catholic poet who died in water. His God is neither taxonomic nor edible; He is a mixture of opposites. Like Shelley's imagination, He is fire, and takes on the qualities of that which He creates. Blaser might have included H. D.'s "Pygmalion" in his notes:

Now am I the power
that has made this fire
as of old I made the gods
start from the rocks?
am I the god?
or does this fire carve me
for its use?

Burning bright, indeed.

Remind yourself that Blaser is gathering voices to make a sequence inside a sequence inside a sequence made by those gatherers gathered. He is assembling a self, a plural self to argue a poetic different from the positivist "I" who plays a role in many reactive poems in many anthologies. If Blaser's notes and the noted are replete with the terms of spiritual language, it is not because this is a poetry designed to praise the transcendent; this is a sacred poetry itself. If paradise is around us in fragments, as Ezra Pound wrote in his Pisan prison, one can assemble those fragments in a poem as they are disbursed in a life. Look at them, perhaps, in Sufism's half-light, defined by Luther as the "being of man," Blaser's "indefinite spiritual condition." What do fragments tell us of syntax?

> Le Paradis n'est pas artificiel
> but spezzato apparently
> it exists only in fragments unexpected excellent sausage
> the smell of mint, for example,
> Ladro the night cat

I am always reminded of "Canto LXXIV" when I read "*lake of souls*" (reading notes".

⁓

J. S. Bach gets onto the last page of the poem because in 1981 Robin Blaser was supposed to be writing *Bach's Belief* for the Curriculum of the Soul series, and he was making reading notes for that. When the booklet finally arrived in 1995, one could see that it is composed in the way in which Blaser's poems and lectures are composed, with a reading mind among a gyre of quoted texts. (When Blaser gave courses at Simon Fraser University he appeared in the classroom with a pile of thick books, bookmarks hanging out of them like tongues.) If Bach knew Luther's definition for the being of man, Blaser will define being as soul. More properly:

> *soul* — that mysterious word, contracted by loss of
> syllables into a single sound and with which Christianity
> grabs at belief with a muscle-bound hand — originally meant
> *life itself, animate existence* — such quickness — subse-
> quently made obsolete by crossdressing in immortality — its
> original sounds
>   *saiwalas* "corresponding formally" to Greek αιολοσ,
> fleeting, flitting movement — of, say, earth, air, water, and
> fire — each of them *lief.*

We know that Blaser is by now that normative 1980s postmodern who sort of believes as Pound did that meanings *inhere* in the language and can be followed and saved by good linguistic order, but that it is at the same time somehow unknowable by the creature participating himself in flux.

And here we are, both in and out of our paradox at last.

We in the North are not creatures of new dawn or twilight, but rather denizens of science's spooky *aurora borealis*, back at the beginning of Blaser's *Syntax*. Ha ha.

The northern lights give their green light to our daytime, but it comes to us out of the blackness at the pole's night. Staying away from upper case letters, Blaser offers us even this mysterious last stanza with its troubled predicate agreement, with shepherd and mother, images that Catholics also appropriated. That black milk, I think, is commodious enough to form a lake of souls, so much so, if you are following Pygmalion-like, that the lake might be *constituted* of souls, our shared life.

If I were to feint and dribble my way out of this essay the way that Blaser departs a poem, turning to give another little wave, I might suggest that you contrast this lake of souls to the sea of faces and limbs and torsos that the racing craft drive through in William Carlos Williams's poem "Yachts."

An apology anyway. This essay of notes has been long and centrifugal because Robin Blaser with his skirl of books *leads* you astray or away to get you here.

Thinking about
Whalley

1.

WHEN I FIRST ran across something written by George Whalley I
recognized him right away as an Atlantic man. I was a Pacific boy.
That is why it is meet that the first extended exposure I had to his
mind was in his book about the Arctic, *The Legend of John Hornby*.

This was forty years ago. Once in a while you would see his name
in the magazines. Somehow you knew he was a scholar of English
literature back east. He wrote poems the way English professors
wrote them in the fifties, lines all the same length, sentences relaxed
and appraisive of life. We animals on the Coast were hoping to grab
the edge of land and tip Canada over, or its poetry, anyway.

We were inwardly tempestuous jazz-riff academics. We found
out about the Canada Council. It was run by an [ex-?]spy with an

English accent. A decade and a half earlier, George Whalley was working for Naval Intelligence, pulling wet Nazis out of the brine. Too good to be true, but who's to be sure? He had a copy of Coleridge in his bunk. We didn't know that.

The Legend of John Hornby is carefully written by a professional who knew research and documentation and so on. But it makes you bite your teeth as it presents Hornby's madness in the snow, and the awful way some people died in the unreachable north because of it.

2.

The only time I ever talked with George Whalley was at the beginning of the eighties, in his room at the old Sylvia Hotel on English Bay in Vancouver. He spoke in a mid-Atlantic accent. I told him that I was writing a novel about the voyages of Captain George Vancouver.

Captain George Vancouver was travelling the Pacific around the time that Samuel Taylor Coleridge was poking around in literature for the story and images that would spook the Ancient Mariner. But we didn't talk about English poetry in the Sylvia Hotel.

Somehow I got the nerve to tell this Navy man about my book, I who used to drive my girlfriend's father's fourteen-foot inboard around the headlands here. Earlier, in high school, I had wooed a girl whose father had been a gunnery officer and boxer in the Royal Navy. Vancouver was a man no one wanted to know about, left to die in neglect in his time, still a footnote to Captain Cook in ours. I did not know what people knew. George Whalley came straight to the point: we discussed the invention that George Vancouver was testing for the Royal Navy, the first device that would inform you, no matter your location on the globe's watery expanses, of your proper longitude.

He had found the theme of my fiction before it was ever published. When that happened I dedicated the book to him. Not just because he was a sailor. I admired him greatly because he tried to write so many different kinds of writing. I also recognized some kind of invisible energy that he emitted. Some rare people have that. My wife just fell in love with him.

I never spoke with him again, and we did not correspond. I wrote about him to the people I corresponded with. I remembered his Atlantic voice when I read his words.

I thought about calling this "The Legend of George Whalley."

3.

One afternoon in Montreal, 1967, I found a hardback copy of George Whalley's book *Poetic Process* and bought it for fifty cents. Soon after I moved to Vancouver, someone stole it, a poet, I think. Then in 1976 my wife Angela bought a copy for fifty dollars. The book was published in England in 1953.

Poetic Process was a wonderful book to find, especially if you were a sort of young poet, and had just been studying Romantic poetry hard for two years. In 1953 the universities were pretty well agreed that the New Criticism had poetry right, that a poem was a self-contained and complex embodiment of truth and/or beauty. In *Poetic Process* the young Whalley said a poem was something that happened, to a poet, to a reader if the reader is sharp and lucky. That a poem is not a thing, but an experience.

George Whalley wrote the book, he said, so that he could begin to understand Coleridge. When I read the book I was the age that Whalley had been when he wrote it. I was amazed and thankful. Also kind of awestruck: that this book was written by a Canadian.

The book is not afraid to say that the poetic experience is like the mystical experience. In fact Whalley goes unashamed into the metaphysical. Yet all the way through 250 pages the voice is measured, orderly, the voice of philosophy. But look: the chapters on metaphor and music will lift the hair on your forearm.

Here are the last words of the book: "Beyond that the reader must work out his own salvation."

4.

Famed Coleridgean Kathleen Coburn composed Whalley's obituary for the *Proceedings of the Royal Society of Canada*. It is reprinted at the beginning of *George Whalley: Remembrances*. Dr. Coburn remarks as everyone does the great breadth of Whalley's interests, and says that "the huge work by which he will be best known throughout the world is his edition of the Coleridge *Marginalia* in five, possibly six volumes."

That is indubitably true. I have never looked at even the first volume, probably never will. But I have heard Coleridge scholars' voices drop to a whisper when they talk about Whalley's work.

I wish God had left him here for a few more years, so he could have looked at the lined-up spines of those great volumes on the shelf. And we could have watched him looking at them.

5.

While you read through George Whalley's essays, especially the ones composed as public addresses, you notice that paragraphs are always finishing with sentences that fall into place like future quotations. How right, you remark, and sometimes how portentous. Listen, for examples, to a few present quotations from his posthumous collection subtitled *Innocence of Intent*.

"Humane studies, at their obscure and subversive best — in the distant past and at this time — are a disease of sanity."

"I claim for criticism a humble and ancillary duty: to seek fidelity, to heighten awareness, to disclose the literature intact and well lighted."

"Language is no mere instrument; and if an instrument at all, the instrument plays on the musician as much as the musician plays on the instrument."

"I take it that imagination is not a 'faculty', but rather an integrated and potent state of the self — a *realising* condition, in which the self and the world are made real."

Old friends were glad to find that in the *Remembrances* there are numerous examples of such Whalleyan vaticisms. I'll give you one.

"Let me be particular by considering my own field of work: the affectionate study of English language and literature."

George Whalley was a wizard at that usually British talent — sounding humble while fashioning sentences you expect from well-prepared prophets.

6.

Remembrances was apparently created at the request of George Whalley's wife Elizabeth. It was printed and bound to resemble the collected poems edited by George Johnston for Quarry Press in 1987. I like the fact that it was published by a Kingston press that has always been in some way connected with Queen's University, where Whalley was head of the English department, member of the architecture committee, instrumental in the shaping of the departments of film and music, etc. The campus, the city and the nearby countryside are felt as environs by anyone who reads this book with innocence.

Whalley was born in Kingston in 1915, and died in his Kingston house in 1983. The cataloguing information at the beginning of *Remembrances* offers "Whalley, George, 1915-" — which seems to be a statement one will happily agree with. He was brought up in Kingston and in the British Empire. His childhood reading, whether *Boy's Own* or Kipling, was British. His father was an Anglican prelate and the son went to an Anglican private school. "Horses and Kings," Whalley's own reminiscence about childhood in Kingston, is framed as a reply to Brits about what Canada might be. The writing is clear and staid and filled with images. I hope that it eventually finds its way into school textbooks.

Whalley went to college (twice) in England, and went to war in England. He was an enthusiastic leader in the Boy Scout movement, in which the future stalwarts of the British Empire were tested and trued. He decided on an English accent as the best way to speak the language he loved. I think that even if one did not know this, one might find oneself "hearing" his printed works in

Oxfordese. His eyewitness account of the attack on the *Bismarck* is an exercise in British understatement.

He exhibited the most attractive features of British idealism. He knew Greek and history and the Arctic and how a motor worked. He wanted to be able to converse intelligently on any topic, eighteenth-century navigation devices or Ontario beer. His memoirists say that no one could stump him, even when the topic was the interlocutor's specialty. We are also told often that he could be visibly wounded by wilful ignorance or complacent mediocrity. He set the highest standards, but he set them for himself too.

Yet we are told by his colleagues and his students that he did not turn the classroom into a forum for his erudition. Rather the opposite: he was there to show the student how to reach down inside and discover that the skill to begin reading Coleridge is right there. Good Romantic. Good teacher.

They all remember his famous long silences during classes, too. Imagine that: students being exposed to thinking rather than the fruits of thought. His ex-students are among the most thankful contributors to his hagiography.

What Whalley taught was that one should try to know everything, but that authority, unity, completion, mastery are not the proper notions to bring to a poem. He would spend as much time on a neophyte's lyric as on a Keats ode. He was interested in poetic *process*. Some memoirists remark that in his last days he did not recognize that he was coming to an end. But he was interested in the ongoing particulars of his condition.

7.

Remembrances is pleasant to read because it does not have a chance to threaten authority or unity or completeness. Here we have many-handed marginalia to Whalley's careers. Only three of the memoirs are by well-known Canadian poets. One can give oneself to sheer pre-critical readability, even when one of the writers appears a little self-serving.

There is some gentle order, though. It is nicely sequenced: when it is time for young Whalley to go to college, we will get memories by college dons and fellow students. Then we hear about the New Brunswick school teacher, the Oxford Rhodes scholar, the Naval officer, the Queen's professor, the radio writer, the poet, and finally the father — the last three entries are by Whalley's two daughters and one son.

The collecting of these pieces from all those times and places and parts of the man's life was a prodigious job well done. In fact it is amazing. Let us congratulate the editor. This is not a book review; let us congratulate the editor. In Canada at least there is no book like *Remembrances*. It would take another person like George Whalley to provoke one. Wouldn't that be something?

Nearly all the contributions are by men. I suppose that reflects the nature of the life, what with Boy Scouts and men's colleges and the Navy and so forth. No matter where they write from they call Whalley a "Renaissance Man." Many of them mention that Whalley would play for hours on the nearest piano or organ. Many point out that this cerebral perfectionist was also an eclectic athlete — he hiked and rowed and ran, played tennis and rugby and hockey. I expect that the hockey was field hockey.

It is interesting to see how many of the contributors end their accounts with a story of some elaborate prank engineered by Whalley. A prank, at private school or Scout camp, is an enlistment in the ranks of the anti-authoritarian. But it is done within the borders of the institution, and dependent on the spirit of the institution. It is meant to teach the institution how to go back and relearn reading.

8.

"Is there anything I can do to help?" he asked the Coleridge people when he came back from the War. They said that the marginalia needed some attention. How Canadian, says D. G. Jones. But how Whalleyan, isn't it? The marginalia were Coleridge's *approaches*. For us they are by their nature debarred from closure and canon. They are the closest thing to sharing of the poet's actual thinking: process. They were a huge job to take on, especially for a person who had to put the shutters on the cottage windows this afternoon and go to a Kingston Symphony meeting tonight.

The poets tend to say that they read *The Legend of John Hornby* as Whalley's most compelling book. The colleagues say that *Poetic Process* will be for them the first book that comes to mind. But it is hard to disagree with Kathleen Coburn's judgement that in terms of the world of English, the *Marginalia* will be what keeps Whalley's name alive. It will be the source of his greatest fame, but it will be his most obscure work because its audience is rarified. That is the kind of paradox one suspects he liked to leap into. He was a John Hornby in the academic world.

9.

In his contribution that is the last in the book, but in no way a summing-up, Christopher Whalley responds as might we all, and quite justly, to that paradox: "It was not that he died slightly before his time, but rather that he did not receive his due. A man of his quality deserved more for his efforts; something broader and more substantial than recognition within a closed circle. I think of modesty as being one aspect of greatness; I think of loneliness being another ..."

Fellow Scout Master Colin Cuttell says, "To be sure, there were few who had kept company with him in academic life, perhaps for years, who tumbled to the fact that they had been walking with greatness. He gave himself away to very few."

That seems to be a truth that is by weight of so many testimonies here contradicted and yet left true. If you follow that you're taking early steps toward seeing George Whalley, or part of him.

10.

I said earlier that his poetry is an English professor's poetry. It is pre-modern, but it does not wail like good Romantic verse. It is competent, but competent at performing a sentiment, with perhaps a smart conceit. It uses phrases such as "we know not," archaisms, inversions, grand descriptive momentous posture. It takes place "on some relentless reef of lamentation."

Really.

But. I think any contemporary poet would be glad to have a frightening muse bring the last poem in *The Collected Poems*. It is designated "Poem in Hospital (6-7 January 1980)." It speaks in the voice of "a great white melancholy snow-braving owl-ferocious bird/ crying in the dark for the cold in its beak/ and the cruel dark light in its huge eyes." Thus frantic the poem begins, but then proud resolve and steadfastness make shape, and the last image is also arctic but still, modest and strong:

> a black spruce in the barren ground
> never flamboyant like brown butterflies or the tiny Alpine
> flower
> rooted in permafrost
> but growing for 400 years, maybe a millimetre of green a year.

Total Organ Transplant

bpNichol's Body

"Felt beeps intensify"

— KENWARD ELMSLIE

A. 1988

Barrie Nichol never had much trouble with his audience. He was witty in an exalted way and a low way. He had the nerve to open his mouth and make barnyard noises on stage. He could slip a pun on a Zoroastrian reference past the PhDs, and he could accurately time a great knock-knock joke. He was a true and tricksome post-modern. He was open and giving, and on stage or next to it an hour later he had the knack of letting newcomers get close.

But if he had ever had trouble with audiences in the eighties, he could have won them over with readings from his ongoing series, *Organ Music*. When he read the first one, "The Vagina," to a group of feminists, they applauded. It's a knack. It's the knack that got us to forgive Nichol the gawd-awful puns we would not accept from, say, David Niven. It's the knack that lets me, for instance, persist against the neo-Nicholists who attack what they call hagiography.

I several times heard Nichol read from *Organ Music*, and once, on the radio, I heard Michael Ondaatje reading the part called "The Hip" at the Harbourfront memorial for bpNichol. I was always, and especially on that last occasion, greatly impressed by the professional writing *éclat* of my small-press friend. *Organ Music* was a hit all through the eighties, and we who heard it kept hoping for more.

2. When in 1988 Black Moss Press published *Selected Organs: Parts of an Autobiography*, we settled in. We did not expect the ongoing phenomenon to be as long as *The Martyrology*. A person has only so many organs, after all. But we did want more. Give us your liver, we said. Or how about your nose? We said this because the parts we did get to see are so well written; or they write so well.

In a short introduction to the book Nichol "explains" the process by which the little book came to be, and tells us that here we will get ten parts of the eleven that had been finished. Here are the parts: the vagina, the mouth, the tonsils, the chest, the lungs, the fingers, the hips, the anus, the toes, and sum of the parts. "I know most of the parts you'll read about in here aren't organs," says their author, "but who could resist a title like *Organ Music*? Not me."

We know that organ music is most likely to be heard in church, or off recordings made in a church. As in *The Martyrology* Nichol will have you thinking of the intent spiritual while showing you the body physical. That is, one happily supposes, a radical plan for the action of poetry. To suggest, further, that the meaty human organs make music is to say that the inspired soul had better not put Descartes before discourse.

Anyway, as so often happened before our eyes and ears, bpNichol had a wonderful idea here. Sometimes we see a friend get such an idea for a book and we mix our congratulations with a little homage of envy. The idea was to reshape autobiography. To make it in parts, and to make the parts body parts. Not to recollect and invent a life leading up to the writer's position in old age, but to write on the run, to make, one might say, a lifelong book. Nichol thought there might be twenty sections, but then he also kept thinking that he had finished *The Martyrology*.

Warren Tallman once described such a book. He called it writing a life rather than writing about one. *Selected Organs* is truly most of an autobio(logy)graphy.

3. I started here by mentioning Nichol's humour. What kind of voice do we hear here? "I miss my tonsils," he says. That is funny, we know right away, and it takes us a while to figure out why it is funny. It is also quite straight, and in fact a nice observation. The voice we get in these prose-poems (is that the right term?) comes from somewhere between Nichol's kids' books and *The Martyrology*.

It is, to place it provisionally, in a recent tradition of serial prose, of lyric analysis of childhood. Think of Frank Davey's *War Poems*, of Fred Wah's *Breathin' My Name with a Sigh*, Robert Kroetsch's *Seed Catalogue*. If you are feeling indulgent think of my book *Autobiology*.

The earliest serial prose I can think of is H. D.'s *Tribute to Freud*. Serial prose is perhaps a variant of serial poetry. It seems perhaps more conscious or the result of something more conscious. It calls for unity provided by discontinuity. That is to say, one paragraph of a piece on the hips will have to be marked off as separate from the previous paragraph, but that very marking off gives us part of the delight in hearing the piece, of knowing its furtherness. This kind of writing glories in an innocent application of modernism's aposiopesis.

4. Typically, each of the parts of *Selected Organs* is made of seven or so numbered paragraphs, ingenuously discontinuous save that all the paragraphs will connect the headbone to the topic, making retrievals from the famous Nichol memory, retrieving stories deposited there by the organ in question.

For instance "The Mouth."

1. Parental admonitions to keep it closed.
2. Mouth as rememberer.
3. First time Barrie was hit on the mouth.
4. Childhood fear of dentists.
5. Relationship between childhood appetites and sex.
6. The poet and the oral tradition.

Here is a delight in this kind of form if the poet is a good poet: the reader gets to see the rimes first, or she feels as if she does.

Yes, there is room in such a book for others, for us. When Michael Ondaatje did such a lovely job of reading a part aloud at Harbourfront, it was partly due to his skill and partly due to the hospitality of the lyric prose. It is an autobiography of a body that became a host, but there is room in it, and it is filled with other bodies, mother's, lover's, sister's. The writing is sumptuous with them.

5. So it is interesting that the series starts with "The Vagina," the organ that bp's body did not possess, but which was his door into the world and back. That is, the rest of the series will be consequent to that absence, that desire. In Wordsworth's writing all the people

we see came out of heaven trailing clouds of glory, and anticipate their return. Here in Nichol's genesis we recognize our loving horny analogy. Our gate of horn.

The conceit presented by the book is that the body is the source of the life story. So naturally the vagina is the source of language, the mouth's mouth:

> I never heard my mother or my sister mention
> them by name. They were an unspoken mouth &
> that was the mouth where real things were
> born. So I came out of that mouth with my mouth
> flapping 'waaah.' Oh I said that. I said that. I said
> 'waaah' Ma again & again after I was born.

In Daphne Marlatt's *Ana Historic*, also published in 1988, there is a climactic scene in which a variegated group of women attends the birth work of another woman:

> And Ana was saying Push, even as she caught a glimpse of
> what she almost failed to recognize: a massive syllable of
> slippery flesh slide out the open mouth ...
> ... What words are there? If *it* could speak! — As indeed it
> did: it spoke the babe.

Ana Historic may be our first good serial novel! In any case, it is very pleasant to see the intertextuality that does exist between these two books. It shows that Nichol, for instance, was right to begin his autobiography intussusceptively. These are my two favourite prose books of 1988.

George Bowering

B. 1944-88

"sometimes you just want to get off one long sentence before you die"

6. That is the first line of part LXXVIII of *Monotones* (1967-70), a poem book that was excluded from bpNichol's *The Martyrology*, but which found its way back in, by way of *Gifts* (1990).

The long sentence, in a commonly-held metaphor, became a life sentence, of course. The poet Nichol was committed to that term, with no time off for good behaviour, though he was, as everyone will tell you, the best-behaved person on the Canadian writing scene.

He died in Toronto General Hospital on September 25, 1988. He left, besides his wife Ellie and daughter Sarah, besides his parents in Victoria and his siblings, an enormous family. Never has the passing of a Canadian writer brought out such shock and grief from human beings *who knew him.*

7. There was a poet who was born in '44, who in his young manhood gave himself over to a lifetime's vocation. In his poetry he spread the boundaries of verse form and enriched the sounds of the English language inside his accomplished works. He was a sound poet. He did not sound like the rest of the poets of his time. At the age of 44 years he died.

His first long poem was about some martyrs, and it was about the relationship between the suffering and singing of those martyrs, and the making of a poem. The poem was "The Wreck of the Deutschland," and the poet was Gerard Manley Hopkins.

a ship in perilous storm
the lover doth compare his state to

often he loses

      (sinking out of view)

wrote young bpNichol in the first book of *The Martyrology*. He too
was born in '44. When he died he was a few days short of 44 years
old.

8. With the literal death of the author, *The Martyrology* is an unfinished poem; but then it always was. It is, in fact, a poem that seems
as if it will never get started, either. A reader opening Book I finds
that she has to pass two dozen pages of variously employed words
before the long work begins: "so many bad beginnings" — and then
the true beginning is a remark about "the poem," found and lost
again.

Here is a nation's famous poem, reluctant to begin but refusing
to exclude, impossible to close but filled with conclusions as nice
as this:

an ending
in itself
unending

Nichol's poem often has a reader thinking again, and thinking: oh,
it also means *that*. So the poem is more than double its length, and
in fact at times it demands measurement, hefting, that has nothing
to do with onward extension. Let's say, though, two thousand pages.

9. As bpNichol was always reminding his dear friend and critic
Steve McCaffery, Nichol was the creator of many things besides
The Martyrology. His first major publication was a package from

Coach House Press, titled *bp*. It contained a book, a record, a flip-book, a little book for burning, a computer card poem, a poster poem, a love letter in an envelope, silver initials, and various other brightly printed things. A treasure trove. A present. One imagined the young author at the funky Coach House, assembling these packages, imagines him there right now. A gift.

Through his career, or rather through his life, and often with his wife, Nichol put together poetry packages and sent them to his friends. For him publication was not part of the career economy; it was part of the gift economy. When it came to publishing more formally, Nichol gave his manuscripts to small presses rather than selling them to big businesses. When he was recognized with a Governor-General's award despite that, the award recognized four books at four small presses.

According to the gift economy, art is not a commodity but rather a presentation. The artist has received the gift called talent, and understands that for art to stay alive it has to be handed on. If you pay some money for a bpNichol book, you are putting groceries in front of a small-press worker's family.

Here is another aspect of the gift economy: there won't be anyone who has acquired all of bpNichol's writings. He gave lines of poetry to many tiny magazines. Sometimes a Nichol "edition" was the same line typed on seven strips of paper, folded, and distributed to fellow artists. The question arose among some fond readers: could a poem typed on bp's typewriter once and given to a friend for his birthday be called a limited edition?

10. "He is a portion of the loveliness/ Which once he made more lovely." Pard-like figures and others, all through the last months of 1988, and all across Canada, came to the places where his spirit

was visiting, and mourned together, and celebrated bpNichol's career of gifts together. There were wakes and mass readings and spiritual services in several cities, several times in some of them. This spontaneous national desire to observe such a loss has never before happened in our literary world, at least not in our lifetimes. It resembles mass sorrows we have heard of from Europe, perhaps, in an earlier time.

bpNichol took the chance of writing a lifelong poem while we all watched. Maybe that has something to do with our passion.

All he had loved, and moulded into thought,
From shape, and hue, and odour, and sweet sound,
Lamented Adonis.

11. *The Martyrology* has been our first great life-poem, yes, and often its subject is death. Readers now reread the books and remark the ironies, the continual treatment of mortality. There are dead animals, dead friends, dead children, dead poets, stanzas of grief and verses of eschatological speculation.

A martyrology must take account of the dead, of course, and let us know about the significance of their passing. Nichol's long poem, though, is *made* of martyrs, the suffering particles of language. It is a poem that like Christendom's most famous martyr, shares our fate rather than transcending it. In a late interview the poet said:

That's my notion of what I'm trying to get at, a writing
which partakes of the human condition in the sense that
we're all vulnerable, we could die at any moment. I
wanted the writing to somehow come to grips with that,
not to stand above it, as though that were not the

> human condition, and pretend to pass on solutions that
> are nonexistent. That's really the project I'm working on.
>
> (Burnham, 295)

In his last few years Nichol was in constant pain, and the chance of death was on his mind. But he continued to fight against cancellation, appearing as much and as often as he could all over the country and sometimes outside it, to encourage all young writers who came to him. At the end of the Writers on Campus Workshop in Red Deer, in July 1987, he raised his arm and commanded that his charges "go forth and publish." In their magazine a year later appeared the poetic sequence he had been writing while the workshop was on. It is called "Read, Dear":

july 5th

things remembered or recalled

the way that old song refuses to
        leave the mind

alone

conversations with gone friends
how it seemed you would all go on
foreverie

/frag/mented/memory of /
beginnings stories of
the world before you came to be

we are all
somebody's dead
baby

eventually

As the years go by, scores of young (and other) writers and editors develop the gifts bpNichol passed freely to them, and in that way his life goes on. We still bitterly resent the absence of his late-life poems. His last work, the radio piece *I Don't Remember This*, showed astonishing maturity and would have promised a wonderful later body of work. From the mental organ.

That is not to be, but all that bpNichol caused to be will be, and as many of us who can be here to hear it, will.

End Notes

Doing our Own Reading

Works consulted:

Barthes, Roland, *The Pleasure of the Text*, New York, Hill & Wang, 1975.

Brossard, Nicole, *Surfaces of Sense*, Toronto, Coach House Press, 1989.

Davenport, Guy, "The Dawn of Erewhon," in *Tatlin!*, Baltimore, Johns Hopkins University Press, 1982.

James, Henry, "The Art of Fiction," in *The Future of the Novel*, New York, Vintage, 1956.

MacLulich, T. D., *Between Europe and America: The Canadian Tradition in Fiction*, Toronto, ECW Press, 1988.

Olson, Charles, "I, Maximus of Gloucester, to You," in *The Maximus Poems*, New York, Jargon/Corinth, 1960.

Ondaatje, Michael, *Coming Through Slaughter*, Toronto, Anansi, 1976.

Vancouver as Postmodern Poetry

Works consulted:

Barthes, Roland, *Image — Music — Text*, New York, Hill and Wang, 1977.

_____, *The Pleasure of the Text*, New York, Hill and Wang, 1975.

Blaser, Robin, *Syntax*, Vancouver, Talonbooks, 1983.

Blonsky, Marshall, ed., *On Signs*, Oxford, Basil Blackwell, 1985.

Bromige, David, *My Poetry*, Berkeley, The Figures, 1980.

Davey, Frank, *Four Myths for Sam Perry*, Vancouver, Talonbooks, 1970.

_____, *From There to Here*, Erin, Press Porcepic, 1974.

_____, ed., *Tish No. 1–19*, Vancouver, Talonbooks, 1975, p. 294.

de la Mare, Walter, "How Sleep the Brave."

Delany, Paul, ed., *Vancouver: Representing the Postmodern City*, Vancouver, Pulp Press, 1994.

Farrell, Dan, *Ape*, Vancouver, Tsunami Editions, 1988.

Hutcheon, Linda, *A Poetics of Postmodernism*, New York, Routledge, 1988.

Janvier, Ludovic, int., *The Review of Contemporary Fiction*, Vol. V, No. 1, Spring 1985.

Kiyooka, Roy, *Stoned Gloves*, Toronto, Coach House Press, n.d.

Marlatt, Daphne, *Net Work*, Vancouver, Talonbooks, 1980.

_____, *Rings*, Vancouver, Georgia Straight Writing Supplement, 1971.

_____, *Steveston*, Vancouver, Talonbooks, 1974.

Olson, Charles and Robert Creeley, *The Complete Correspondence*, Volume 7, Santa Rosa, Black Sparrow Press, 1987.

Olson, Charles, *The Distances*, New York, Grove Press, 1960.

_____, *Human Universe and Other Essays*, New York, Grove Press, 1967.

_____, *A Special View of History*, Berkeley, Oyez, 1970.

Pound, Ezra, ABC *of Reading*, London, Faber and Faber, 1961.

Rilke, Rainer Maria, *Letters of Cézanne*, New York, Fromm, 1985.

Robertson, Lisa, *The Apothecary*, Vancouver, Tsunami Editions, 1991.

Scholes, Robert, *Structuralism in Literature*, New Haven, Yale University Press, 1974.

Sylvestre, Guy and H. Gordon Green, eds., A *Century of Canadian Literature*, Toronto, Ryerson, 1967.

Stein, Gertrude, *Narration*, Chicago, University of Chicago Press, 1969.

Tallman, Warren, *Godawful Streets of Man*, Toronto, Coach House Press, 1977.

Wah, Fred, *Among*, Toronto, Coach House Press, 1972.

Waldman, Anne and Marilyn Webb, eds., *Talking Poetics from Naropa Institute*, Volume One, Boulder, Shambala, 1978.

Atwood's Hook

Works consulted:

Atwood, Margaret, *Bodily Harm*, Toronto, McClelland & Stewart, 1981.

_____, *Power Politics*, Toronto, House of Anansi, 1971.

_____, *Selected Poems 1966–1984*, Toronto, Oxford, 1990.

_____, *Surfacing*, Toronto, McClelland & Stewart, 1972.

_____, *Survival*, Toronto, House of Anansi, 1972.

Davidson, Arnold E. and Cathy N. Davidson, eds., *The Art of Margaret Atwood*, Toronto, House of Anansi, 1981.

Frazer, Sir James, *The Golden Bough*, Abridged edition in one volume, London, Macmillan, 1959.

Kroetsch, Robert, *The Sad Phoenician*, Toronto, Coach House Press, 1979.

Pound, Ezra, "In a Station of the Metro," in *Poetry*, II, 1 (April 1913).

Watson, Sheila, *A Collection*, Toronto, (*Open Letter*, 3rd Series, No. 1, Winter 1974–1975).

_____, *The Double Hook*, Toronto, McClelland & Stewart, 1959.

Weston, Jessie, *From Ritual to Romance*, Cambridge, Cambridge University Press, 1957.

Woodcock, George, ed., *The Canadian Novel in the Twentieth Century*, Toronto, McClelland & Stewart, New Canadian Library, 1975.

Once Upon a Time in the South: Ondaatje and Genre

1. I am grateful to my colleague Richard M. Coe for this note.

Works consulted:

Frye, Northrop, *Anatomy of Criticism*, New York, Atheneum, 1968, p. 98.

Ondaatje, Michael, *Leonard Cohen*, Toronto, McClelland & Stewart, Canadian Writers No. 8, 1970, p. 23.

_____, *Leonard Cohen*, pp. 44–45.

Solecki, Sam, "An Interview with Michael Ondaatje (1974)," in *Spider Blues*, ed. Sam Solecki, Montreal, Véhicule Press, 1985, p. 20.

Hutcheon, Linda, "*Running in the Family*: The Postmodernist Challenge," in *Spider Blues*, p. 303.

Kamboureli, Smaro, "The Alphabet of Self," in *Reflections: Autobiography and Canadian Literature*, ed. K. P. Stich, Ottawa, University of Ottawa Press, 1988, p. 83.

The Autobiographings of Mourning Dove

1. On the U.S. side of the border the spelling is Okanogan, while on the Canadian side it is Okanagan.

2. The Colville Reservation in northeastern Washington is populated by several Salishan peoples. One group is called the Colviles, the spelling changed to avoid confusion between place and tribe.

3. The term "tribe" is used in the U.S. In Canada we tend to use such terms as "band" or "community" or "nation."

Works consulted:

Armstrong, Jeanette, *Slash*, Penticton, Theytus Books, 1985.

Barthes, Roland, *Image — Music — Text*, New York, Hill and Wang, 1977.

Dybikowski, Ann et al., eds., *In the Feminine: Women and Words Conference Proceedings 1983*, Edmonton, Longspoon Press, 1985.

Gunn, Janet Varner, *Autobiography: Toward a Poetics of Experience*, Philadelphia, University of Pennsylvania Press, 1982.

Jelinek, Estelle C., *The Tradition of Women's Autobiography: From Antiquity to the Present*, Boston, Twayne Publishers, 1986.

Larson, Charles R., *American Indian Fiction*, Albuquerque, University of New Mexico Press, 1978.

Mourning Dove, *Cogewea: The Half-Blood*, Lincoln, University of Nebraska Press, 1981. Reprint of the 1927 ed. published by Four Seas Co., Boston.

_____, *Coyote Stories*, ed. Heister Dean Guie, Lincoln, University of Nebraska Press, 1990. Reprint of the 1933 ed. published by The Caxton Printers, Caldwell, Idaho.

_____, *Mourning Dove: A Salishan Autobiography*, ed. Jay Miller, Lincoln, University of Nebraska Press, 1990.

I would also like to express my appreciation of the extensive work and publications of Dr. Alanna Kathleen Brown of Montana State University. Dr. Brown is the leading scholar of Mourning Dove's writing and life, and a trusted friend of the Quintasket family. I encourage readers to seek out her work.

Robin Blaser at Lake Paradox
Works consulted:

Blaser, Robin, *Bach's Belief*, Canton, N.Y., The Institute of Further Studies, Glover Publishing, 1995.

_____, *The Holy Forest*, Toronto, Coach House Press, 1993.

_____, *Syntax*, Vancouver, Talonbooks, 1983.

D[oolittle], H[ilda], *Collected Poems 1912–1944*, New York, New Directions, 1983.

Duncan, Robert, *The Opening of the Field*, New York, Grove Press, 1960.

Olson, Charles, *The Maximus Poems*, Berkeley, University of California, 1983.

Pound, Ezra, *The Cantos of Ezra Pound*, London, Faber & Faber, 1954.

Webber, Jean and the En'owkin Centre, eds., *Okanagan Sources*, Penticton, Theytus Books, 1990.

Total Organ Transplant: bpNichol's Body

Works consulted:

Burnham, Clint, "Nichol Interviewed: on *Book 6 books*" in *Tracing the Paths: Reading & Writing* The Martyrolog, ed. Roy Miki, Vancouver, Talonbooks, 1988.

Nichol, bp, *Organ Music*, Windsor, Black Moss Press, 1988.

_____, "Read, Dear," *Secrets from the Orange Couch*, Vol. 1, No. 2 (August 1988): 19.

Acknowledgements

"17 Questions," *Communications World*, Volume 10, Number 4, June-July 2003.

"Atwood's Hook," *Open Letter*, Series 8, Number 2, Winter 1992.

"Backyard Burgers" was a talk at Cleveland State University sometime in the 90s.

"British Columbia, What Did You Expect?" is from a talk given to the annual convention of Fluids Engineers, Vancouver, June 1997.

"Diamond in the Rain" was commissioned by the *Neue Zürcher Zeitung* for April 2004, and appeared in English in the New Zealand journal *Jacket* in April 2005.

"Doing Our Own Reading" is adapted from my introduction to *And Other Stories*, Vancouver, Talonbooks, 2001.

"Ethel Wilson's Maggie" was the afterword to Wilson's novel *Swamp Angel*, Toronto, New Canadian Library, McClelland & Stewart, 1990.

"God Only Knows" was a talk given at the Surrey International Writers' Festival in 2004.

"Let Me Get Back to You on That" was commissioned for a book of essays on the subject "What is a Canadian?" McClelland & Stewart, 2005.

"Man with Pencil" was written for a conference on Greg Curnoe, at the Art Gallery of Ontario. It was published in *Open Letter*, Series 11, Number 5, Summer 2002.

"Milton Acorn" was in *Canadian Literature* 112, Spring 1987.

"Off Their Map" was a talk at Western Washington University, 2002, and published in *Borderblur*, ed. Alper, Western Washington University Press, 2003.

"Once Upon a Time in the South" was a lecture at University of Paris VI, in 1997, and published in *Re-Constructing the Fragments of Michael Ondaatje's Works*, ed. Jean-Michel LaCroix, Paris, the Sorbonne, 1999.

"Purdy's Purple," *West Coast Review*, Volume 25, Number 2, Fall 1991.

"Remember Appropriation?" *Books in Canada*, Jan/Feb 1991; *The Globe & Mail*, May 5, 1990.

"Robin Blaser at Lake Paradox," in *Even on Sunday*, ed. Miriam Nichols, Orono, National Poetry Foundation, 2002.

"The Autobiographings of Mourning Dove," *Canadian Literature* 144, Spring 1995.

"The Grand Tour of Gleis-Binario," *Rampike*, Volume 10, Number 2, 1999.

"The Struggle for Pork," [ed. D.M.R. Bentley] Galt, Press Porcépic, 1996.

"Total Organ Transplant," *Canadian Literature* 122–123, Autumn-Winter 1989.

"Vancouver as Postmodern Poetry," in *Vancouver Representing the Post-Modern City*, ed. Paul Delany, Vancouver, Pulp Press, 1994.

"VVVVVVV," in *The Véhicule Poets Now*, ed. Tom Konyves and Steven Morrissey, Winnipeg, The Muses' Company, 2004.

INDEX